PLAZA

NEW WASHINGTON HOTEL

SEATTLE

Chicago

NORTH WESTERN

LINE

GREAT SALT LAKE
CUT-OFF

30 MILES from SHORE to SHORE

AMERICAN CANYON ROUTE VIA OGDEN

12-'22

Sun Valley IDAHO

RATES AND INFORMATION
(All rates are European plan—Meals not included)
JUNE 1 TO OCTOBER 15, 1953

BROADMOOR HOTEL, COLORADO SPRINGS, COLO.

AMERICA

National Parks and Destinations

Table of Contents

LEGEND

BOUNDARIES

- - - International border
——— State border
••••• Continental Divide

WATER FEATURES

——— Major river
——— River
——— Seasonal stream
Swamp
••••••• Intracoastal Waterway

CITIES

⊛ Capital city

○ City dot. Size relative to population.

HIGHWAYS

(80) Interstate highway
(89) Federal highway
(29) State highway
G3 County highway
(14) Tribal road

INTERNATIONAL

2 Mexico
1 Canada

STATE MAPS

——— Interstate highway
——— Federal highway
——— State highway
——— Scenic route
National park
Forest/grassland
Indian land
Subject state
Non-subject area

REGIONAL THEME MAPS

——— Interstate highway
——— Federal highway
——— State/county highway
——— Unpaved road
Scenic route
Tunnel
- - - Foot trail
- - - Major/historic trail
+ + + Railroad
••••••• Ferry line
National park/area/site
Forest/grassland
Indian land
Area of interest
Other land

NATIONAL PARK MAPS

——— Paved road
•••••• Unpaved road
- - - Horse carriage road
——— Major/historic trail
••••••• Foot trail
+ + + Railroad
Tunnel
••••••• Ferry line
National park
Forest/grassland
Other natural area
Indian land
Glacier
Shoal/coral reef
Other land

CITY MAPS

——— Major road
——— Minor road
← One-way road
——— Scenic route
Tunnel
Park/golf course
Area of interest
Airport with runway
Other land

LEGEND

SYMBOLS

	Air Force base		Horse riding/stable		Ruin
	Battlefield		Hospital		Sailing
	Beach		Hunting		Sand dunes
	Bike trail		International airport		Shipwreck
	Bird watching		Lighthouse		Snorkeling/diving
	Boating		Local airport		Snowmobile trail
	Campground		Marina		Surfing
	Canoeing		Mission		Trailhead
	Church		Museum		Tram
	Covered bridge		Music festival		University
	Cross-country ski trail		Nature preserve		Viewpoint
	Downhill ski area		Pass		Visitor center
	Ferry		Peak		Waterfall
	Fishing		Picnic area		Whalewatching
	Four-wheel vehicle trail		Plantation/mansion		Whitewater rafting
	Golf course		Point of interest		Wild horses
	Hiking		Pueblo		Wildlife viewing area
	Historic seaport		Ranger station		Winery
	Horse racing		Rock/mountain climbing		

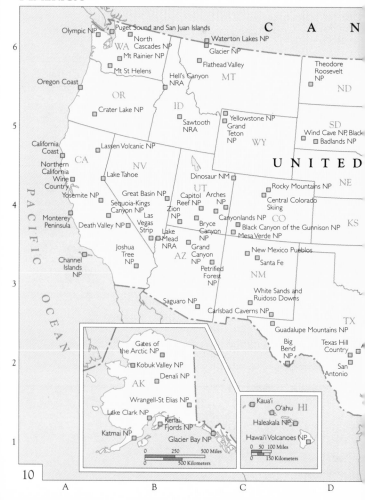

Olympic NP
Puget Sound and San Juan Islands
Waterton Lakes NP
North Cascades NP
WA
Glacier NP
Mt Rainier
Flathead Valley
Mt St Helens
Hell's Canyon NRA
MT
Oregon Coast
OR
Crater Lake NP
ID
Sawtooth NRA
Yellowstone NP
Grand Teton NP
WY
California Coast
Lassen Volcanic NP
Northern California Wine Country
CA
NV
Lake Tahoe
Dinosaur NM
Yosemite NP
Great Basin NP
UT
Capitol Reef NP
Arches NP
Rocky Mountains NP
Sequoia-Kings Canyon NP
Las Vegas Strip
Zion NP
Canyonlands NP
CO
Central Colorado Skiing
Monterey Peninsula
Lake Mead NRA
Bryce Canyon NP
Black Canyon of the Gunnison NP
Death Valley NP
Mesa Verde NP
Channel Islands NP
Joshua Tree NP
AZ
Grand Canyon NP
New Mexico Pueblos
Santa Fe
Petrified Forest NP
NM
White Sands and Ruidoso Downs
Saguaro NP
Carlsbad Caverns NP
TX
Guadalupe Mountains NP
Texas Hill Country
Big Bend NP
San Antonio

C   A   N
Theodore Roosevelt NP
ND
SD
Wind Cave NP, Black
Badlands NP
UNITED
NE
KS

PACIFIC

OCEAN

Gates of the Arctic NP
Kobuk Valley NP
Denali NP
AK
Wrangell-St Elias NP
Lake Clark NP
Kenai Fjords NP
Katmai NP
Glacier Bay NP

0   250   500 Miles
0   500 Kilometers

Kaua'i
O'ahu   HI
Haleakala NP
Hawai'i Volcanoes NP

0 50 100 Miles
0   130 Kilometers

10

A   B   C   D

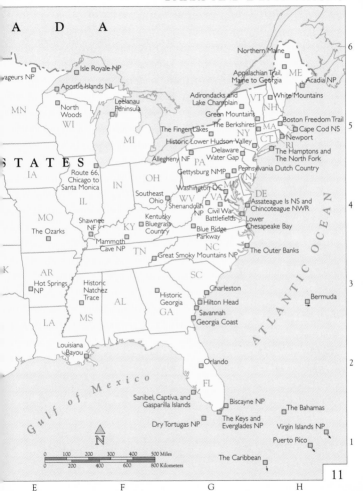

NATIONAL TRAILS

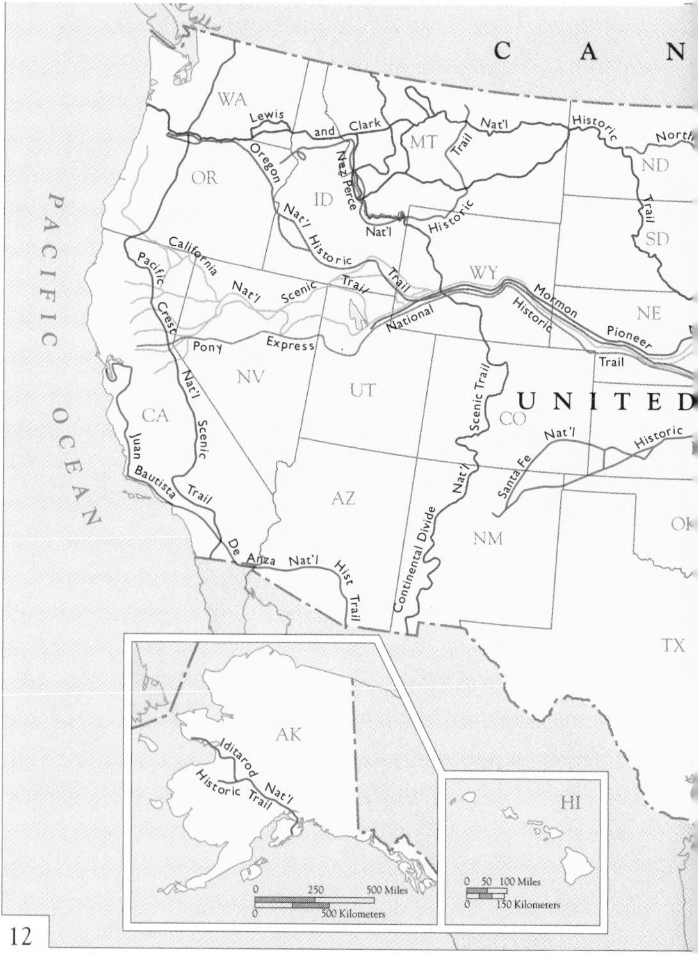

PACIFIC OCEAN

C A N

WA

Lewis and Clark Nat'l Historic North

OR

Oregon

Nez Perce

MT

ND

ID

Nat'l Historic

Trail

SD

California

Nat'l Scenic Trail

WY

Mormon

NE

Pacific Crest

Pony Express

National

Historic

Pioneer

Trail

NV

UT

U N I T E D

CA

Nat'l Scenic

CO

Nat'l

Historic

Juan Bautista Trail

AZ

Santa Fe

Continental Divide Nat'l Scenic Trail

NM

OK

De Anza Nat'l Hist. Trail

TX

AK

Iditarod Nat'l

Historic Trail

HI

| 0 | 250 | 500 Miles |
| 0 | 500 Kilometers | |

| 0 | 50 | 100 Miles |
| 0 | 150 Kilometers | |

12

A   B   C   D

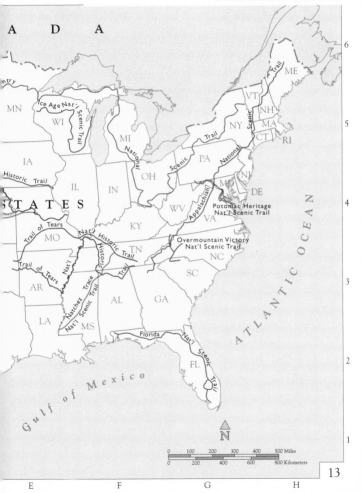

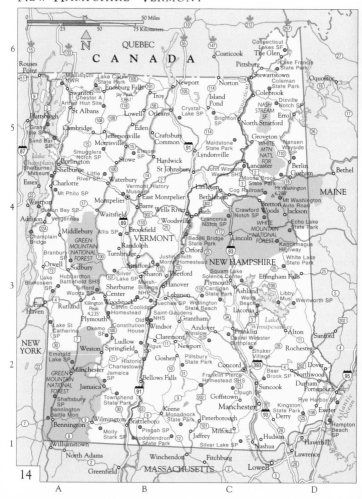

14

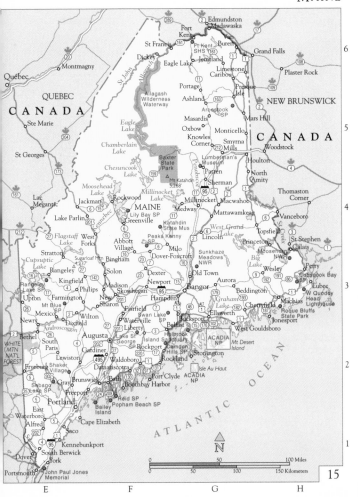

Acadia NP MAINE

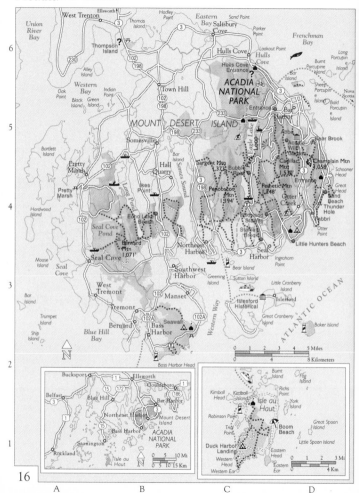

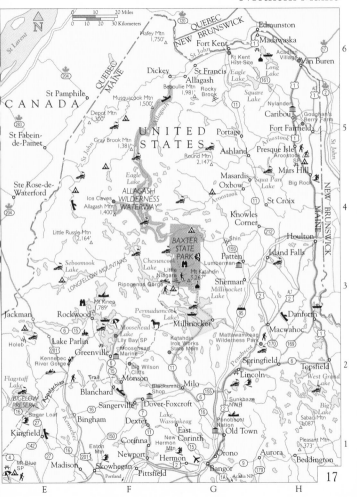

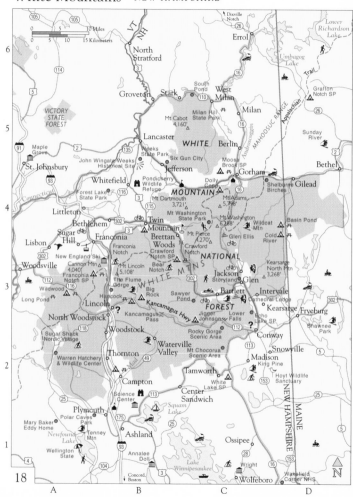

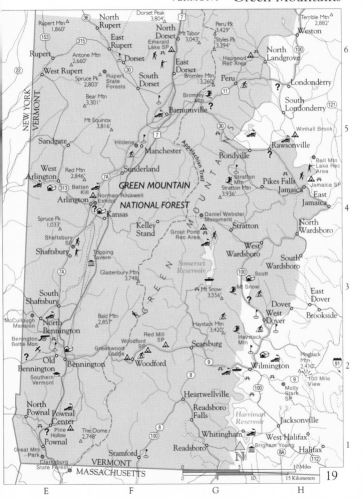

19

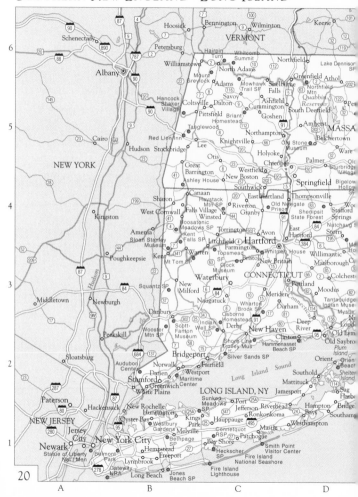

20

A   B   C   D

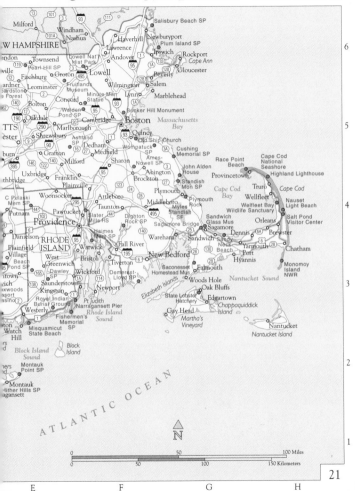

E   F   G   H

Cape Cod NS MASSACHUSETTS

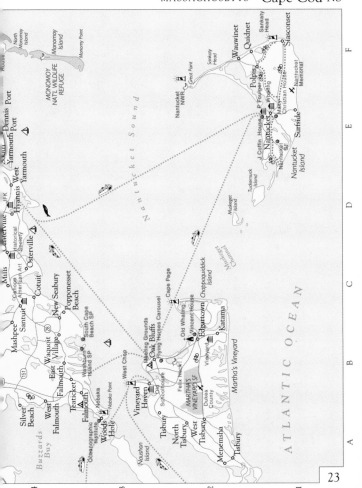

Boston Freedom Trail MASSACHUSETTS

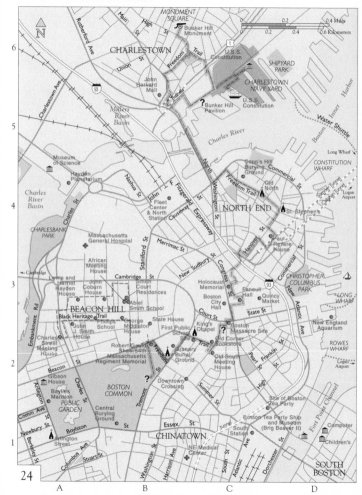

24

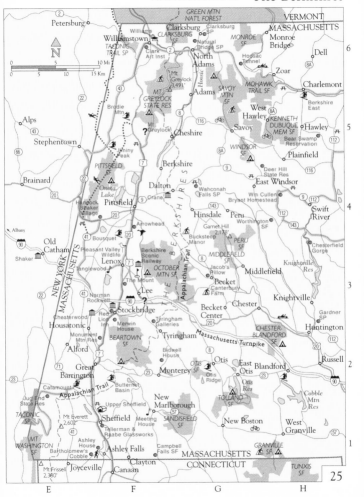

Newport RHODE ISLAND

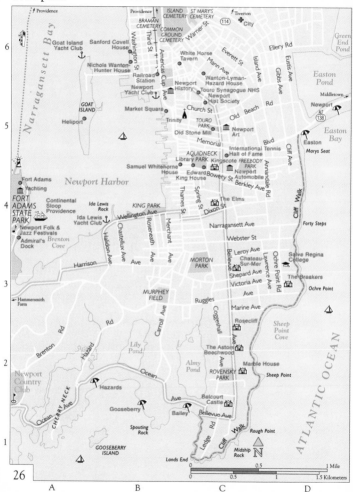

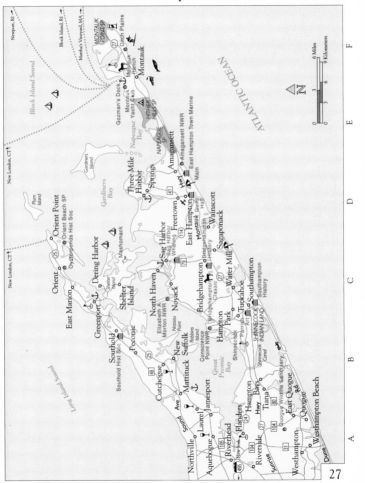

27

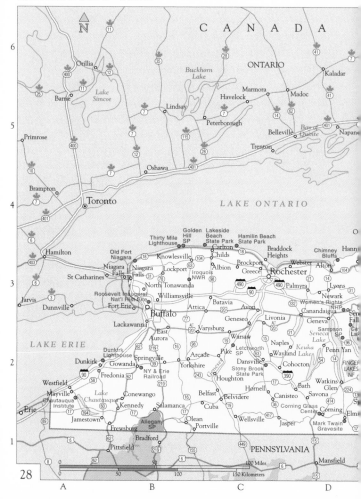

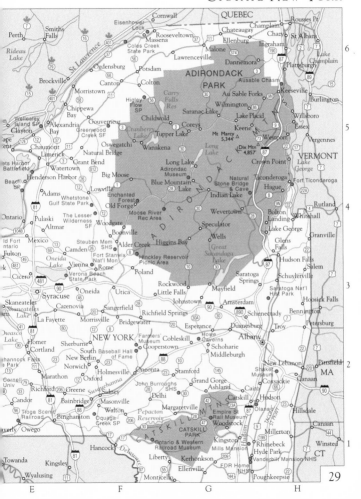

QUEBEC

Eisenhower Lock
Cornwall
Roosevelttown
Chateaugay
Champlain
Chazy
St Albans
Rousses Pt

Perth
Smiths Falls
Coles Creek State Park
Ellenburg
Ingraham
Lake Champlain

Rideau Lake
Ogdensburg
Lawrenceville
Malone
Dannemora
Plattsburgh

Brockville
Potsdam
ADIRONDACK PARK
Au Sable Forks
Keeseville

Morristown
Canton
Colton
Carry Falls Res
Wilmington
Ausable Chasm

Alexandria Bay
Chippewa Bay
Higley Flow SP
Childwold
Saranac Lake
Lake Placid
Burlington

Clayton
Gouverneur
Greenwood Creek SF
Cranberry Lake
Tupper Lake
Coreys
Mt Marcy 5,344'
Keene
Willsboro

Chaumont
Natural Bridge
Oswegatchie
Wanakena
Dix Mtn 4,857'
Westport
Essex

Limerick
Grant Bend
Long Lake
Adirondack Museum
Crown Point
Vergennes

Watertown
Big Moose
VERMONT
Lake George

Henderson Harbor
Lowville
Blue Mountain Lake
Natural Stone Bridge & Cave
Ticonderoga
Fort Ticonderoga

Adams
Whetstone Gulf State Park
Enchanted Forest
Old Forge
Indian Lake
Hague
Rutland

Pulaski
Altmar
The Lesser Wilderness SF
Woodgate
Moose River Rec Area
Wevertown
Bolton Landing
Whitehall

Mexico
Boonville
Speculator
Lake George
Granville

Camden
Steuben Mem SHS
Alder Creek
Wells
Glens Falls

Fulton
Fort Stanwix Nat'l Mon
Hinckley Reservoir Picnic Area
Great Sacandaga Lake
Hudson Falls
Salem

Cicero
Vienna
Rome
Poland
Saratoga Springs
Schuylerville

Oneida Lake
Verona Beach State Park
Rockwood
Mayfield
Saratoga Nat'l Hist Park
Hoosick Falls

Syracuse
Oneida
Utica
Little Falls
Johnstown
Amsterdam
Bennington

Cazenovia
Sangerfield
Richfield Springs
Schenectady
Troy
Petersburg

Skaneateles
La Fayette
Morrisville
Bridgewater
Esperance
Duanesburg
Albany
New Lebanon
Pittsfield

Homer
Sherburne
NEW YORK
Farmers' Museum
Cobleskill
Howe Caverns
Schoharie
Shaker Museum
Canaan
MA

Cortland
South Baseball Hall of Fame
Cooperstown
Middleburgh
Coxsackie

New Berlin
Holmesville
Stamford
Grand Gorge
Ashland
Cairo
Catskill

Marathon
Norwich
Oxford
Oneonta
John Burroughs SHS
Delhi
Margaretville
CATSKILL MTNS
Empire St Rail Museum
Olana SHS
Hillsdale

Richford
Bainbridge
Masonville
Walton
Pepacton Reservoir
Woodstock
Kingston
Rhinebeck
Millerton
CT

Binghamton
Ouaquaga Creek SP
CATSKILL PARK
Ontario & Western Railroad Museum
Mills Mansion
Hyde Park
Winsted

Hancock
Liberty
Kerhonkson
Ellenville
FDR Home NHS
Vanderbilt Mansion NHS

Monticello
Poughkeepsie

29

Adirondacks and Lake Champlain NEW YORK

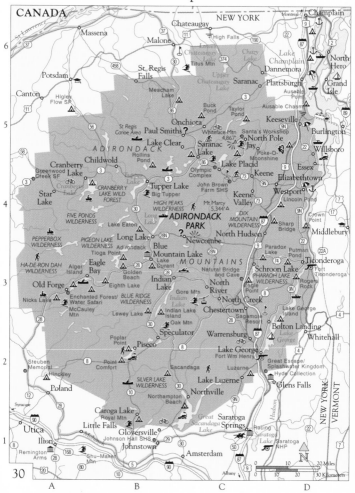

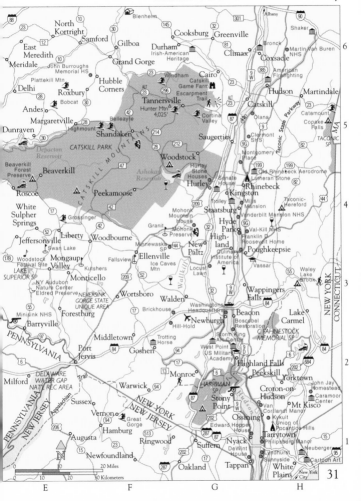

31

Finger Lakes NEW YORK

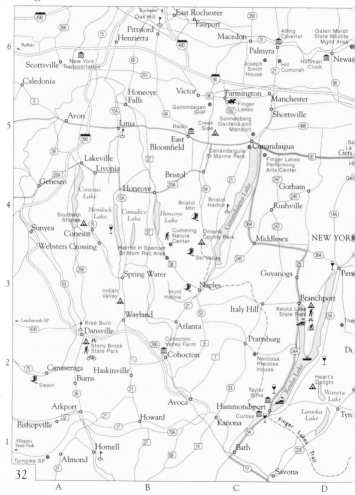

32

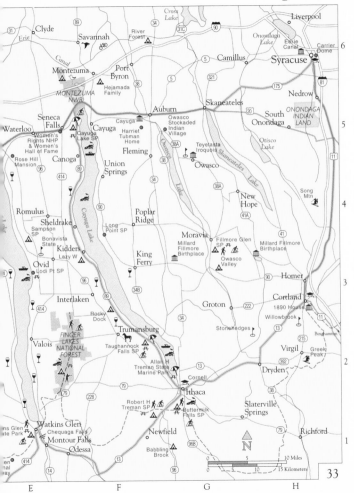

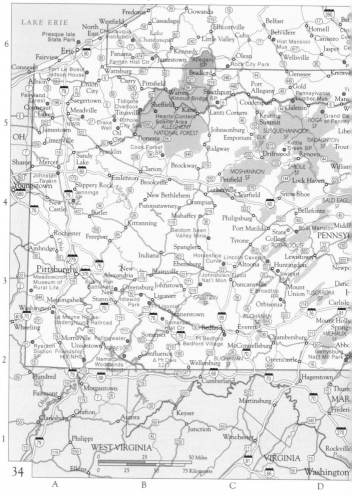

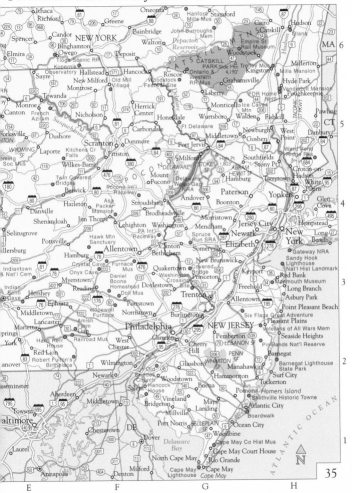

Pennsylvania Dutch Country

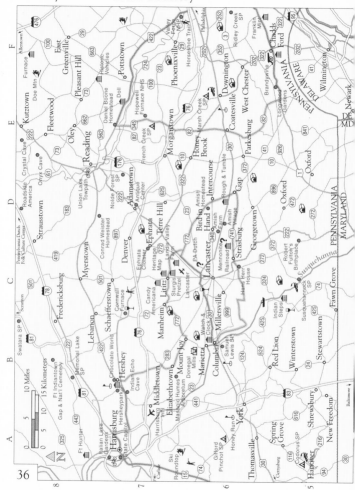

36

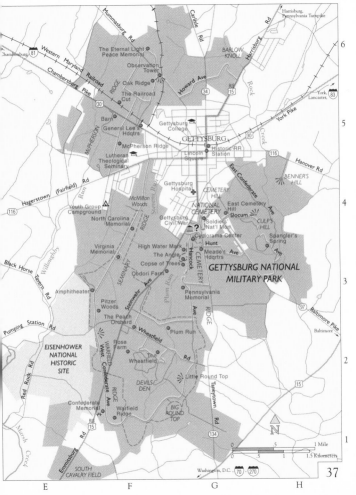

EISENHOWER
NATIONAL
HISTORIC
SITE

GETTYSBURG NATIONAL
MILITARY PARK

Allegheny NF PENNSYLVANIA

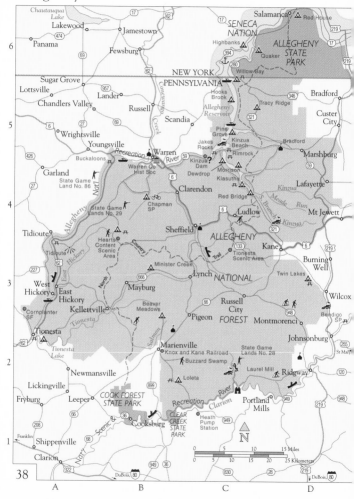

38

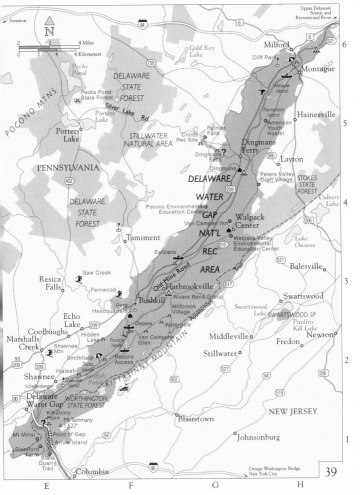

39

Appalachian Trail MAINE TO GEORGIA

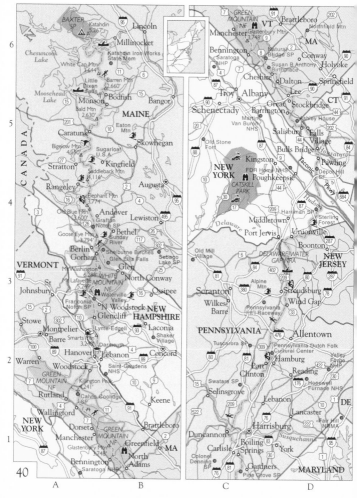

40

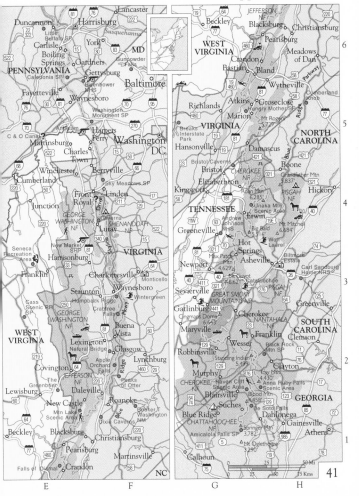

MID-ATLANTIC STATES

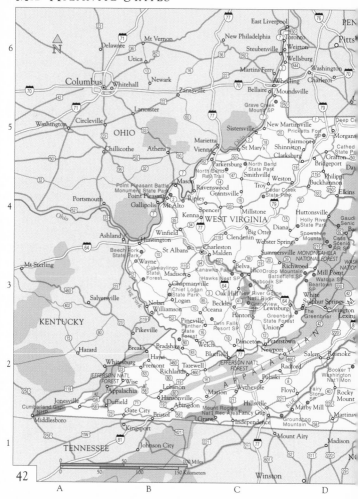

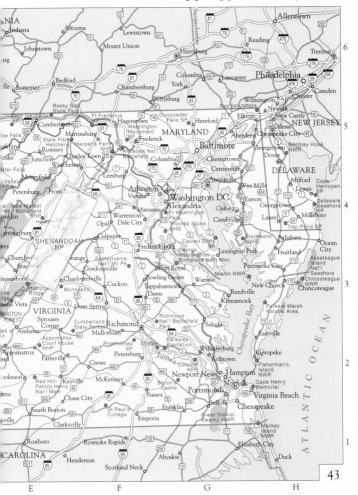

Washington DISTRICT OF COLUMBIA

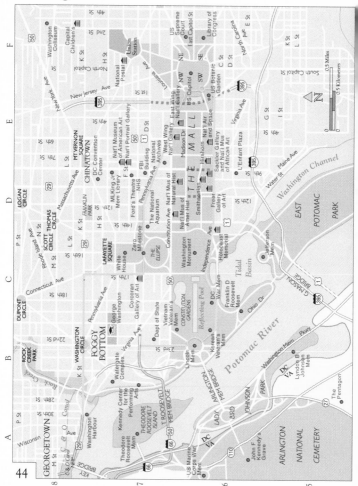

44

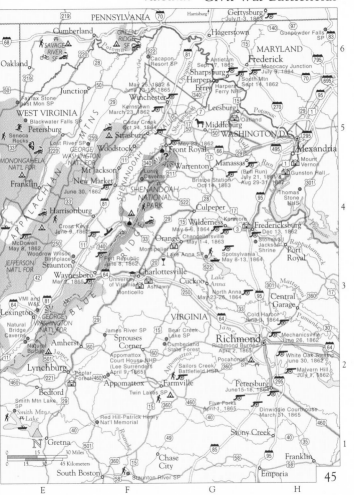

VIRGINIA Civil War Battlefields

VIRGINIA

PENNSYLVANIA

Harrisburg

Gettysburg
July 1-3, 1863

Gunpowder Falls
SP

Cumberland

GREEN
RIDGE
SF

Hagerstown

MARYLAND

Frederick

SAVAGE
RIVER
SF

Oakland

Antietam
Sept 17, 1862

Sharpsburg

Monocacy Junction
July 9, 1864

Fairfax Stone
Hist Mon SP

Junction

Harpers
Ferry

South Mtn
Sept 14, 1862

Harpers Ferry NHP

May 25, 1862 &
June 13-15, 1865

WEST VIRGINIA

Blackwater Falls SP

Kernstown
March 23, 1862

Winchester

Leesburg

Oatland

Petersburg

Seneca
Rocks

Cedar Creek
Oct 14, 1864

Middleburg

WASHINGTON D.C.

Strasburg

MONONGAHELA
NAT'L FOR

Lost River SP

Woodstock

GEORGE
WASHINGTON
NAT'L FOR

Front Royal

Manassas

Alexandria

Franklin

Mt Jackson

Luray
Caverns

Warrenton

May 23, 1862

Mount
Vernon

Gunston Hall

New Market
June 30, 1862

SHENANDOAH
NATIONAL
PARK

Bristoe Station
Oct 14, 1863

Manassas
(Bull Run)
July 21, 1861
Aug 29-31, 1862

Thomas
Stone
NHS

Harrisonburg

Culpeper

Cross Keys
June 9, 1862

Wilderness
May 5-6, 1864

Kenmore

Fredericksburg
Dec 13, 1862

McDowell
May 8, 1862

Orange

Chancellorsville
May 1-4, 1863

Stonewall
Jackson
Shrine

Port
Royal

Woodrow Wilson
Birthplace

Montpelier

Lake Anna SP

Spotsylvania
May 8-13, 1864

JEFFERSON
NAT'L FOR

Staunton

Port Republic
June 8, 1862

Charlottesville

Cuckoo

North Anna
May 23-26, 1864

Waynesboro
Mar 2, 1865

University
of Virginia

Ashlawn

Central
Garage

VMI
W&L

Monticello

Cold Harbor
June 3, 1864

Lexington

GEORGE
WASHINGTON
NAT'L FOR

Natural
Bridge
Caverns

James River SP

Bear Creek
Lake SP

Richmond
Richmond Burned
April 2, 1865

Mechanicsville
June 26, 1862

White Oak Swamp
June 30, 1862

Natural
Bridge

Sprouses
Corner

Amherst

Cumberland
State Forest

Pocahontas
SP

VIRGINIA

Malvern Hill
July 1, 1862

Lynchburg

Poplar
Forest

Appomattox
Court House NHP
(Lee Surrenders
April 9, 1865)

Sailors Creek
Battlefield HSP

Petersburg
June 15-18, 1864

Bedford

Appomattox

Farmville

Five Forks
April 1, 1865

Smith Mtn Lake
SP

Twin Lakes
SP

Dinwiddie Courthouse
March 31, 1865

Smith Mtn
Lake

Red Hill-Patrick Henry
Nat'l Memorial

Stony Creek

Gretna

Chase
City

Franklin

0   15   30 Miles

Staunton River SP

South Boston

Emporia

45

Blue Ridge Parkway NORTH CAROLINA–VIRGINIA

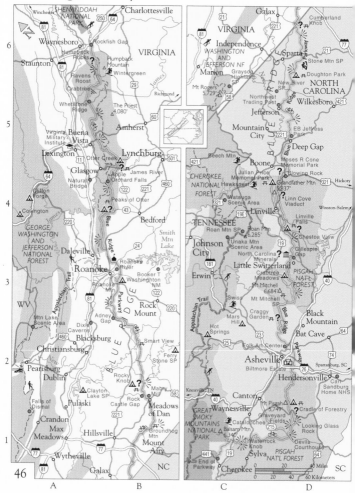

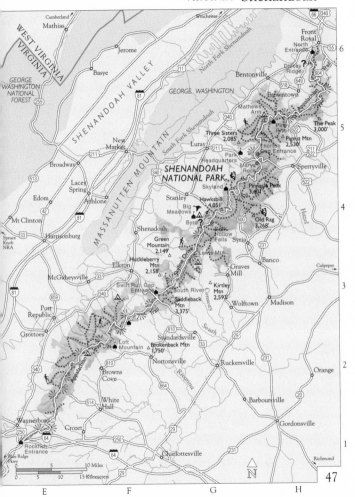

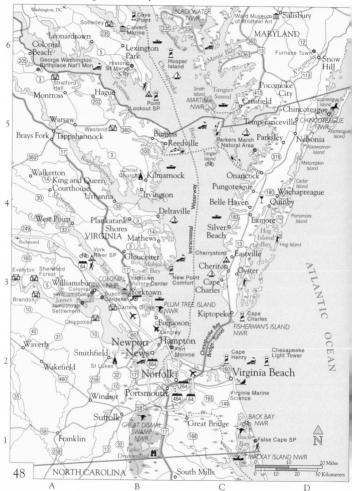

Lower Chesapeake Bay VIRGINIA

Washington, DC

MARYLAND

BLACKWATER NWR

Ward Museum of Wildfowl Art · Salisbury

Sotterley

Cove Point

Calvert Marine

Leonardtown

Colonial Beach

George Washington Birthplace Nat'l Mon.

Lexington Park

Historic St Mary's City

Hooper Island

Furnace Town

Snow Hill

Stratford Hall

Hague

Point Lookout SP

MARTIN NWR

Smith Island

Tangier Sound

Pocomoke City

Crisfield

Chincoteague

CHINCOTEAGUE NWR

Montross

Warsaw

Westend

Burgess

Reedville

Tangier Island

Temperanceville

Nelsonia

Assowoman Island

Brays Fork · Tappahannock

Harkers Marsh Natural Area

Parksley

Metompkin Island

Christ Church

Kilmarnock

Onancock

Pungoteague

Wachapreague

Cedar Island

Walkerton

King and Queen Courthouse

Urbanna

Irvington

Belle Haven

Quinby

Paramore Island

West Point

Plankatank Shores

VIRGINIA

Deltaville

Exmore

Silver Beach

Hog Island NWR

Hog Island

Richmond

Evelyton

Sherwood Forest

Mathews

York River SP

Gloucester

Mobjack Bay

Cherrystons

Eastville

ATLANTIC OCEAN

Williamsburg

Colonial Williamsburg

Busch Gardens

COLONIAL NHP

Yorktown Victory Center

Yorktown

New Point Comfort

Cheriton

Oyster

Cape Charles

Brandon

Jamestown Settlement

Carters Grove

PLUM TREE ISLAND NWR

Kiptopeke

Cape Charles

Chippokes

Poquoson

Langley

FISHERMAN'S ISLAND NWR

Waverly

Smithfield

Newport News

Hampton

Fort Monroe

Cape Henry

Chesapeake Light Tower

Wakefield

St Lukes

Norfolk

Virginia Beach

Windsor

Portsmouth

Virginia Marine Science

Suffolk

GREAT DISMAL SWAMP NWR

Great Bridge

BACK BAY NWR

Franklin

Lake Drummond

False Cape SP

Back Bay

MACKAY ISLAND NWR

48

NORTH CAROLINA

South Mills

N

20 Miles

10   20   30 Kilometers

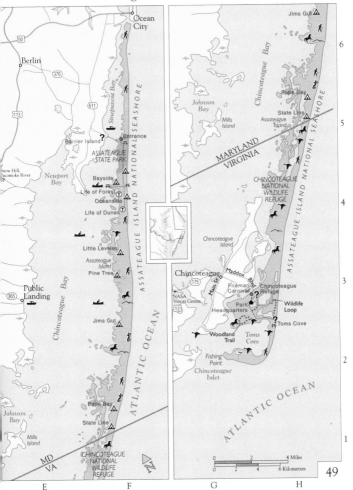

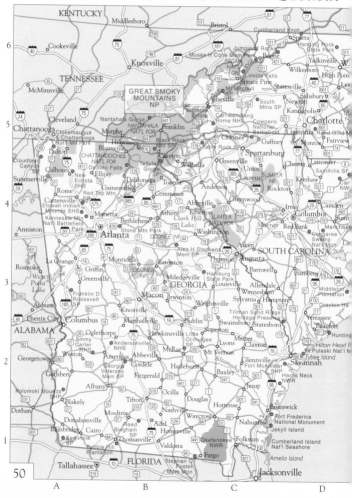

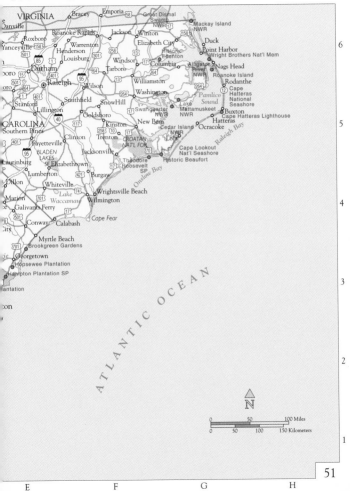

ATLANTIC OCEAN

VIRGINIA
Danville
Bracey
Emporia
58
Great Dismal
Swamp
NWR
17
Mackay Island
NWR
Roxboro
Roanoke Rapids
Jackson
Whiton
158
Duck
Yanceyville
158
Henderson
Warrenton
301
Elizabeth City
Point Harbor
Wright Brothers Nat'l Mem
501
85
1
Louisburg
301
Windsor
Historic
Edenton
Nags Head
boro
15
Durham
64
Tarboro
17
Columbia
Alligato
River
NWR
264
Roanoke Island
oro
501
Raleigh
95
Wilson
13
Williamston
64
Rodanthe
1
401
Washington
264
Cape
Hatteras
National
Seashore
Smithfield
SnowHill
Pamlico
Sound
CAROLINA
40
Goldsboro
117
Swanquarter
NWR
Lake
Mattamuskeet
NWR
Hatteras
Southern Pines
Lillington
258
10
Kinston
New Bern
Cedar Island
Ocracoke
Cape Hatteras Lighthouse
Buxton
401
Clinton
Trenton
17
Lola
Fayetteville
95
BLADEN
LAKES
SE Elizabethtown
Jacksonville
CROATAN
NAT'L FOR
70
Cape Lookout
Nat'l Seashore
Raleigh Bay
aurinburg
Lumberton
421
Burgaw
Theodore
Roosevelt
SP
Historic Beaufort
Dillon
Whiteville
74
Wrightsville Beach
Onslow Bay
Marion
e
Galivants Ferry
Lake
Waccamaw
17
Wilmington
81
City
501
Conway
Calabash
Cape Fear
Myrtle Beach
Brookgreen Gardens
701
Georgetown
Hopsewee Plantation
Hampton Plantation SP
ie
lantation
N
ton

100 Miles
0   50   100
0   50   100   150 Kilometers

6

5

4

3

2

1

E   F   G   H

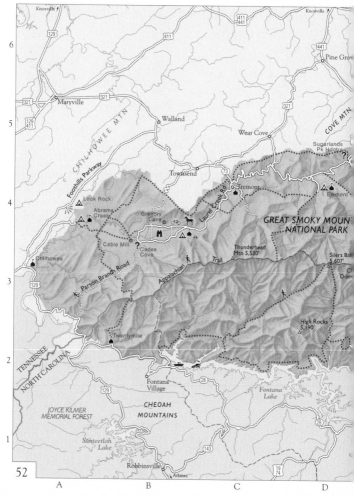

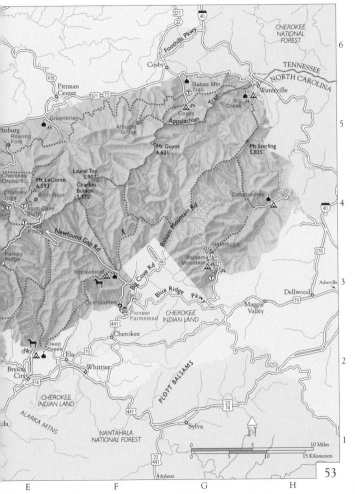

The Outer Banks   NORTH CAROLINA

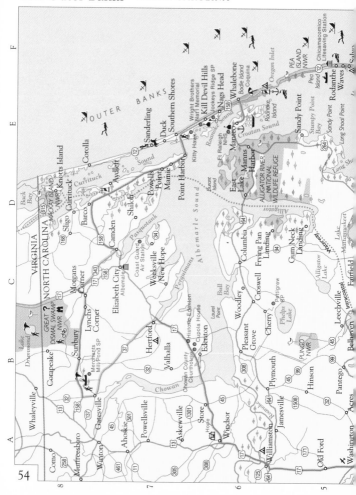

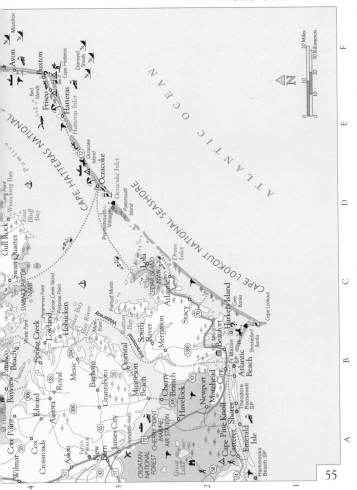

55

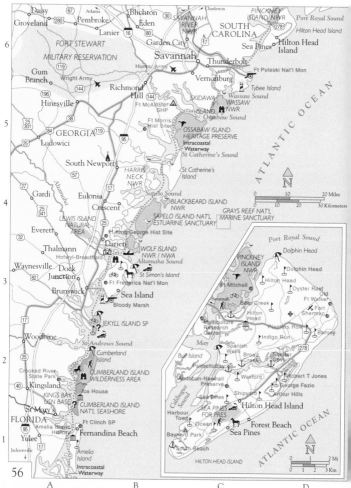

Georgia Coast and Hilton Head SOUTH CAROLINA

56

Historic Georgia

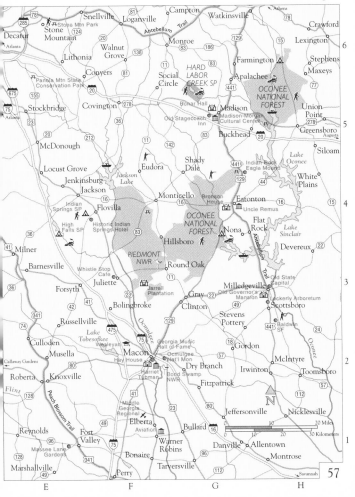

57

Savannah GEORGIA

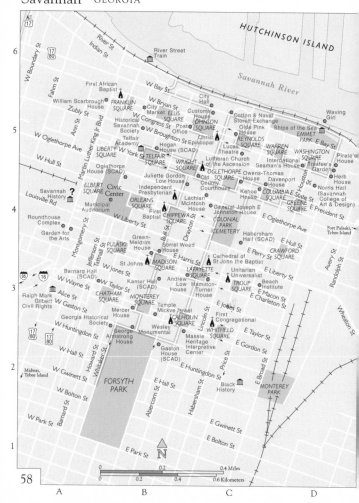

HUTCHINSON ISLAND

Savannah River

ALT 17

17 80

River St

Indian St

6

W Boundary St

Farm St

Zubly St

Ann St

W Bay St

Ship Street Train

First African Baptist

FRANKLIN SQUARE

William Scarbrough House

Historical Savannah Society

Telfair Academy

W Oglethorpe Ave

5

W Hull St

Martin Luther King Jr Blvd

City Market

W Bryan St

W Congress St

Post Office

W Broughton St

ELLIS SQUARE

JOHNSON SQUARE

City Hall

Customs House

Christ Episcopal

Cotton & Naval Stores Exchange

Olde Pink House

REYNOLDS SQUARE

Waving Girl

Ships of the Sea

EMMET PARK E Bay St

Pirate's House

LIBERTY SQUARE

W York St

Hogan House (SCAD)

Telfair

WRIGHT SQUARE

Lucas Theatre

Lutheran Church of the Ascension

WARREN SQUARE

WASHINGTON SQUARE

International Seaman's House

Trustee's Garden

Herb House

Oglethorpe House (SCAD)

Juliette Gordon Low House

Independent Presbyterian

Old County Courthouse

OGLETHORPE SQUARE

Owens-Thomas House

Davenport House

Norris Hall (Savannah College of Art & Design)

ELBERT SQUARE

Savannah History

Civic Center

ORLEANS SQUARE

Lachlan McIntosh House

Kehoe House

COLUMBIA SQUARE

E State St

E President St

Louisville Rd

?

Municipal Auditorium

W Liberty St

First Baptist

CHIPPEWA SQUARE

General Joseph E Johnston House

E Oglethorpe Ave

GREENE SQUARE

Fort Pulaski, Tybee Island

4

Roundhouse Complex

Garden for the Arts

Montgomery St

Jefferson St

Tattnall St

Barnard St

PULASKI SQUARE

Green-Meldrim House

Gorrel Weed House

Bull St

Drayton

COLONIAL PARK CEMETERY

Habersham St

Cathedral of St John the Baptist

Habersham Hall (SCAD)

E Hull St

E Perry St

CRAWFORD SQUARE

Avery St

Randolph St

95

16

W Jones St

St Johns

MADISON SQUARE

E Harris St

LAFAYETTE SQUARE

Unitarian Universalist

E Liberty St

Wheaton St

3

Ralph Mark Gilbert Civil Rights

Barnard Hall (SCAD)

W Wayne St

Alice St

W Gaston St

Kanter Hall (SCAD)

CHATHAM SQUARE

Andrew Low House

Hamilton-Turner House

TROUP SQUARE

Beach Institute

E Macon St

E Charlton St

17 80

Georgia Historical Society

Mercer House

MONTEREY SQUARE

Temple Mickve Israel

E Jones St

Lincoln St

CALHOUN SQUARE

First Congregational

17 80

17 80

W Huntingdon St

George Armstrong House

Wesley Monumental

WHITFIELD SQUARE

E Taylor St

2

Midway, Tybee Island

W Hall St

W Gwinnett St

Howard St

Whitaker St

Gaston House (SCAD)

Massie Heritage Interpretive Center

E Gordon St

Price St

E Broad St

MONTEREY PARK

W Bolton St

FORSYTH PARK

E Huntingdon St

Habersham St

Black History

E Gwinnett St

1

W Park St

Barnard St

Abercorn St

E Park St

E Hall St

E Bolton St

N

58

0   0.2   0.4 Miles

0   0.2   0.4   0.6 Kilometers

A   B   C   D

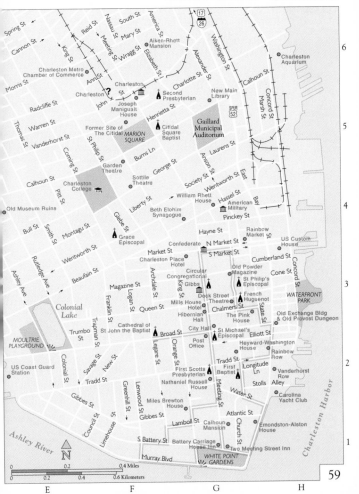

FLORIDA

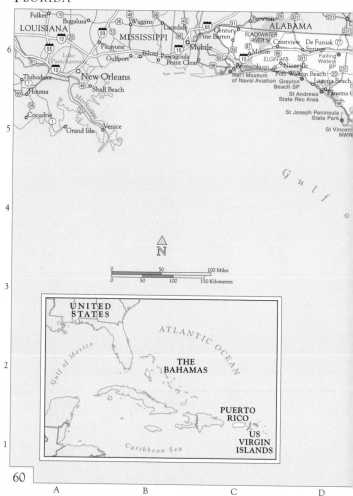

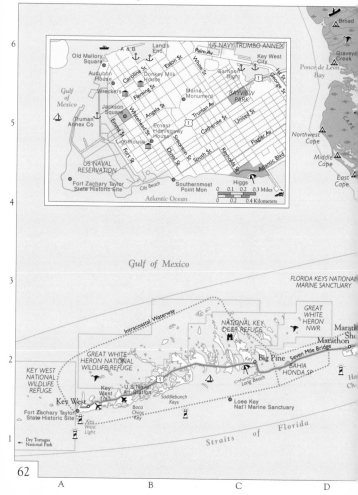

Inset map — Key West:

US NAVY TRUMBO ANNEX

Old Mallory Square
A & B
Land's End
Palm Av
Key West City

Audubon House
Caroline St
White St
Eaton St
Garrison Bight

Wreckers
Fleming St
Donkey Milk House
George St

Gulf of Mexico

Jackson Square
Truman Annex Co
Angela St
Maine Monument
BAYVIEW PARK

Ernest Hemingway House
Truman Av
Catherine St
United St

Lighthouse
Whitehead St
Duval St
Smathers St
South St
Catherine St
Flagler Av

Emma St
Fort St
Reynolds St
Atlantic Blvd

US NAVAL RESERVATION

Fort Zachary Taylor State Historic Site

City Beach

Southernmost Point Mon

Higgs

Atlantic Ocean

0   0.1   0.2   0.3 Miles
0   0.2   0.4 Kilometers

Main map:

Broad

Graveyard Creek

Ponce de Leon Bay

Northwest Cape

CAPE

Middle Cape

East Cape

Gulf of Mexico

FLORIDA KEYS NATIONAL MARINE SANCTUARY

Intracoastal Waterway

NATIONAL KEY DEER REFUGE

GREAT WHITE HERON NWR

Marathon
Marathon Shores

GREAT WHITE HERON NATIONAL WILDLIFE REFUGE

Big Pine Key

Big Pine

Seven Mile Bridge

KEY WEST NATIONAL WILDLIFE REFUGE

BAHIA HONDA SP

Long Beach

Ho
Ch

Key West
Key West Intl
U.S. Naval Air Station

Saddlebunch Keys

Loee Key Nat'l Marine Sanctuary

Fort Zachary Taylor State Historic Site

Boca Chica Key

Key West Light

Dry Tortugas National Park

Straits of Florida

62

A   B   C   D

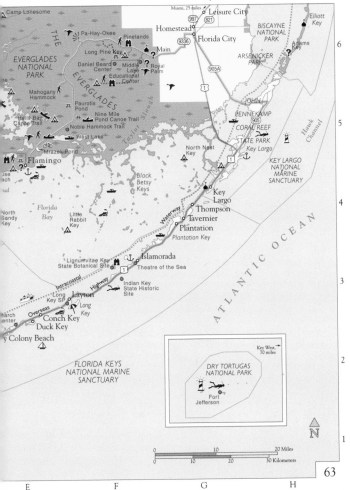

Camp Lonesome

THE

EVERGLADES
NATIONAL
PARK

Pa-Hay-Okee

Pinelands

Long Pine Key

Daniel Beard
Center

Middle
Lake
Educational
Center

Royal
Palm

Mahogany
Hammock

Paurotis
Pond

Nine Mile
Pond Canoe Trail

Noble Hammock Trail

Hells Bay
Canoe Trail

West Lake

Mrazek Pond

Flamingo

THE EVERGLADES

Taylor Slough

Miami, 25 miles

997 821

Homestead

9336

Main

Florida City

Leisure City

BISCAYNE
NATIONAL
PARK

Elliott
Key

Adams
Key

ARSENICKER
PARK

905A

1

JOHN
PENNEKAMP
CORAL REEF
STATE PARK

905

North Nest
Key

Key Largo

Hawk Channel

KEY LARGO
NATIONAL
MARINE
SANCTUARY

North Sandy
Key

Florida
Bay

Little
Rabbit
Key

Black Betsy
Keys

Waterway

Key
Largo

Thompson

Tavernier

Plantation

Plantation Key

ATLANTIC OCEAN

Lignumvitae Key
State Botanical Site

Islamorada

Theatre of the Sea

1

Intracoastal

Highway

Indian Key
State Historic
Site

Long
Key SP

Layton

Long
Key

Conch Key

Duck Key

Colony Beach

Overseas

arch
center

FLORIDA KEYS
NATIONAL MARINE
SANCTUARY

Key West,
70 miles

DRY TORTUGAS
NATIONAL PARK

Fort
Jefferson

N

0   10   20 Miles

0   10   20   30 Kilometers

63

E   F   G   H

Sanibel, Captiva, and Gasparilla Islands   FLORIDA

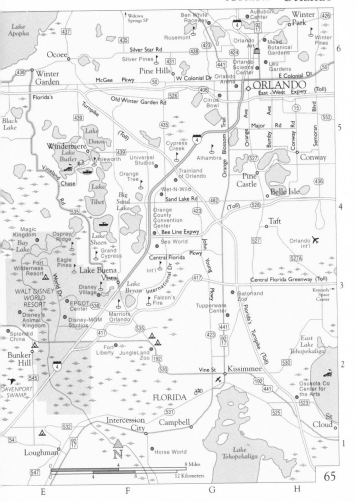

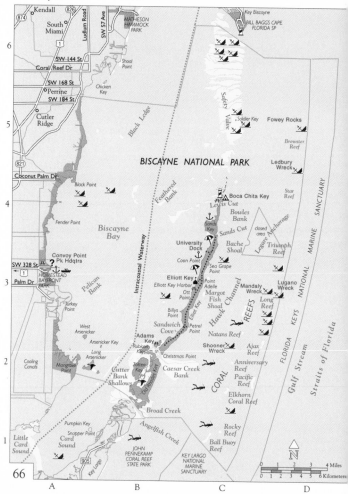

Biscayne NP FLORIDA

Kendall

South
Miami

SW 144 St

Coral Reef Dr

SW 168 St

Perrine

SW 184 St

Cutler
Ridge

Coconut Palm Dr

Black Point

SW 328 St

Convoy Point
Pk Hdqtrs

HOMESTEAD
BAYFRONT
PARK

Palm Dr

Turkey Pt

West
Arsenicker

Cooling
Canals

Mangrove
Point

Long Arsenicker

Arsenicker Key

Pumpkin Key

Snapper Point

Little
Card
Sound

Card
Sound

Key Largo

JOHN PENNEKAMP
CORAL REEF STATE PARK

Ludlum Road

SW 57 Ave

MATHESON
HAMMOCK PARK

Shoal
Point

Chicken
Key

Black Ledge

Shoal
Point

Biscayne
Bay

Fender Point

Pelican Bank

Intracoastal Waterway

Feathered
Bank

BISCAYNE NATIONAL PARK

Key Biscayne

BILL BAGGS CAPE
FLORIDA SP

Safety Valve

Soldier Key

Fowey Rocks

Brewster
Reef

Ledbury
Wreck

Boca Chita Key

Lewis Cut

Bowles
Bank

Sands
Key

Sands Cut

Bache
Shoal

closed
area

Legare Anchorage

Star
Reef

Triumph
Reef

University
Dock

Coon Point

Sea Grape
Point

Elliott Key

Point
Adelle

Elliott Key Harbor

Ott
Point

Margot
Fish
Shoal

Mandaly
Wreck

Lugano
Wreck

Long
Reef

Billys Point

Petrel
Point

Hawk Channel

Natans Reef

CORAL

REEFS

Sandwich Cove

Adams
Key

Rubicon
Keys

Christmas Point

Shooner
Wreck

Ajax
Reef

Cutter Bank
Shallows

Totten
Key

Old Rhodes Key

Caesar Creek
Bank

Anniversary
Reef

Pacific
Reef

Elkhorn
Coral Reef

Broad Creek

Rocky
Reef

Ball Buoy
Reef

Angelfish Creek

KEY LARGO
NATIONAL
MARINE
SANCTUARY

FLORIDA KEYS NATIONAL MARINE SANCTUARY

Gulf Stream

Straits of Florida

66

A   B   C   D

0   1   2   3   4 Miles
0 1 2 3 4 5 6 Kilometers

N

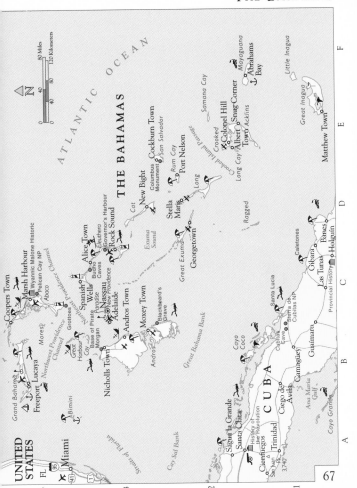

THE BAHAMAS

ATLANTIC OCEAN

UNITED STATES

FL

Miami

Grand Bahama

Freeport Lucaya

Bimini

Coopers Town

Marsh Harbour

Wyannie Malone Historic

Pelican Cay NP

Abaco

Great Harbour Cay

Mores?

Northwest Providence Channel

Northeast Providence Channel

Great Bahama Bank

Cay Sal Bank

Straits of Florida

Alice Town

Eleuthera

Governor's Harbour

Rock Sound

Budho Caves

Spanish Wells

Nassau

New Providence

Paradise

Base of Pirate Morgan

Adelaide

Blackbeard's Grave

Andros Town

Andros

Moxey Town

Nicholls Town

Cat

New Bight

Columbus Monument

Cockburn Town

San Salvador

Rum Cay

Port Nelson

Stella Maris

Long

Georgetown

Great Exuma

Exuma Sound

Ragged

Crooked Island Passage

Samana Cay

Crooked

Colonel Hill

Long Cay Albert Town

Acklins

Snug Corner

Mayaguana

Abrahams Bay

Little Inagua

Great Inagua

Matthew Town

CUBA

Sagua la Grande

Santa Clara

History of the Revolution

Cienfuegos

Trinidad

San Juan 3,740

Santa Lucia

Sierra de Cubitas NP

Cayo Coco

Cayo Guillén?

Cueva

Camagüey

Ciego de Avila

Ana María Gulf

Cayo Grande

Guáimaro

Las Tunas

Caletones

Gibara

Holguín

Provincial History

Banes

THE BAHAMAS

N

0   40   80 Miles
0   40   80   120 Kilometers

67

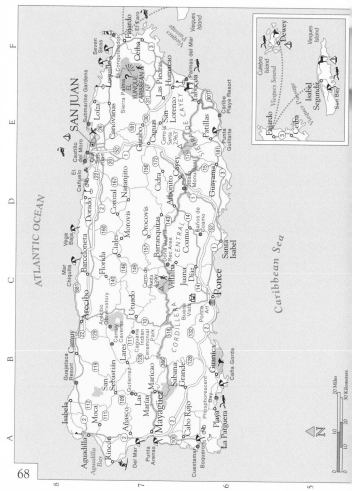

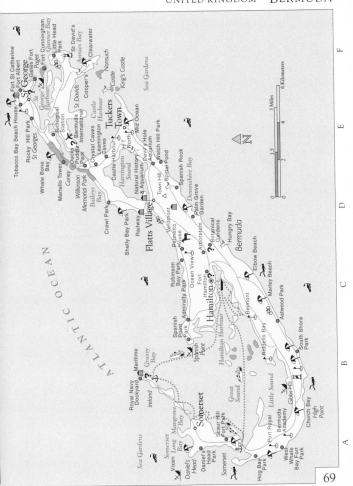

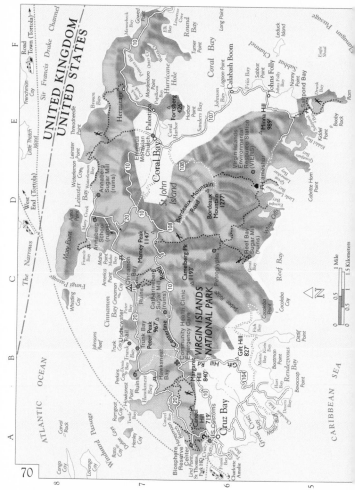

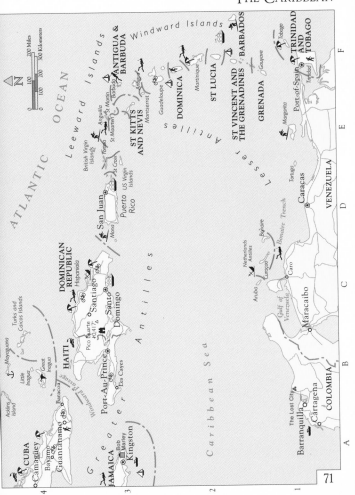

ATLANTIC OCEAN

Windward Islands

Leeward Islands

ANTIGUA & BARBUDA

Antigua

Barbuda

Montserrat

St Martin / St Maarten

Anguilla

British Virgin Islands

Tortola

ST KITTS AND NEVIS

St Croix

US Virgin Islands

San Juan

Puerto Rico

Mona

Guadeloupe

DOMINICA

Martinique

ST LUCIA

BARBADOS

Gouyave

ST VINCENT AND THE GRENADINES

GRENADA

Margarita

TRINIDAD AND TOBAGO

Tobago

Port-of-Spain

Trinid

VENEZUELA

Caracas

Tortuga

Bonaire Trench

Bonaire

Netherlands Antilles

Curaçao

Aruba

Caro

Gulf of Venezuela

Maracaibo

COLOMBIA

Barranquilla

Cartagena

The Lost City

Lesser Antilles

Caribbean Sea

Greater Antilles

JAMAICA

Kingston

Bob Marley

Les Cayes

Port-Au-Prince

HAITI

Pico Duarte 3,141/2

DOMINICAN REPUBLIC

Santo Domingo

Santiago

Hispaniola

Windward Passage

Baracoa

Guantánamo

CUBA

Bayamo

Camagüey

Great Inagua

Little Inagua

Turks and Caicos Islands

Mayaguana

Acklins Island

N

0 100 200 Miles

0 100 200 300 Kilometers

71

F E D C B A

4 3 2 1

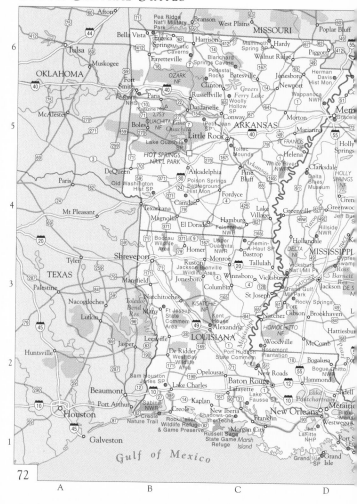

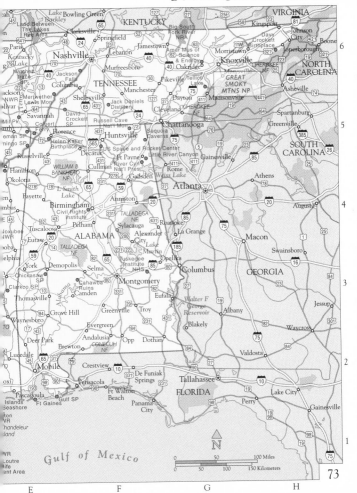

Louisiana Bayou

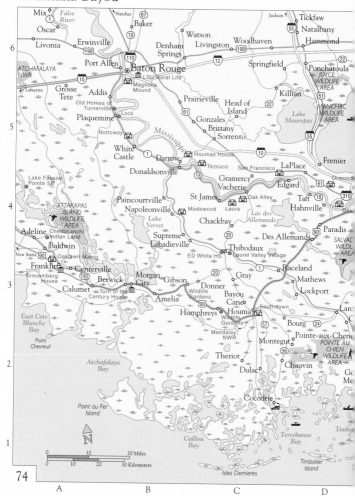

Historic Natchez Trace

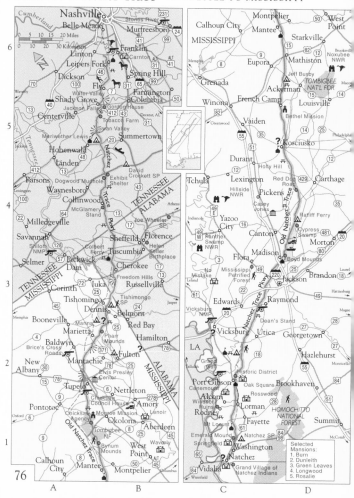

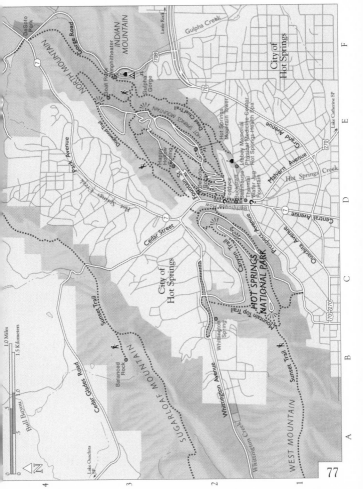

ILLINOIS ✦ INDIANA ✦ OHIO ✦ KENTUCKY

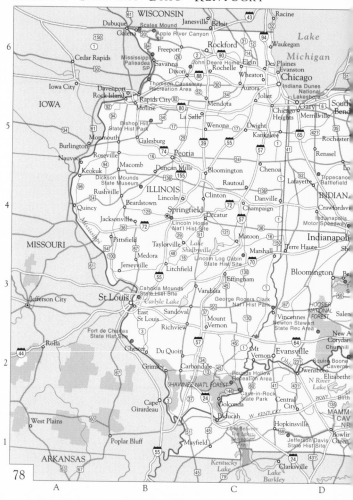

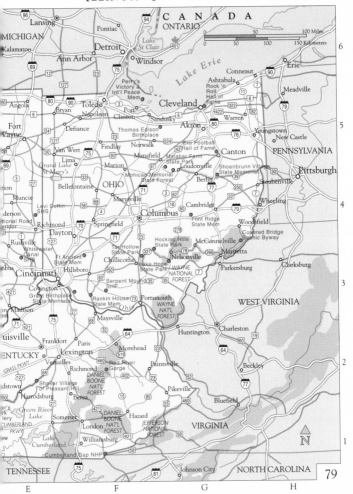

Mammoth Cave NP KENTUCKY

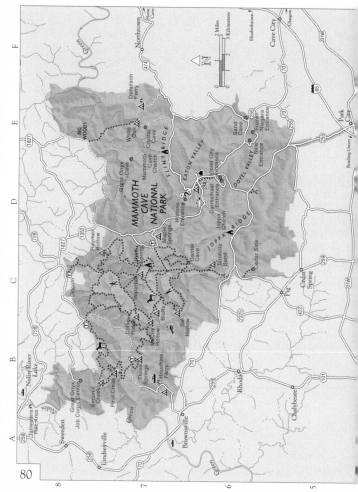

Kentucky Bluegrass Country

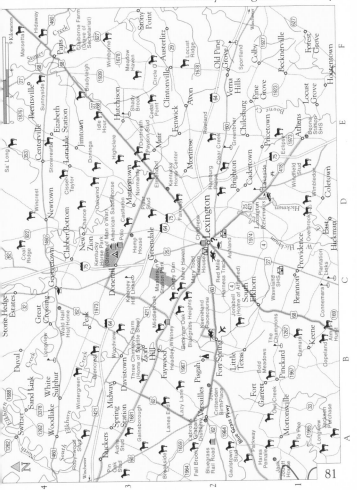

81

Shawnee NF ILLINOIS

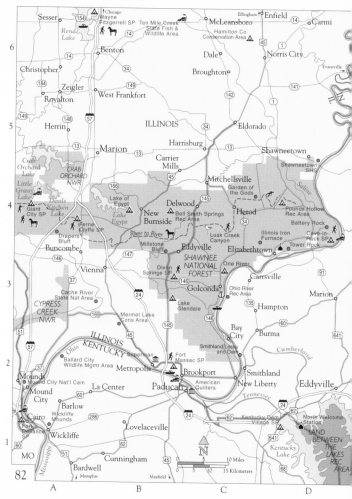

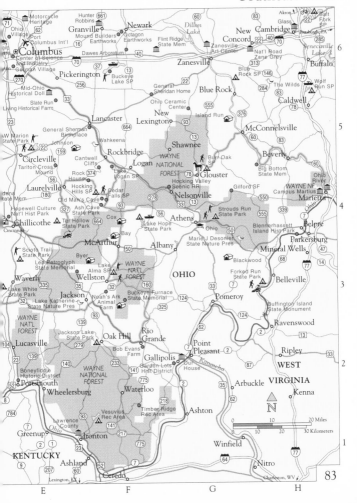

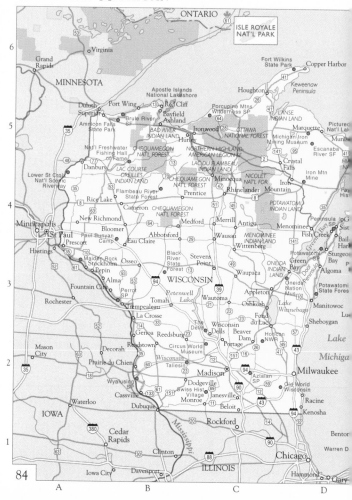

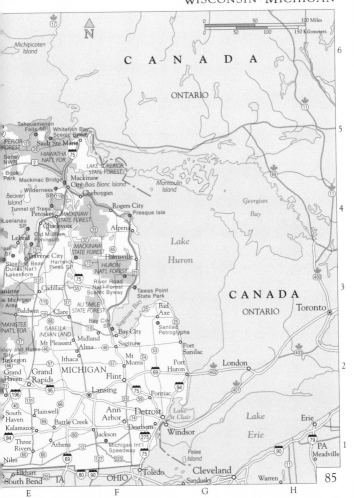

85

E   F   G   H

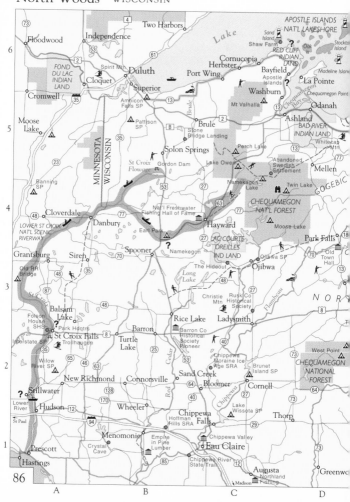

North Woods WISCONSIN

A   B   C   D

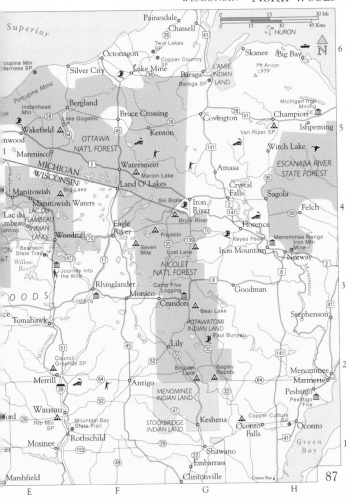

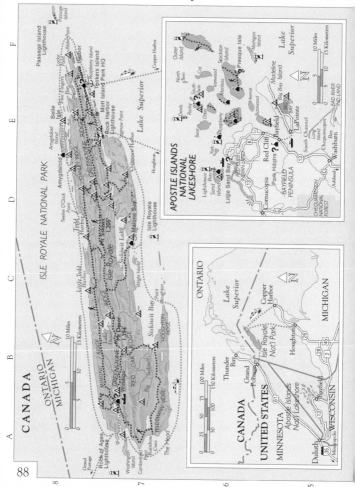

88

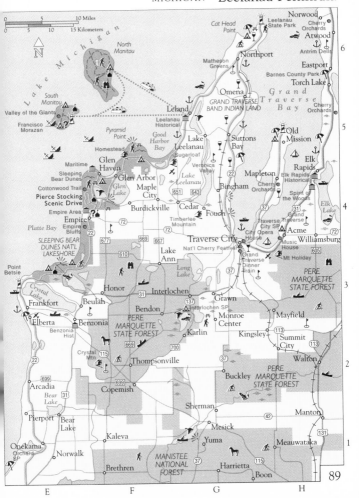

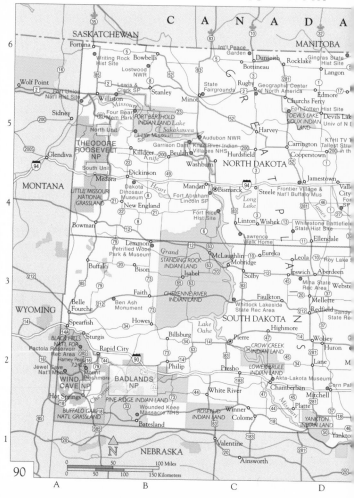

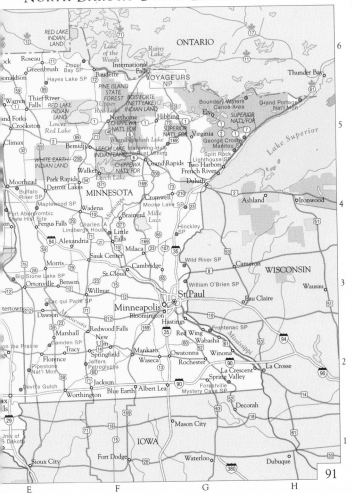

Theodore Roosevelt NP   NORTH DAKOTA

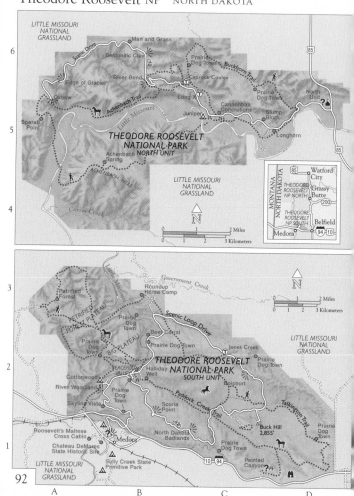

LITTLE MISSOURI
NATIONAL
GRASSLAND

Scenic Drive

Man and Grass

Bentonitic Clay

River Bend

Edge of Glacier

Oxbow

Achenbach Trail

Spendid
Point

Achenbach
Spring

ACHENBACH HILLS

Little Missouri

Prairie
Dog Town

Caprock Coulee

Buckhorn Trail

Long X

Juniper

Cannonball
Concretions

Prairie
Dog Town

North
Unit

Slump
Block

Longhorn

THEODORE ROOSEVELT
NATIONAL PARK
NORTH UNIT

LITTLE MISSOURI
NATIONAL
GRASSLAND

N

0   1   2 Miles
0   1   2   3 Kilometers

MONTANA   NORTH DAKOTA

85

Watford
City

THEODORE
ROOSEVELT
NP NORTH

Grassy
Butte

200

Belfield

Medora

94   10

Little Missouri

Government Creek

Petrified
Forest

Roundup
Horse Camp

Scenic Loop Drive

N

0   1   2 Miles
0   1   2   3 Kilometers

PETRIFIED
FOREST PLATEAU

Prairie
Dog Town

Prairie
Dog Town

BIG PLATEAU

Beef Corral

Prairie Dog Town

Jones Creek

LITTLE MISSOURI
NATIONAL
GRASSLAND

Cottonwood

River Woodlands

Skyline Vista

PEACEFUL
VALLEY

Halliday
Well

Prairie
Dog Town

Scoria
Point

Paddock Creek Trail

Boicourt

THEODORE ROOSEVELT
NATIONAL PARK
SOUTH UNIT

Prairie
Dog Town

Talkington Trail

Prairie
Dog Town

Roosevelt's Maltese
Cross Cabin

Chateau DeMores
State Historic Site

Medora

North Dakota
Badlands

Buck Hill
2,855'

Prairie
Dog Town

Sully Creek State
Primitive Park

Painted
Canyon

10   94

LITTLE MISSOURI
NATIONAL
GRASSLAND

92

A   B   C   D

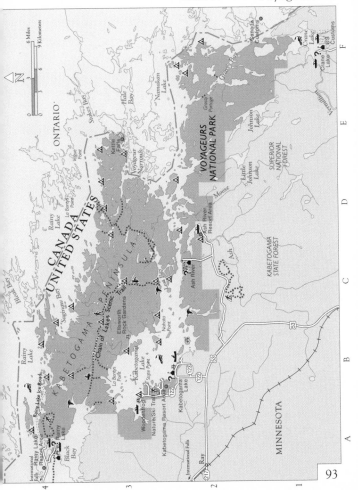

Wind Cave NP, Black Hills SOUTH DAKOTA

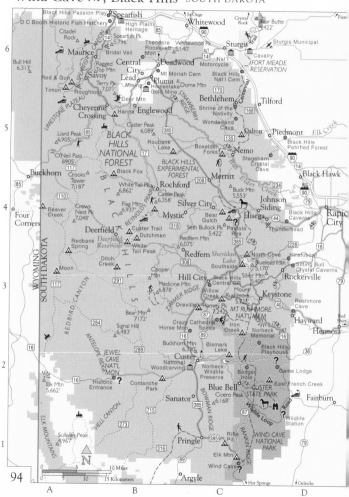

St Onge

Black Hills Passion Play — Spearfish
D C Booth Historic Fish Hatchery — High Plains Heritage
Citadel Rock
14 Spearfish Pk △5,796'
Maurice
Ragged Top Mtn
Bridal Veil
Savoy
Rod & Gun
Timon
Roughlock
Hanna
Terry Pk 7,071'
Top Mtn
Deer Mtn
Mining
Homestake Gold Mine
Pluma
Lead
Central City
Deadwood
Mt Moriah Cem
Theodore Roosevelt Mon △5,140'
Whitewood Pk
Whitewood
Bear Butte △1,422'
Sturgis
Sturgis Municipal
Cavalry FORT MEADE RESERVATION
Nat'l Motorcycle
Crystal Rock
Pierr
Bull Hill 6,313'
Cheyenne Crossing
Custer Peak △6,089'
Englewood
Roubank Lake
Nemo
Bethlehem
Shrine of the Nativity
Wonderland Cave
Dalton
Tilford
Piedmont
Elk Creek
Liard Peak △6,905'
O'Neil Pass △6,905'
Crooks Tower △7,187'
Black Fox
White Tail Pk △6,862'
Castle Creek △6,358'
Flag Mtn △6,937'
Crows Nest Pk △7,048'
Rochford
Silver City
Buck Mtn △5,553'
Boxelder Forks
Merritt
Black Hills Experimental Forest
Stagebarn Crystal Cave
Black Hills Petrified Forest
Black Hawk
Buckhorn
BLACK HILLS NATIONAL FOREST
LIMESTONE PLATEAU
SPEARFISH CANYON
STRAWBERRY RIDGE
BEAR BUTTE CREEK
Four Corners
Beaver Creek
Deerfield
Custer Trail
Dutchman
Deerfield Reservoir
Redbank Spring
Ditch Creek
Moon
Mystic
White Tail Peak
Seth Bullock Tr △5,422'
Redfern Mtn △6,075'
Bear Gulch
Pactola Res
Johnson Siding
Hisega
Thunderhead
Black Hills Caverns
Rapid City
WYOMING
SOUTH DAKOTA
REDBIRD CANYON
ZIMMER RIDGE
REYNOLDS PRAIRIE
Redfern
Cooper Mtn
Hill City
Black Hills Central RR
Medicine Mtn △6,878'
Oreville
Willow Creek
Bear Mtn △7,172'
Signal Hill △6,483'
Crazy Horse Mon
Cathedral Spires
Buckhorn Mtn △6,392'
Bismarck Lake
Harney Pk △7,242'
Mount Rushmore
MT RUSHMORE NAT'L MEM
Iron Creek
Norbeck Memorial
Sheridan Lake
Southside
North Cove
Bluelead Mtn △5,170'
Silver Mtn △6,405'
Stratobowl
Sitting Bull Crystal Caverns
Rockerville
Keystone
Rushmore Cave
Hayward
Hermosa
Red Shirt
JEWEL CAVE NAT'L MON
Historic Entrance
Contanche Park
Sanator
Custer
National Woodcarving
Norbeck Wildlife Preserve
Blue Bell
Cicero Peak △6,168'
CUSTER STATE PARK
Badger Hole
Game Lodge
East French Creek
Wildlife Station
Fairburn
Elk Mtn △5,662'
Pringle
Rifle Pit
Elk Mtn
Wind Cave
WIND CAVE NATIONAL PARK
Wildlife Loop
RANKIN RIDGE
BOWMAN RIDGE
ANTELOPE RIDGE
HELL CANYON
ELK MOUNTAINS
Sullivan Peak △4,967'
Black Hills Playhouse
Argyle
Hot Springs
Oelrichs

94

N

0 5 10 Miles
0 5 10 15 Kilometers

6
5
4
3
2
1

A   B   C   D

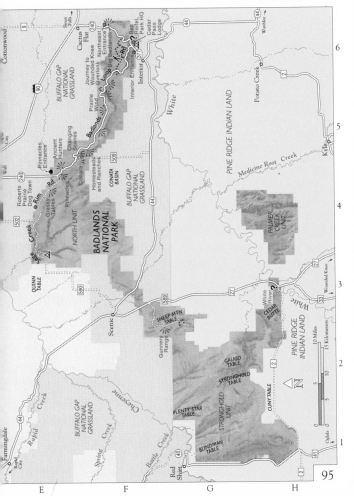

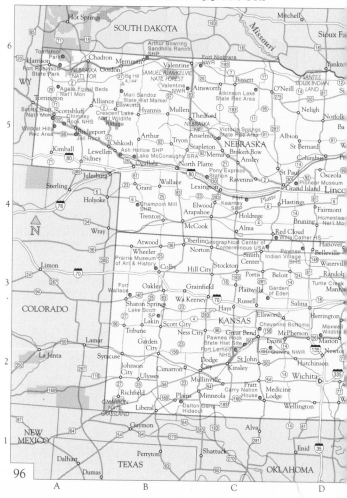

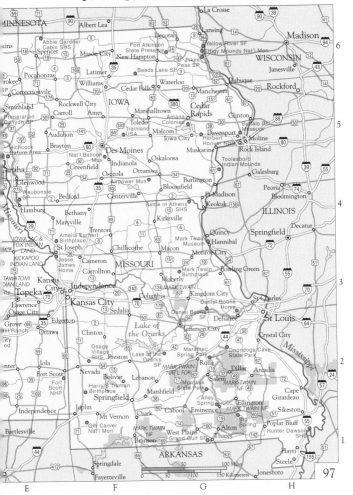

The Ozarks MISSOURI

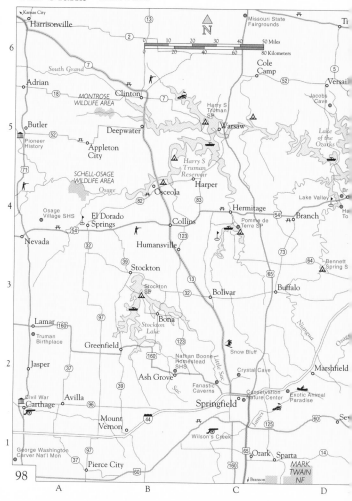

98

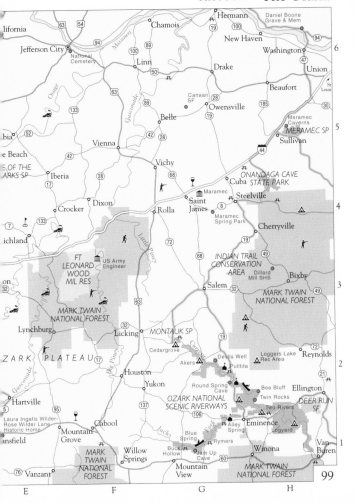

The Mother Road, Historic Route 66

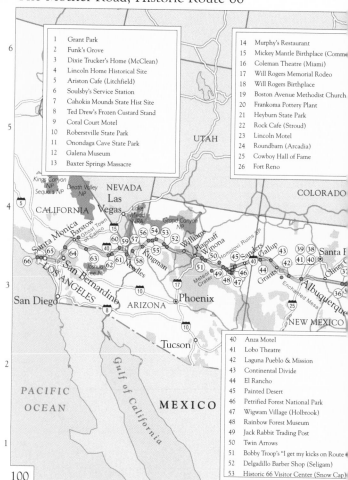

1	Grant Park
2	Funk's Grove
3	Dixie Trucker's Home (McClean)
4	Lincoln Home Historical Site
5	Ariston Cafe (Litchfield)
6	Soulsby's Service Station
7	Cahokia Mounds State Hist Site
8	Ted Drew's Frozen Custard Stand
9	Coral Court Motel
10	Robertsville State Park
11	Onondaga Cave State Park
12	Galena Museum
13	Baxter Springs Massacre

14	Murphy's Restaurant
15	Mickey Mantle Birthplace (Comme
16	Coleman Theatre (Miami)
17	Will Rogers Memorial Rodeo
18	Will Rogers Birthplace
19	Boston Avenue Methodist Church
20	Frankoma Pottery Plant
21	Heyburn State Park
22	Rock Cafe (Stroud)
23	Lincoln Motel
24	Roundbarn (Arcadia)
25	Cowboy Hall of Fame
26	Fort Reno

40	Anza Motel
41	Lobo Theatre
42	Laguna Pueblo & Mission
43	Continental Divide
44	El Rancho
45	Painted Desert
46	Petrified Forest National Park
47	Wigwam Village (Holbrook)
48	Rainbow Forest Museum
49	Jack Rabbit Trading Post
50	Twin Arrows
51	Bobby Troop's "I get my kicks on Route
52	Delgadillo Barber Shop (Seligam)
53	Historic 66 Visitor Center (Snow Cap)

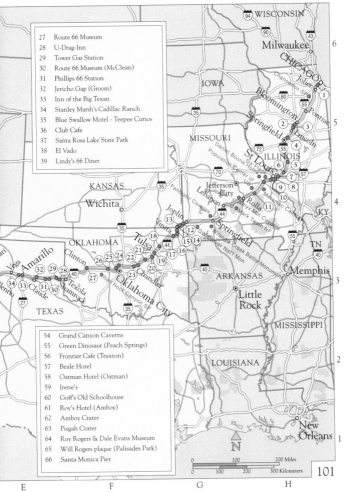

The Mother Road, Historic Route 66

27 Route 66 Museum
28 U-Drag-Inn
29 Tower Gas Station
30 Route 66 Museum (McClean)
31 Phillips 66 Station
32 Jericho Gap (Groom)
33 Inn of the Big Texan
34 Stanley Marsh's Cadillac Ranch
35 Blue Swallow Motel - Teepee Curios
36 Club Cafe
37 Santa Rosa Lake State Park
38 El Vado
39 Lindy's 66 Diner

54 Grand Canyon Caverns
55 Green Dinosaur (Peach Springs)
56 Frontier Cafe (Truxton)
57 Beale Hotel
58 Oatman Hotel (Oatman)
59 Irene's
60 Goff's Old Schoolhouse
61 Roy's Hotel (Amboy)
62 Amboy Crater
63 Pisgah Crater
64 Roy Rogers & Dale Evans Museum
65 Will Rogers plaque (Palisades Park)
66 Santa Monica Pier

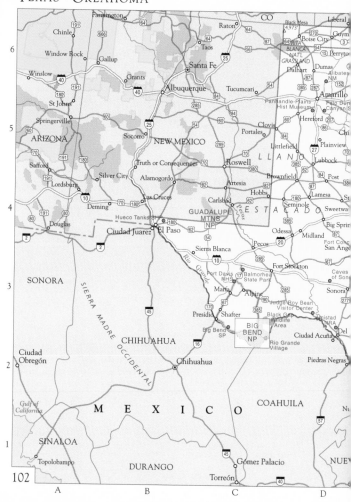

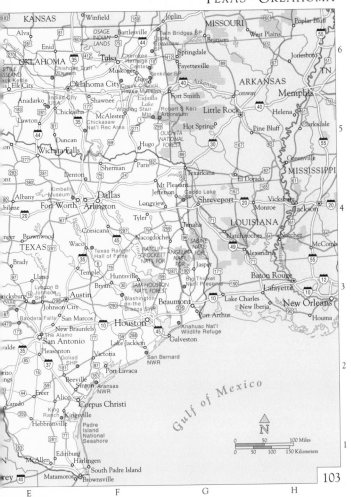

Guadalupe Mountains NP TEXAS

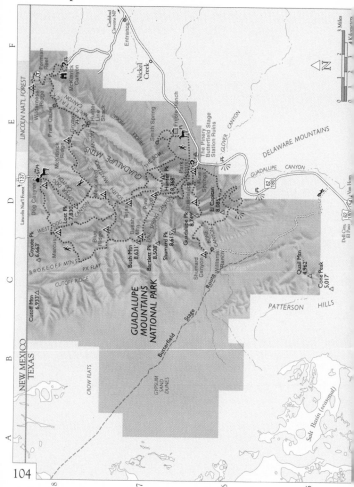

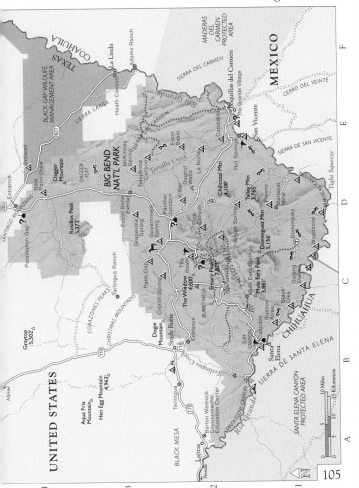

Texas Hill Country

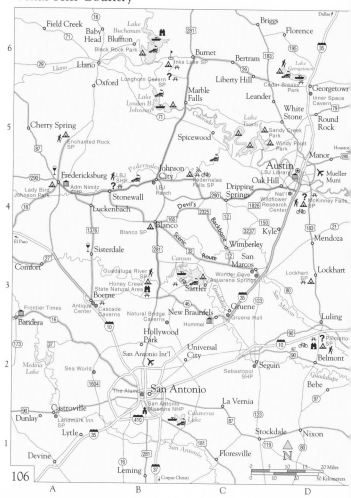

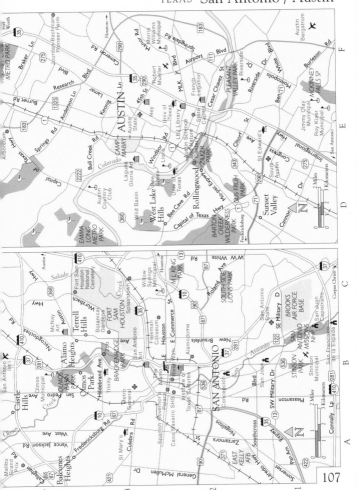

107

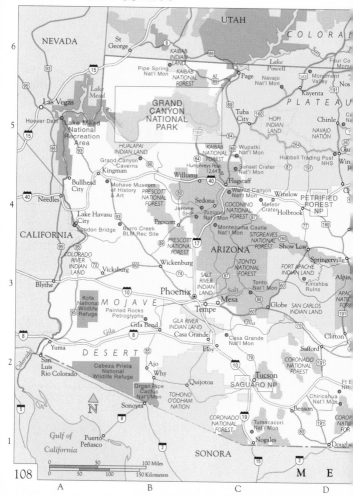

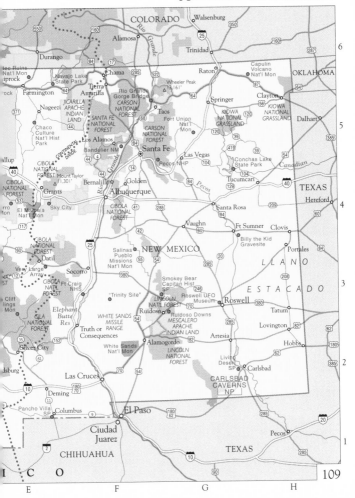

New Mexico Pueblos

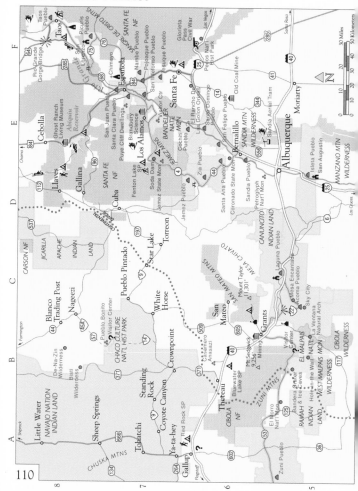

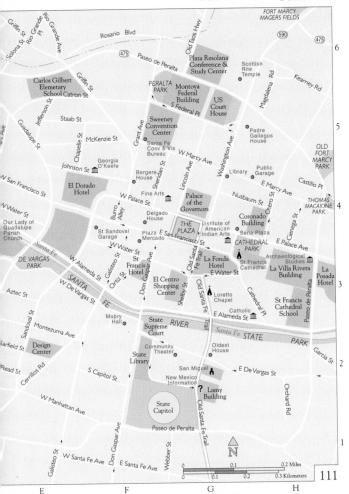

Carlsbad Caverns NP NEW MEXICO

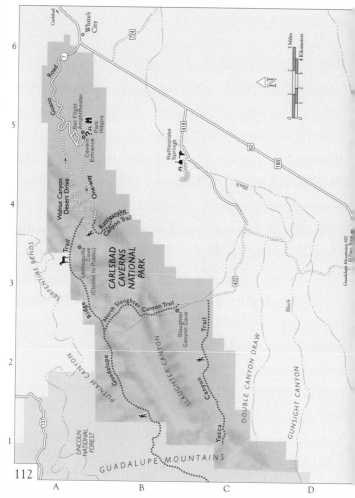

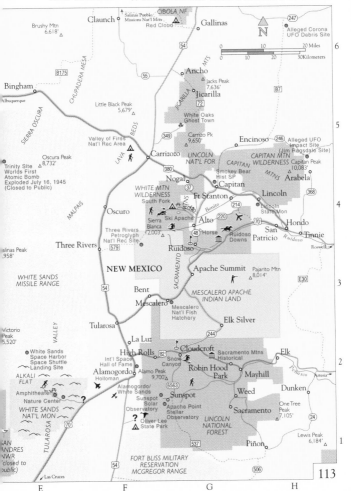

113

Petrified Forest NP ARIZONA

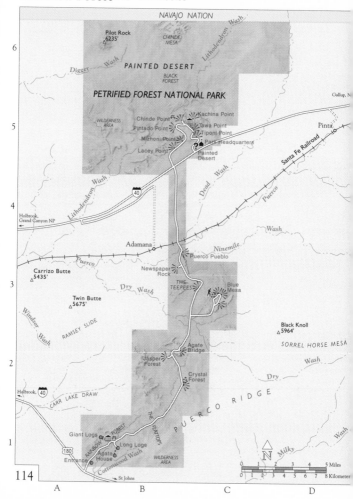

NAVAJO NATION

Pilot Rock
6235'

CHINDE MESA

PAINTED DESERT

BLACK FOREST

PETRIFIED FOREST NATIONAL PARK

Digger Wash

Lithodendron Wash

Gallup, N

WILDERNESS AREA

Chinde Point   Kachina Point
Pintado Point   Tawa Point
Nizhoni Point   Tiponi Point
Lacey Point   Park Headquarters
                Painted Desert

Pinta

Santa Fe Railroad

Lithodendron Wash

Dead Wash

Puerco

Wash

Holbrook,
Grand Canyon NP

Adamana

Ninemile

Wash

Puerco Pueblo

Carrizo Butte
△5435'

Puerco

Newspaper Rock

THE TEEPEES   Blue Mesa

Twin Butte
△5675'

Dry Wash

RAMSEY SLIDE

Black Knoll
△5964'

SORREL HORSE MESA

Agate Bridge

Wash

Jasper Forest

Crystal Forest

Dry

Wash

Holbrook

PUERCO RIDGE

CARR LAKE DRAW

THE FLATTOPS

Milky

Wash

Giant Logs

RAINBOW FOREST

Long Logs

180   Agate House

Entrance

Cottonwood Wash

WILDERNESS AREA

St Johns

N

0   1   2   3   4   5 Miles
0   1   2   3   4   5   6   7   8 Kilometer

114

A   B   C   D

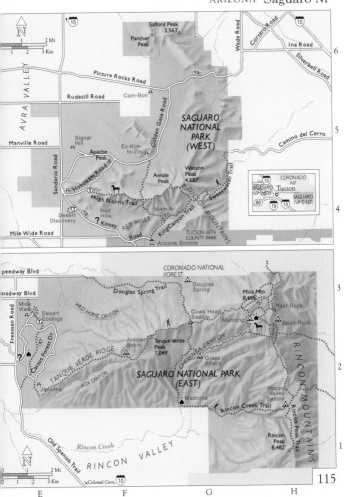

Grand Canyon NP ARIZONA

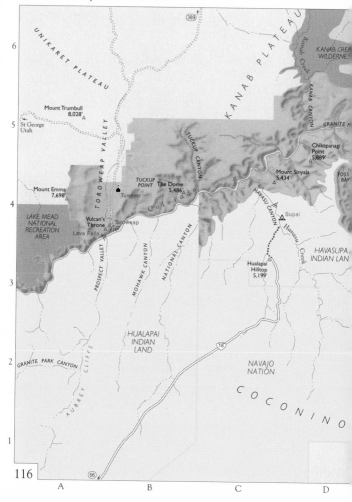

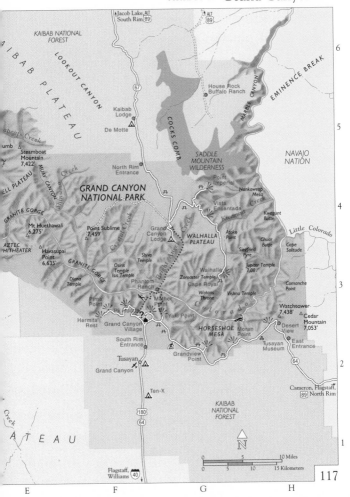

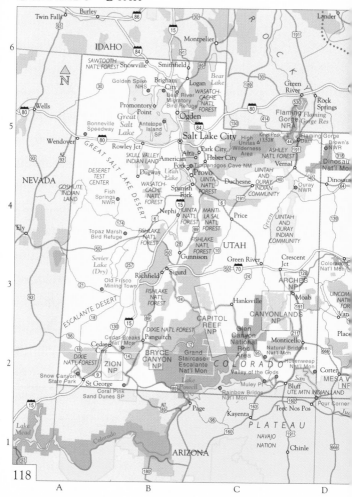

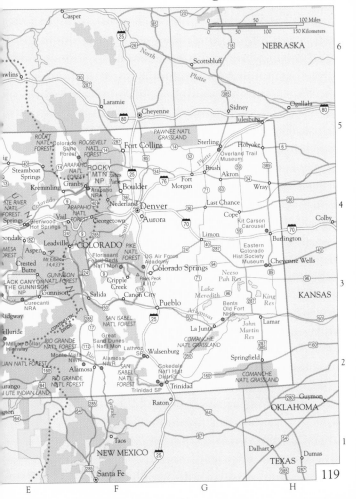

Central Colorado Skiing

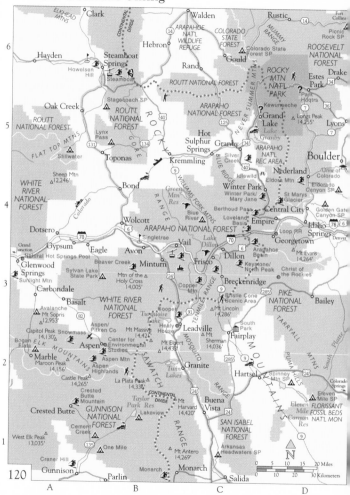

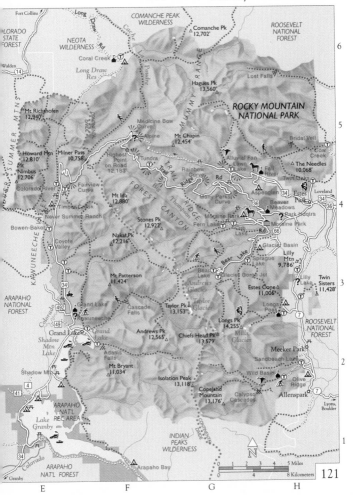

Fort Collins

COLORADO STATE FOREST

Walden

14

NEOTA WILDERNESS

Long Draw Rd

Long Draw Res

COMANCHE PEAK WILDERNESS

Comanche Pk 12,702'

ROOSEVELT NATIONAL FOREST

6

Coral Creek

Hagues Pk 13,560'

Lost Falls

Twin Lakes

5

Mt Richthofen 12,940'

Milner Pass 10,758'

Howard Mtn 12,810'

Mt Nimbus 12,706'

Medicine Bow Curve

Alpine

Highest Point on Road 12,183'

Mt Chapin 12,454'

Tundra

Rainbow Curve

Alluvial Fan

Lawn Lake

Fall River

MUMMY RANGE

ROCKY MOUNTAIN NATIONAL PARK

Bridal Veil

Cow Creek

The Needles 10,068'

Colorado River

Fairview Curve

Never Summer Ranch

Mt Ida 12,880'

FOREST CANYON

Trail Ridge Rd

Many Parks Curve

Aspenglen

Fall River Rd

Beaver Meadows

Park Headqtrs

Moraine Park

Estes Park

Loveland

34

36

4

Coyote Valley

Stones Pk 12,922'

Nakai Pk 12,216'

Bear Lake Rd

Fern Lake

Moraine Park

Sprague Lake

Glacier Basin

Lilly Mtn 9,786'

Lily Lake

36

66

Bowen-Baker

34

492

Grand Lake

Kawuneeche

Mt Patterson 11,424'

Cascade Falls

Taylor Pk 13,153'

Bear Lake

Andrews Glacier

Taylor Glacier

Glacier Gorge Jct

Estes Cone 11,006'

Longs Pk

Twin Sisters 11,428'

3

ARAPAHO NATIONAL FOREST

KAWUNEECHE

49

Grand Lake

Shadow Mtn Lake

Adams Falls

Andrews Pk 12,565'

Chiefs Head Pk 13,579'

Longs Pk 14,255'

Mills Glacier

Longs Peak

7

Meeker Park

ROOSEVELT NATIONAL FOREST

2

Shadow Mtn

41

4

ARAPAHO NAT'L REC AREA

Mt Bryant 11,034'

Isolation Peak 13,118'

Copeland Mountain 13,176'

Calypso Cascades

Sandbeach Lake

Wild Basin

Olive Ridge

Allenspark

7

Lyons, Boulder

Lake Granby

INDIAN PEAKS WILDERNESS

1

34

Colorado

Granby

ARAPAHO NAT'L FOREST

Arapaho Bay

0 1 2 3 4 5 Miles
0   4   8 Kilometers

N

121

E   F   G   H

Mesa Verde NP COLORADO

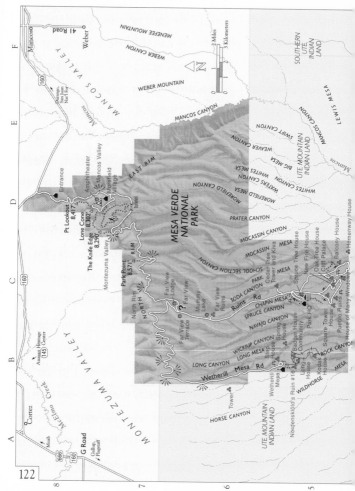

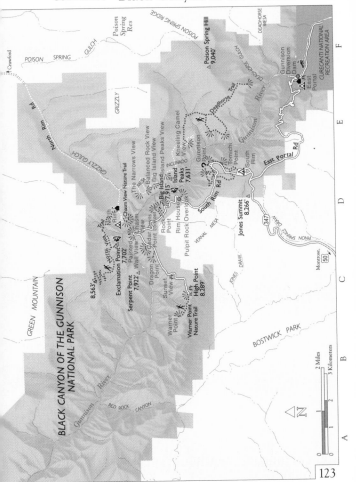

BLACK CANYON OF THE GUNNISON NATIONAL PARK

GREEN MOUNTAIN

Gunnison River

RED ROCK CANYON

BOSTWICK PARK

Montrose 50

PIÑON DRAW

JONES DRAW

347

Jones Summit 8,266'

South Rim Rd

East Portal Rd

VERNAL MESA

Warner Point Nature Trail

Warner Point 7,177'

High Point 8,289'

Sunset View

Dragon Point

Cedar Point

Rock Point

Rim House

Pulpit Rock Overlook

Painted Wall View

Chasm View

Serpent Point 7,922'

Exclamation Point 7,702'

North Vista Trail

8,563'

North Rim

Cliami View Nature Trail

The Narrows View

Balanced Rock View

Big Island View

Island Peaks View

Kneeling Camel View

Gunnison Point

Tomichi Point

South Rim

Big Island 7,915'

Island Peaks 7,631'

GRIZZLY GULCH

North Rim Rd

POISON SPRING GULCH

GRIZZLY

Poison Spring Res

POISON SPRING GULCH

Crawford

Deadhorse Trail

Deadhorse Gulch

Poison Spring Hill 9,040'

Gunnison River

DEADHORSE MESA

Gunnison Diversion Dam

East Portal

CURECANTI NATIONAL RECREATION AREA

0 Miles 2
0 Kilometers 3

N

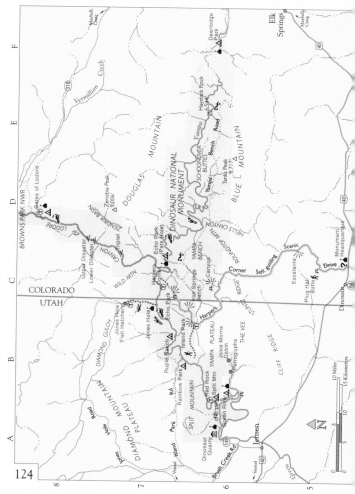

Dinosaur NM UTAH-COLORADO

Morwell Craig

Elk Springs

40

Deerlodge Park

BROWNS PARK NWR

318

Vermillion Creek

Gates of Lodore

LODORE

Zenobia Peak 9,006'

ZENOBIA BASIN

DOUGLAS MOUNTAIN

Haystack Rock 6,544'

Yampa Road

SCHOONOVER BUTTE

Yampa Bench

Tanks Peak 8,717'

BLUE MOUNTAIN

DINOSAUR NATIONAL MONUMENT

Hells Canyon

Upper Disaster
Lower Disaster

CANYON

Triplet

WILD MTN

Echo Park (Pats Hole)

Haldens Camp

ROUNDTOP MTN

Corner

YAMPA BENCH

Monument Headquarters

COLORADO

UTAH

Pool Creek

Warm Springs Bench

Scenic

Self-guiding

Escalante

Plug Hat Butte

DINOSAUR

40

DIAMOND GULCH

Jones Hole Fish Hatchery

Jones Hole

Echo Park

Canyon

STUNTZ RIDGE

Drive

64

HOLE

DIAMOND MOUNTAIN PLATEAU

Jones Hole Rd

Rupie Ranch

Rainbow Park

Island Park

Split Mtn

Harpers

YAMPA PLATEAU

THE VEE

Petroglyphs

Josie Morris Cabin

CLIFF RIDGE

Vernal Island

SPLIT MOUNTAIN

Red Rock

Green River

Dinosaur Quarry

149

Jensen

Brush Creek Rd.

40

Vernal

Green

124

N

10 Miles

15 Kilometers

5   10   15

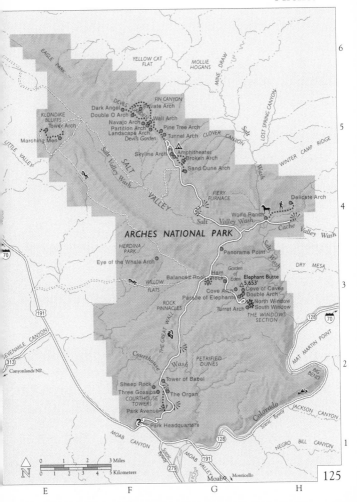

Bryce Canyon NP UTAH

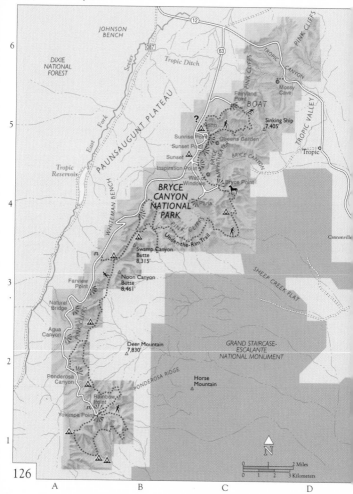

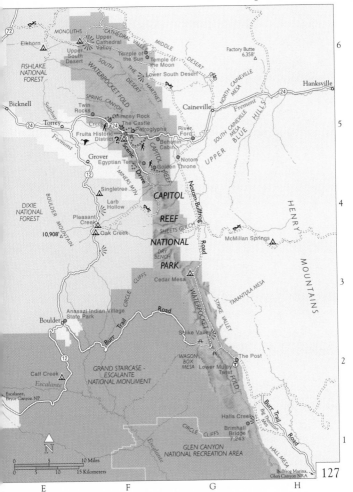

Zion NP UTAH

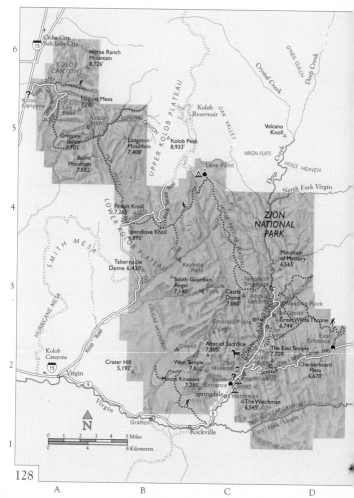

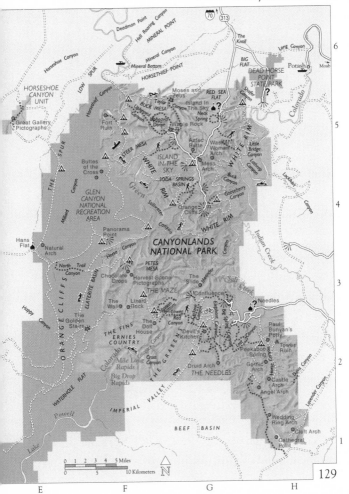

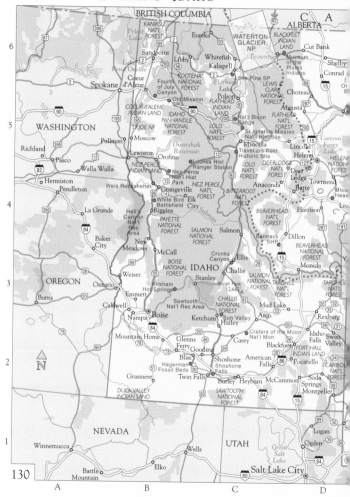

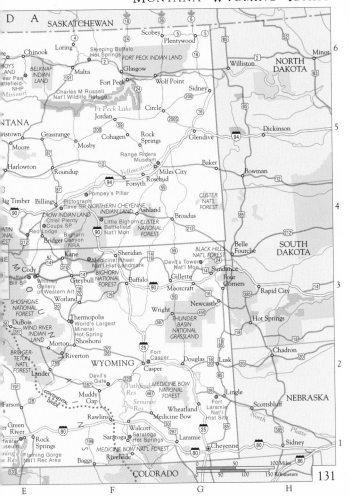

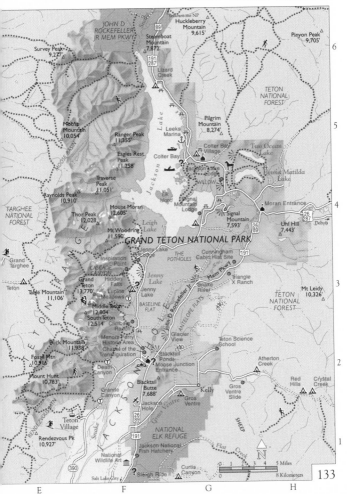

JOHN D
ROCKEFELLER
JR MEM PKWY

Huckleberry
Mountain
9,615'

Steamboat
Mountain
7,872'

Survey Peak
9,227'

Pinyon Peak
9,705'

Lizard
Creek

TETON
NATIONAL
FOREST

Moose
Mountain
10,054'

Ranger Peak
11,355'

Pilgrim
Mountain
8,274'

Leeks
Marina

Colter Bay
Village

Two Ocean
Lake

Eagles Rest
Peak
11,258'

Colter Bay

Jackson Lake
Lodge

Emma Matilda
Lake

Traverse
Peak
11,051'

Elk
Island

Signal
Mountain
Lodge

Moran Entrance

Reynolds Peak
10,910'

TARGHEE
NATIONAL
FOREST

Thor Peak
12,028'

Mount Moran
12,605'

Leigh
Lake

GRAND TETON NATIONAL PARK

Signal
Mountain
7,593'

Uhl Hill
7,443'

Dubois

Mt Woodring
11,590'

THE
POTHOLES

Cunningham
Cabin Hist Site

Grand
Targhee

Jenny Lake

Inspiration
Point

CASCADE
CANYON

Grand
Teton
13,770'

Hidden
Falls

Lupine
Meadows

Jenny
Lake

Snake
River

Triangle
X Ranch

Mt Leidy
10,326'

Table Mountain
11,106'

Teton

BASELINE
FLAT

TETON
NATIONAL
FOREST

Middle Teton
12,804'

South Teton
12,514'

Climbers'
Ranch

Menors Ferry
Historic Area

Chapel of the
Transfiguration

Glacier
View

Teton Science
School

Buck Mountain
11,938'

Blacktail
Ponds

Atherton
Creek

Fossil Mtn
10,916'

Death
Canyon

Moose Junction
Entrance

Mount Hunt
10,783'

Blacktail
Butte
7,688'

Red
Hills

Crystal
Creek

Granite
Canyon

Kelly

Gros
Ventre
Slide

Teton
Village

Gros
Ventre

SHEEP

Rendezvous Pk
10,927'

NATIONAL
ELK REFUGE

Jackson Hole

Flat
Creek

National
Wildlife Art

Jackson National
Fish Hatchery

Curtis
Canyon

Salt Lake City

Sleigh Ride

N

0   1   2   3   4   5 Miles

0   8 Kilometers

E   F   G   H

Hell's Canyon NRA IDAHO–OREGON

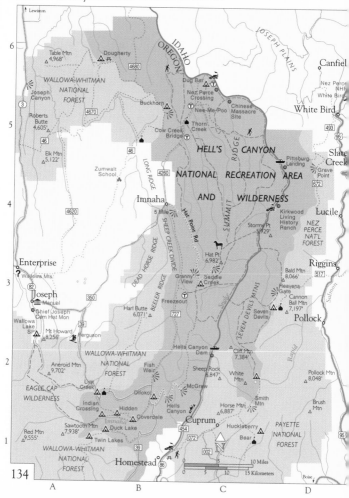

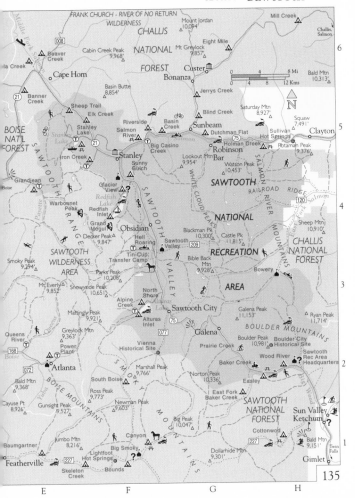

FRANK CHURCH - RIVER OF NO RETURN
WILDERNESS

CHALLIS

Mount Jordan
10,094'

Eight Mile

Mill Creek

Challis,
Salmon

008

Cabin Creek Peak
9,968'

Mt Greylock
9,857'

Custer

NATIONAL

Beaver Creek

Cape Horn

Bonanza

FOREST

8 Mi

Bald Mtn
10,313'

0   4   8   12 Kms

21

Banner
Creek

Basin Butte
8,854'

Jerrys Creek

Blind Creek

Saturday Mtn
8,927'

Squaw
7,491'

N

BOISE
NAT'L
FOREST

Sheep Trail

Elk Creek

Riverside

Salmon River

Basin
Creek

Sunbeam

Dutchman Flat

Sullivan
Hot Springs

Clayton

la Creek

Stanley
Lake

Stanley
Lake

21

Stanley

Big Casino
Creek

Robinson
Bar

Holman Creek

Potaman Peak
9,376'

Iron Creek

Sunny
Gulch

Lookout Mtn
9,954'

Watson Peak
10,453'

SAWTOOTH

Grandjean

Boise

Glacier
View

Redfish
Lake

SAWTOOTH RANGE

NATIONAL

Warbonnet
Peak

Redfish Inlet

Obsidian

Hell
Roaring

Blackman Pk
10,300'

Castle Pk
11,815'

RAILROAD RIDGE

East Fork Salmon

120

Sheep Mtn
10,910'

CHALLIS

Grand
Mogul

Decker Peak
9,847'

Sawtooth
Valley

209

Bible Back
Mtn
9,928'

RECREATION

NATIONAL

Smoky Peak
9,294'

SAWTOOTH
WILDERNESS
AREA

Tin-Cup
Transfer Camp

Parks Peak
9,208'

AREA

Bowery

FOREST

Mt Everly
9,852'

Snowyside Peak
10,651'

North
Shore

Rising
Lake

Galena Peak
11,153'

Ryan Peak
11,714'

Mattingly Peak
9,921'

Alpine
Creek

Alturas Inlet

Sawtooth City

Galena

Boulder Peak
10,981'

Boulder City
Historical Site

BOULDER MOUNTAINS

Sawtooth
Rec Area
Headquarters

Queens
River

168

Greylock Mtn
9,363'

075

Prairie Creek

Baker Creek

Wood River

Boise

072

Power
Plant

Atlanta

Vienna
Historical Site

SMOKY

Marshall Creek

Norton Peak
10,336'

Easley

SAWTOOTH

Bald Mtn
9,368'

BOISE MOUNTAINS

South Boise

Mattingly Peak
9,766'

East Fork
Baker Creek

NATIONAL

Sun Valley
Ketchum

Cayuse Pt
8,926'

Gunsight Peak
9,527'

Ross Peak
9,773'

Newman Peak
9,603'

Big Peak
10,047'

FOREST

Cottonwod

Bald Mtn
9,151'

MOUNTAINS

Canyon

227

Wood River

Baumgartner

Jumbo Mtn
8,216'

Big Smoky

Dollarhide Mtn
9,301'

Gimlet

Featherville

227

Lightfoot
Hot Springs

Bounds

Twin
Falls

Skeleton
Creek

E   F   G   H

135

Glacier NP MONTANA

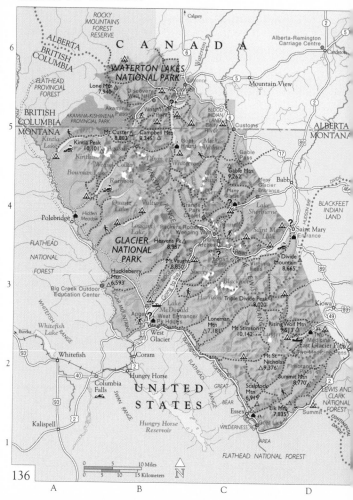

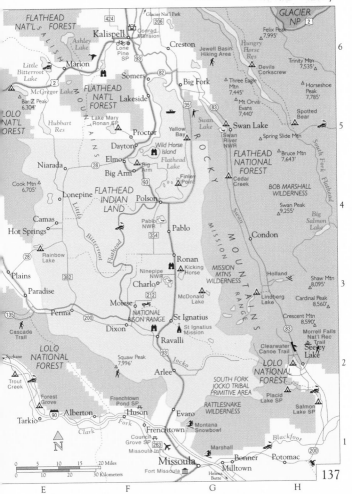

FLATHEAD NAT'L FOREST

Glacier Nat'l Park

GLACIER NP

424

206

Kalispell

Ashley Lake

Conrad Mansion

Creston

Felix Peak 7,995'

Little Bitterroot Lake 6,304'

Marion

2

Somers

Jewell Basin Hiking Area

Hungry Horse Res

Trinity Mtn 7,535'

Devils Corkscrew

McGregor Lake

82

Bar Z Peak 6,304'

FLATHEAD NAT'L FOREST

Lakeside

Big Fork

Three Eagle Mtn 7,445'

Horseshoe Peak 7,785'

OLO NAT'L OREST

Hubbart Res

Lake Mary Ronan SP

35

Yellow Bay

Mt Orvis Evans 7,440'

Spotted Bear

Proctor

Swan Lake

Swan Lake

Spring Slide Mtn

Dayton

Wild Horse Island

Swan River NWR

FLATHEAD NATIONAL FOREST

Elmo

Big Arm

Flathead Lake

Cedar Creek

Bruce Mtn 7,643'

Niarada

28

Big Arm

Finley Points

BOB MARSHALL WILDERNESS

Cook Mtn 6,705'

Lonepine

FLATHEAD INDIAN LAND

Polson

Swan Peak 9,255'

Big Salmon Lake

Camas

Little Bitterroot

93

Pablo NWR

354

Pablo

MISSION MOUNTAINS RANGE

Hot Springs

Rainbow Lake

Flathead

Condon

28

Ronan

Kicking Horse

Holland

382

Shaw Mtn 8,095'

Plains

Charlo

Ninepipe NWR

MISSION MTNS WILDERNESS

Lindberg Lake

Cardinal Peak 8,560'

Paradise

Moiese

212

McDonald Lake

Crescent Mtn 8,590'

135

Perma

NATIONAL BISON RANGE

St Ignatius

Morrell Falls Nat'l Rec Trail

Cascade Trail

Dixon

St Ignatius Mission

83

Clearwater Canoe Trail

Seeley Lake

Ravalli

93

Jocko

LOLO NATIONAL FOREST

Spokane

Perma

Squaw Peak 7,996'

Arlee

SOUTH FORK JOCKO TRIBAL PRIMITIVE AREA

Trout Creek

Forest Grove

Frenchtown Pond SP

Evaro

RATTLESNAKE WILDERNESS

Placid Lake SP

Salmon Lake SP

Tarkio

Alberton

90

Huson

Frenchtown

Montana Snowbowl

200

Clark

Fork

Council Grove SP

263

Missoula Int'l

Marshall

N

Missoula

Fort Missoula

Milltown

Bonner

Potomac

Helena, Butte

137

0 5 10 15 20 Miles

0 10 20 30 Kilometers

E F G H

6

5

4

3

2

1

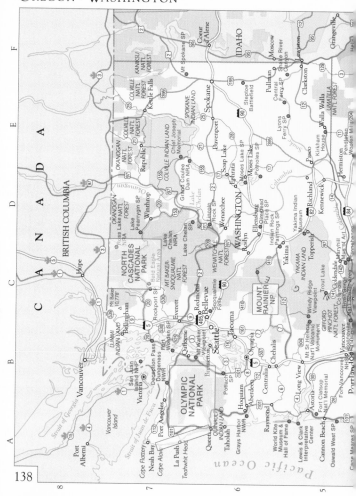

OREGON • WASHINGTON

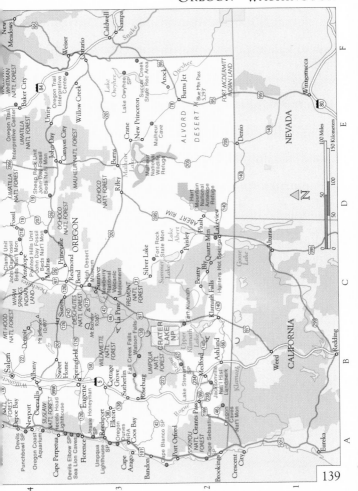

139

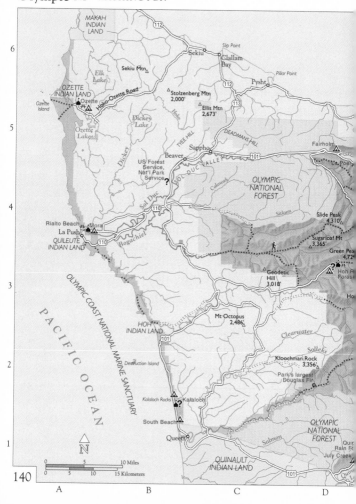

MAKAH
INDIAN LAND

112

Sekiu

Slip Point

Clallam
Bay

Pysht

Pillar Point

112

Elk
Lake

Sekiu Mtn

Ozette
Island

OZETTE
INDIAN LAND

Ozette

Hoko-Ozette Road

Stolzenberg Mtn
2,000'

113

Ellis Mtn
2,673'

DEADMANS HILL

Fairholm

La Poel

Ozette
Lake

Dickey
Lake

TYEE HILL

Sappho

Beaver

101

OLYMPIC
NATIONAL
FOREST

Dickey

US Forest
Service,
Nat'l Park
Service?

SOL DUC VALLEY

Calawah

Sitkum

Slide Peak
4,310'

Rialto Beach
Mora
La Push

110

Sol Duc

110

Sugarloaf Mt
3,365'

QUILEUTE
INDIAN LAND

Bogachiel

Green Peak
4,720'

Hoh R
Forest

OLYMPIC COAST NATIONAL MARINE SANCTUARY

Geodetic
Hill
3,018'

Ho

PACIFIC   OCEAN

HOH
INDIAN LAND

101

Mt Octopus
2,486'

Clearwater

Destruction Island

Solleks

Kloochman Rock
3,356'

Park's largest
Douglas Fir

Kalaloch Rocks

Kalaloch?

South Beach

Queets

Salmon

OLYMPIC
NATIONAL
FOREST

Quir

Rain Fc

July Creek

QUINAULT
INDIAN LAND

101

Quin

N

0   5   10 Miles

0   5   10   15 Kilometers

A   B   C   D

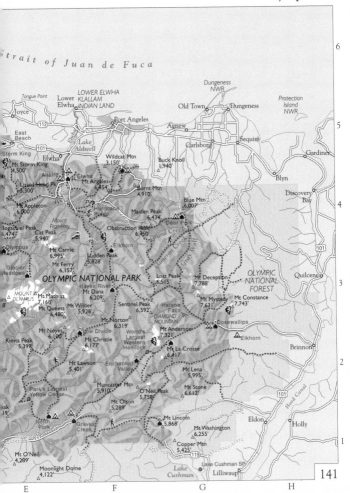

Strait of Juan de Fuca

6

LOWER ELWHA
Tongue Point   KLALLAM
Lower   INDIAN LAND
Elwha   Dungeness
                                    NWR   Protection
                          Old Town   Dungeness   Island
Joyce   NWR
                    Port Angeles   5
East   Agnew
Beach   112
Storm King   Lake   Carlsborg   Sequim
         Elwha   Aldwell   Gardiner
Mt Storm King   Wildcat Mtn   Buck Knoll
4,500'   Altaire   3,150'   1,940'   Blyn
Lizard Head Pk   Elwha   Discovery
5,300'   Mt Angeles   Bay
Mt Appleton   6,454'   Burnt Mtn
6,000'   Mount   4,910'
         Fitzhenry   Hurricane   Blue Mtn
Bogachiel Peak   Ridge   Maiden Peak   6,007'
5,474'   Cat Peak   Obstruction Point 6,434'   Deer Park   101
Olympus 5,940'   6,450'   Grand Creek
         Mt Carrie   Gray Wolf   OLYMPIC
Glacier 6,995'   Elkhorn   NATIONAL
Meadows Mt Ferry   Lillian Peak   Cameron Creek FOREST
         6,157'   5,828'   Lost Peak   Mt Constance
MOUNT   OLYMPIC NATIONAL PARK 6,515' Mt Deception   Quilcene 4
OLYMPUS Mt Mathias   Hayes River   7,788'
7,168'   7,168'   Mt Dana   Mt Mystery   Mt Constance
Mt Queets 5,928'   6,209' Sentinel Peak 7,631' 7,743'
6,480'   Mt Wilder   6,592' Hatana   Dosewallips
         Mt Norton Falls DIAMOND   Elkhorn   Brinnon 3
Mt Noyes   6,319'   MOUNTAIN
Kimta Peak 6,100' Low Divide World's   Mt Anderson
5,399'   Mt Christie Largest 7,321'
         6,177' Western Mt La Crosse
                 Hemlock 6,417'   Mt Lena
         Mt Lawson   Enchanted   5,995'
         5,401'   Valley   Mt Stone 2
Park's Largest   Muncaster Mtn 6,612'
Yellow Cedar   5,910'   O'Neil Peak
                    Mt Olson 5,758'   Hood Canal
North   5,289'   Mt Lincoln   Eldon   Holly
Fork   Graves   5,868'   Mt Washington
         Creek   6,255'   101
Mt O'Neil   Copper Mtn   1
4,289'   Moonlight Dome   5,425'   119
         4,122'   Lake   Lake Cushman SP
                  Cushman   Lilliwaup

141

E   F   G   H

Puget Sound and San Juan Islands WASHINGTON

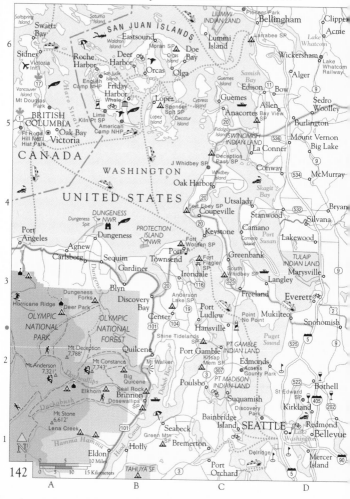

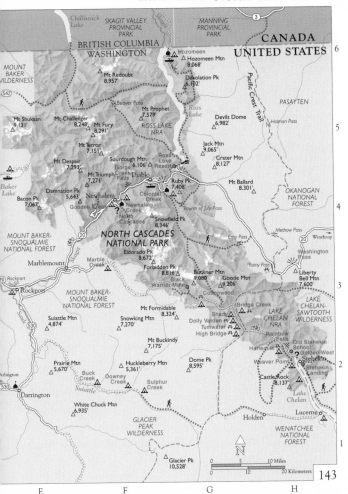

Chilliwack Lake

SKAGIT VALLEY PROVINCIAL PARK

MANNING PROVINCIAL PARK

3

BRITISH COLUMBIA
WASHINGTON

CANADA
UNITED STATES 6

MOUNT BAKER WILDERNESS

Hozomeen
Hozomeen Mtn 8,068'

Mt Redoubt 8,957'

Desolation Pk 6,102'

PASAYTEN

542

Beaver Pass

Ross Lake

Holman Pass

Pacific Crest Trail

Devils Dome 6,982'

5

Mt Shuksan 9,131'

Mt Challenger 8,248'

Mt Prophet 7,579'

Mt Fury 8,291'

ROSS LAKE NRA

Jack Mtn 9,065'

Mt Terror 7,151'

Crater Mtn 8,127'

Sourdough Mtn 6,106'

Ross Lake Resort

Mt Despair 7,293'

Gorge Creek Falls

Diablo

Ruby Pk 7,408'

Mt Ballard 8,301'

OKANOGAN NATIONAL FOREST

Baker Lake

Mt Triumph 7,271'

Colonial Creek

Damnation Pk 5,643'

Newhalem

Fourth of July Pass

Bacon Pk 7,067'

Goodell Creek

Newhalem Creek North Cascades

Snowfield Pk 8,346'

4

NORTH CASCADES NATIONAL PARK

Eldorado Pk 8,672'

Easy Pass

Methow Pass

20 Winthrop

MOUNT BAKER-SNOQUALMIE NATIONAL FOREST

Marblemount

Marble Creek

Forbidden Pk 8,816'

Buckner Mtn 9,080'

Goode Mtn 9,206'

Rainy Pass

20

Washington Pass

Liberty Bell Mtn 7,600'

Rockport SP

Black Warrior Mine

Cottonwood

LAKE CHELAN-SAWTOOTH WILDERNESS

3

20 Rockport

MOUNT BAKER-SNOQUALMIE NATIONAL FOREST

Mt Formidable 8,324'

Bridge Creek

Shady

LAKE CHELAN NRA

530

Suiattle Mtn 4,874'

Snowking Mtn 7,270'

Dolly Varden

Tumwater

Rainbow Falls

Rainbow Falls

Old Stehekin School

Golden West

Mt Buckindy 7,175'

High Bridge

Harlequin

Stehekin

Stehekin Landing

2

Arlington

Prairie Mtn 5,670'

Buck Creek

Downey Creek

Dome Pk 8,595'

Weaver Point

Castle Rock 8,137'

530 Darrington

Suiattle

Huckleberry Mtn 5,361'

Sulphur Creek

Lake Chelan

Lucerne

White Chuck Mtn 6,935'

GLACIER PEAK WILDERNESS

Holden

WENATCHEE NATIONAL FOREST

1

Glacier Pk 10,528'

N

0   5   10 Miles

0   10   20 Kilometers

143

E   F   G   H

Mt. Rainier NP WASHINGTON

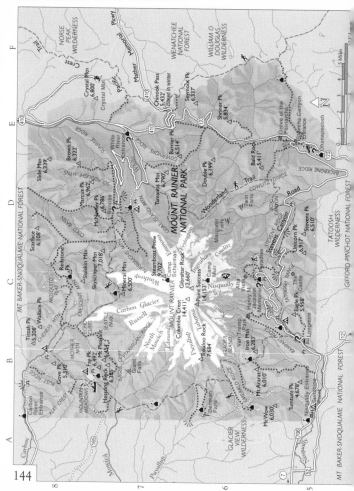

144

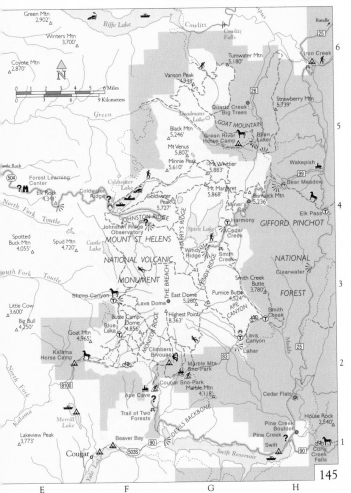

Oregon Coast

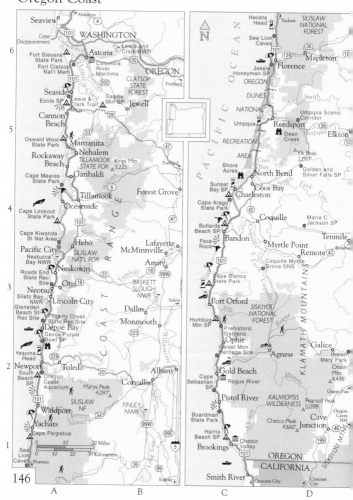

WASHINGTON

Seaview
Cape Disappointment
Fort Stevens State Park
Fort Clatsop Nat'l Mem
Astoria
Columbia River Maritime
Lewis and Clark NWR
Aberdeen
Seaside
Ecola SP
Lewis & Clark Trail
Cannon Beach
Saddle Mtn SP
Jewell
Oswald West State Park
Manzanita
Nehalem
Rockaway Beach
Garibaldi
TILLAMOOK STATE FOR
Kings Mtn 3,225'
Cape Meares State Park
Tillamook
Forest Grove
Oceanside
Cape Lookout State Park
Cape Kiwanda St Nat Area
Pacific City
Hebo
McMinnville
Lafayette
Nestucca Bay NWR
SIUSLAW NAT'L FOR
Roads End Rec Site
Neskowin
Amity
Oris
Neotsu
Siletz Bay NWR
Lincoln City
BASKETT SLOUGH NWR
Gleneden Beach St Rec Site
Fogarty Creek State Rec Site
Dallas
Depoe Bay
Devils Punch Bowl SP
Monmouth
Yaquina Head
Newport
Toledo
South Beach SP
Oregon Coast Aquarium
Marys Peak 4,097'
Corvallis
Albany
Waldport
SIUSLAW NF
Yachats
FINLEY NWR
Cape Perpetua
Sea Lion Caves
Florence

OREGON

Heceta Head
Yachats
SIUSLAW NATIONAL FOREST
Sea Lion Caves
Jessie Honeyman SP
Florence
Mapleton
OREGON DUNES
NATIONAL RECREATION AREA
Umpqua Scenic Corridor
Umpqua
Reedsport
Elkton
Dean Creek
Elk Peak 2,097'
Golden and Silver Falls SP
Shore Acres
Coos Bay
North Bend
Sunset Bay SP
Charleston
Coos Bay
Cape Arago State Park
Coquille
Maria C Jackson SP
Bullards Beach SP
Bandon
Myrtle Point
Remote
Tenmile
Face Rock
Coquille Myrtle Grove SNS
Cape Blanco State Park
SISKIYOU NATIONAL FOREST
Port Orford
Humbug Mtn SP
Prehistoric Gardens
Ophir
Geisel Mon Heritage Site
Agness
Galice
Indian Mary Park
Onion Mtn 4,438'
Cape Sebastian SP
Gold Beach
Rogue River
Grants Pass
Pistol River
KALMIOPSIS WILDERNESS
Pearsoll Peak 5,098'
Cave Junction
Oregon Caves NM
Boardman State Park
Chetco Peak 4,660'
Harris Beach SP
Chetco Valley
Brookings
SISKIYOU MTNS
OREGON
CALIFORNIA
Smith River
Crescent City

COAST RANGE

PACIFIC OCEAN

KLAMATH MOUNTAINS

20 Miles
30 Kilometers

A   B   C   D

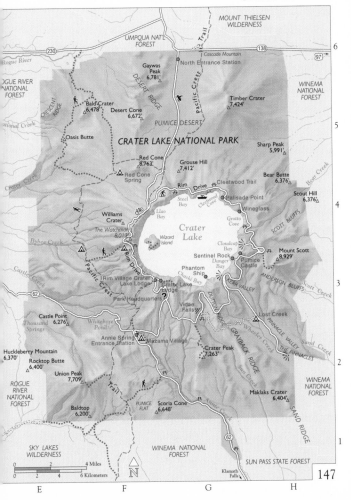

MOUNT THIELSEN
WILDERNESS

UMPQUA NAT'L
FOREST

230

Rogue River

North Entrance Station

Cascade Mountain

138

97

6

WINEMA
NATIONAL
FOREST

ROGUE RIVER
NATIONAL
FOREST

Gaywas
Peak
6,781'

DESERT RIDGE

Timber Crater
7,424'

Bald Crater
6,478'

Desert Cone
6,672'

Oasis Butte

PUMICE DESERT

CRATER LAKE NATIONAL PARK

Sharp Peak
5,991'

Red Cone
8,763'

Grouse Hill
7,412'

Red Cone
Spring

Rim
Drive

Cleetwood Trail

Bear Butte
6,376'

Bear Creek

Williams
Crater

The Watchman
8,013'

Steel
Bay

Llao
Bay

Cleetwood Cove

Palisade Point

Wineglass

Scout Hill
6,376'

SCOTT BLUFFS

Bybee Creek

Crater
Lake

Wizard Island

Grotto
Cove

Castle Creek

Pacific Crest

Rim Drive

Cloudcap
Bay

Sentinel Rock

Pumice
Castle

Mount Scott
8,929'

ANDERSON BLUFFS

Phantom
Ship

Chaski Bay

Danger
Bay

62

Rim Village Crater
Lake Lodge

Crater
Lake
Lodge

Park Headquarters

Vidae
Falls

KERR VALLEY

DUTTON CREEK

GRAYBACK RIDGE

Wheeler Creek

Lost Creek

PINNACLE VALLEY

THE PINNACLES

Sand Creek

Scott Creek

Castle Point
6,276'

Thousand
Springs

Whitehorse
Pond

Annie Spring
Entrance Station

Mazama Village

Crater Peak
7,263'

Huckleberry Mountain
6,370'

Rocktop Butte
6,400'

Union Peak
7,709'

ROGUE RIVER
NATIONAL
FOREST

Pacific Crest Trail

PUMICE
FLAT

Scoria Cone
6,648'

Annie Creek

Maklaks Crater
6,404'

WINEMA
NATIONAL
FOREST

SAND RIDGE

Baldtop
6,200'

SKY LAKES
WILDERNESS

62

WINEMA NATIONAL
FOREST

SUN PASS STATE FOREST

Klamath
Falls

0   2   4 Miles
0   2   4   6 Kilometers

N

147

E   F   G   H

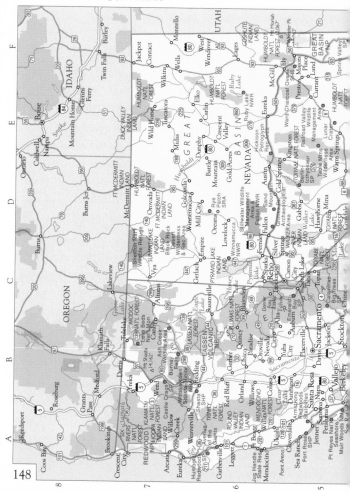

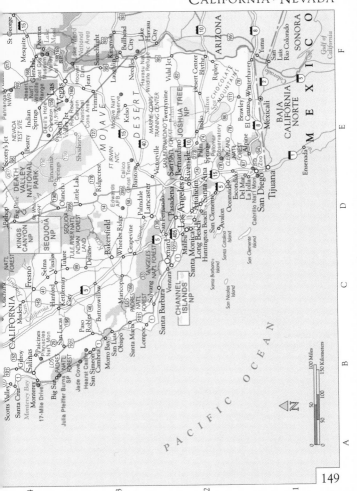

California Coast

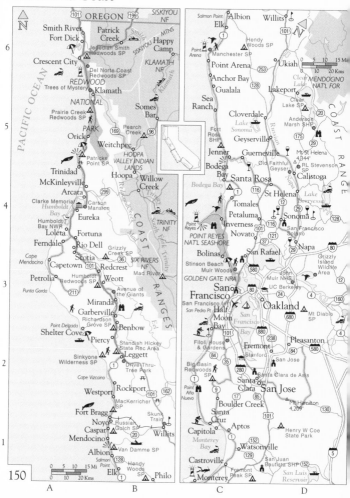

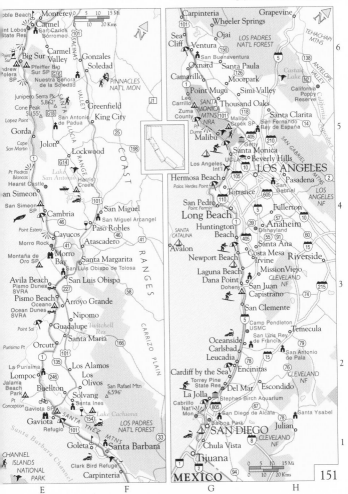

California Coast

Lassen Volcanic NP CALIFORNIA

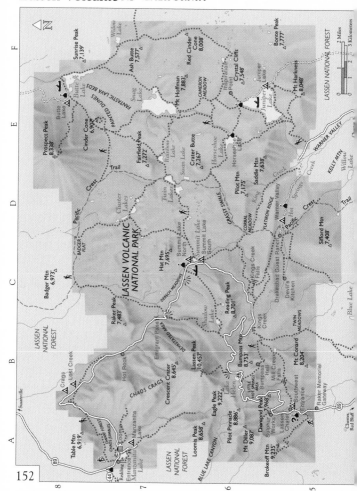

Northern California Wine Country

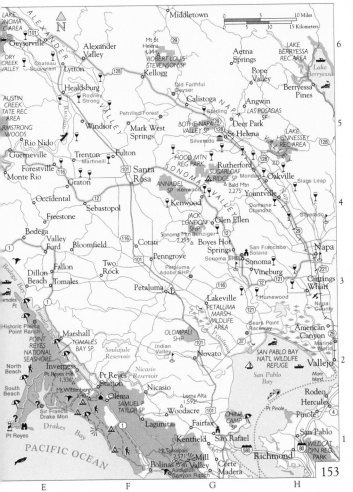

Yosemite NP CALIFORNIA

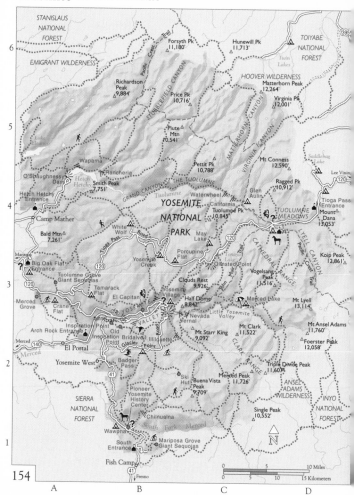

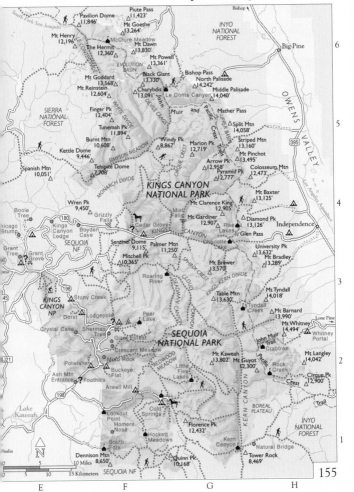

South Fork San Joaquin

Piute Pass
11,423'

Mt Goethe
13,264'

Bishop

Pavilion Dome
11,846'

Mt Henry
12,196'

McClure Meadow
Mt Dawn
13,830'

The Hermit
12,360'

*INYO
NATIONAL
FOREST*

Big Pine

*EVOLUTION
BASIN*

Mt Powell
13,361'

Black Giant
13,330'

Bishop Pass

North Palisade
14,242'

Mt Goddard
13,568'

Charybdis
13,091'

Middle Palisade
14,040'

Mt Reinstein
12,604'

Le Conte Canyon

Mather Pass

**SIERRA
NATIONAL
FOREST**

Finger Pk
12,404'

Split Mtn
14,058'

OWENS VALLEY

Tunemah Pk
11,894'

Windy Pk
8,867'

Marion Pk
12,719'

Striped Mtn
13,160'

395

Burnt Mtn
10,608'

Mt Pinchot
13,495'

Kettle Dome
9,446'

Arrow Pk
12,958'

Colosseum Mtn
12,473'

Tehipite Dome
7,708'

Pyramid Pk
12,777'

Spanish Mtn
10,051'

MONARCH DIVIDE

**KINGS CANYON
NATIONAL PARK**

Mt Baxter
13,125'

Wren Pk
9,450'

Mt Clarence King
12,905'

Diamond Pk
13,126'

Independence

Boole
Tree

Grizzly
Falls

Mist
Falls

Mt Gardiner
12,907'

Rae
Lakes

Glen Pass

Chicago
Stump

180

Kings
Canyon
Lodge

Boyden
Cave

Cedar Grove

Charlotte
Lake

University Pk
13,632'

Grant
Tree

**SEQUOIA
NF**

Sentinel Dome
9,115'

Palmer Mtn
11,250'

Mt Bradley
13,289'

Grant
Grove

Mitchell Pk
10,365'

Mt Brewer
13,570'

Roaring
River

Table Mtn
13,630'

**KINGS
CANYON NP**

Stony Creek

Mt Tyndall
14,018'

Dorst

Lodgepole

Pear
Lake

Tyndall
Creek

Mt Barnard
13,990'

Lone Pine

Crystal Cave

Sherman
Tree

Glen
Forest

**SEQUOIA
NATIONAL
PARK**

Mt Whitney
14,494'

Whitney
Portal

Potwisha

Crescent Meadow

Moro Rock

Mt Kaweah
13,802'

John Muir Trail

Grabtree

Ash Mtn
Entrance

Buckeye
Flat

Foothills

198

Mt Guyot
12,300'

Mt Langley
14,042'

Rock
Creek

Cirque Pk
12,900'

Lake
Kaweah

Atwell Mill

Little
Five
Lakes

**BOREAL
PLATEAU**

Lookout
Point

Homers
Nose

Cold
Springs

Florence Pk
12,432'

South
Fork

Hockett
Meadows

Kern
Canyon

Natural Bridge

*INYO
NATIONAL
FOREST*

Visalia

Dennison Mtn
8,650'

Quinn Pk
10,168'

Tower Rock
8,469'

SEQUOIA NF

N

5   10 Miles

5   10   15 Kilometers

E   F   G   H

Monterey Peninsula CALIFORNIA

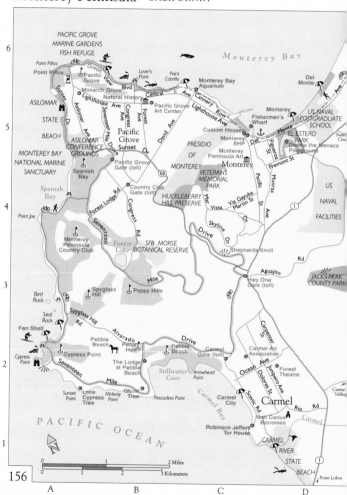

PACIFIC GROVE
MARINE GARDENS
FISH REFUGE

Monterey Bay

Point Piños
Point Piños
Ocean View
Pacific Grove
Monarch Grove
Natural History
Lover's Point
Point Cabrillo
Monterey Bay
Aquarium
Cannery Row
Del
Monte

ASILOMAR

Lighthouse Ave
Congress Ave
Forest
Central
Lighthouse Ave
Pacific Grove
Art Center
Monterey
Fisherman's
Wharf
US NAVAL
POSTGRADUATE
SCHOOL
Santa Cruz

STATE

BEACH

Pacific Grove
Sunset

Seventeen Mile Drive
David Ave
Custom House
PRESIDIO
OF
MONTEREY
Monterey SHP
Monterey
Peninsula Art
Monterey
Del Monte
EL ESTERO
PARK
Dennis the Menace
Playground

MONTEREY BAY
NATIONAL MARINE
SANCTUARY

Spanish Bay
Pacific Grove
Gate (toll)
VETERANS
MEMORIAL
PARK
Figueroa St
Pacific Ave
Fremont St

Spanish
Bay
Country Club
Gate (toll)
HUCKLEBERRY
HILL PRESERVE
Mar
Vista
Via Gayuba
Martin St
Munras Ave

Point Joe
Forest Lodge Rd
Congress Rd
Skyline
US
NAVAL
FACILITIES

Seventeen
Drive
1

Monterey
Peninsula
Country Club
Forest
Lake
SFB MORSE
BOTANICAL RESERVE
Shepherds Knoll

Mile
Aguajito
Rd
JACKS PEAK
COUNTY PARK

Bird
Rock
Spyglass
Hill
Poppy Hills
Hwy One
Gate (toll)

Seal
Rock
Spyglass Hill
Rd
Alvarado
Peter Hay
Pebble
Beach
Carmel Gate (toll)
Carpenter St.
Carmel Art
Association
Forest
Theatre

Fan Shell

Cypress
Point
Cypress Point
The Lodge
at Pebble
Beach
Stillwater
Cove
Arrowhead
Point
Ocean Ave
Junipero Ave
Dolores St.
Carmel

Seventeen
Mile
Ghost
Tree
Carmel
City
Scenic Rd
Carmel
Valley

Sunset
Point
Lone Cypress
Tree
Midway
Point
Pescadero Point
Carmel Bay
San Carlos
Borromeo
Rio
Rd
Carmel

PACIFIC OCEAN
Robinson Jeffers
Tor House
CARMEL
RIVER
STATE
BEACH

0   1   2 Miles
0   1   2   3 Kilometers

156

A   B   C   D

Point Lobos

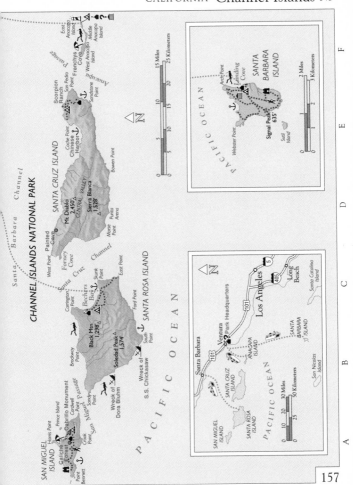

CHANNEL ISLANDS NATIONAL PARK

Santa Barbara Channel

SANTA CRUZ ISLAND

Mt Diablo 2,450'
Sierra Blanca 1,528'
CENTRAL VALLEY
Painted Cave
West Point
Forney Cove
Santa Cruz Channel
Punta Arena
Morse Point
Bowen Point

Scorpion Ranch
Coche Point
Chinese Harbor
Sandstone Point
San Pedro Point
Frenchys Cove
Prisoners Harbor

East Anacapa Island
West Anacapa Island
Middle Anacapa Island

Anacapa Passage

SANTA ROSA ISLAND

Black Mtn 1,298'
Soledad Peak 1,574'
Bechers Bay
Carrington Point
Skunk Point
East Point
Ford Point
South Point
Wreck of Dora Bluhm
Wreck of S.S. Chickasaw
Brockway Point

SAN MIGUEL ISLAND

Harris Point
Prince Island
Cardwell Point
Crook Point
Point Bennett
Cabrillo Monument
Caliche Forest
Simonton Cove
Sandy Point
San Miguel Passage

PACIFIC OCEAN

N

0   5   10   15 Miles
0   5   10   15   20   25 Kilometers

SANTA BARBARA ISLAND

Arch Point
Landing Cove
Webster Point
Signal Peak 635'
Sutil Island

PACIFIC OCEAN

N

0   1   2 Miles
0   1   2   3 Kilometers

Santa Barbara
Ventura
Park Headquarters
Los Angeles
Long Beach
101
5
405
SAN MIGUEL ISLAND
SANTA ROSA ISLAND
SANTA CRUZ ISLAND
ANACAPA ISLAND
SANTA BARBARA ISLAND
Santa Catalina Island
San Nicolas Island

PACIFIC OCEAN

N

0   10   20   30 Miles
0   25   50 Kilometers

157

Death Valley NP CALIFORNIA

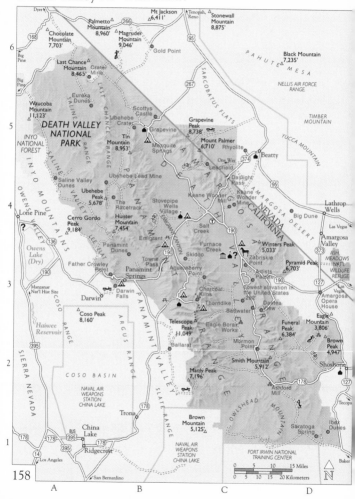

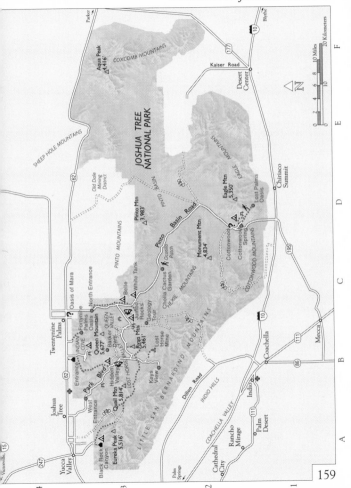

Lake Tahoe CALIFORNIA–NEVADA

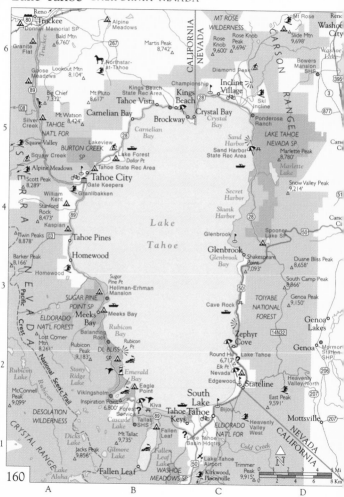

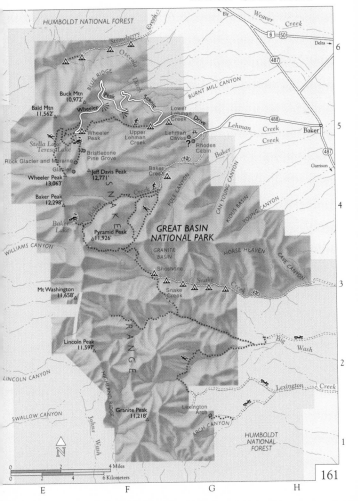

HUMBOLDT NATIONAL FOREST

Ely

Weaver

Creek

6

50

Delta

487

Strawberry

Creek

BLUE RIDGE

Oscosla

Buck Mtn
10,972'

Wheeler
Peak

BURNT MILL CANYON

488

Baker

Bald Mtn
11,562'

Lehman Creek

Lehman

Creek

5

Wheeler
Peak

Upper
Lehman
Creek

Lower
Lehman
Creek

Scenic

Drive

Lehman
Caves

Stella Lake
Teresa Lake

Rock Glacier and Moraine

Bristlecone
Pine Grove

Rhodes
Cabin

Garrison

Glacier

Jeff Davis Peak
12,771'

Baker
Creek

487

Wheeler Peak
13,063'

Baker
Creek

Baker Peak
12,298'

JOLE CANYON

Baker
Lake

Pyramid Peak
11,926'

GREAT BASIN
NATIONAL PARK

WILLIAMS CANYON

GRANITE
BASIN

Shoshone

CAN YOUNG CANYON

KIOUS BASIN

YOUNG CANYON

HORSE HEAVEN

CAVE CANYON

4

Mt Washington
11,658'

Snake
Creek

Snake
Creek

3

RANGE

Lincoln Peak
11,597'

Big
Wash

2

LINCOLN CANYON

HIGHLAND RIDGE

Lexington
Creek

SWALLOW CANYON

Johns Wash

Granite Peak
11,218'

Lexington
Arch

ARCH CANYON

HUMBOLDT
NATIONAL
FOREST

1

N

0   4 Miles

0   2   4   6 Kilometers

161

E   F   G   H

Las Vegas Strip   NEVADA

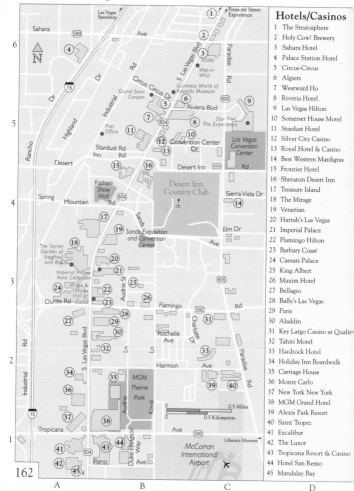

Sahara

Las Vegas
Speedway

Fremont Street
Experience

Las Vegas Blvd

Ave

589

Circus Circus Dr

Grand Slam
Canyon

Guinness World of
Records Museum

Wet-n-Wild

Riviera Blvd

Star Trek:
The Experience

Post
Office

Stardust Rd

Convention Center
Dr

Las Vegas
Convention
Center

Stardust
Inn

Rd

Desert

Spring

Mountain

Desert Inn

Rd

Fashion
Show
Mall

Desert Inn
Country Club

Sierra Vista Dr

Sands

Sands Exposition
and Convention
Center

Elm Dr

Ave

The Secret
Garden of
Siegfried
and Roy

Imperial Palace
Auto Collection

Magic &
Movie
Hall of
Fame

Audrie St

Dunes Rd

Flamingo

Rochelle
Ave

Charlotte Dr

Rd

Harmon

Ave

MGM
Theme
Park

Audrie

Royal

0.5 Miles

0.5 Kilometers

Tropicana

Duke Ellington Way

Reno

Ave

McCarran
International
Airport

Liberace Museum

Industrial

Rancho

Rd

Highland

Dr

Industrial

Rd

Paradise

Rd

Paradise

Rd

15

162

A   B   C   D

6

5

4

3

2

1

N

Hotels/Casinos

1 The Stratosphere
2 Holy Cow! Brewery
3 Sahara Hotel
4 Palace Station Hotel
5 Circus-Circus
6 Algiers
7 Westward Ho
8 Riviera Hotel
9 Las Vegas Hilton
10 Somerset House Motel
11 Stardust Hotel
12 Silver City Casino
13 Royal Hotel & Casino
14 Best Western Mardigras
15 Frontier Hotel
16 Sheraton Desert Inn
17 Treasure Island
18 The Mirage
19 Venetian
20 Harrah's Las Vegas
21 Imperial Palace
22 Flamingo Hilton
23 Barbary Coast
24 Caesars Palace
25 King Albert
26 Maxim Hotel
27 Bellagio
28 Bally's Las Vegas
29 Paris
30 Aladdin
31 Key Largo Casino at Qualit
32 Tahiti Motel
33 Hardrock Hotel
34 Holiday Inn Boardwalk
35 Carriage House
36 Monte Carlo
37 New York New York
38 MGM Grand Hotel
39 Alexis Park Resort
40 Saint Tropez
41 Excalibur
42 The Luxor
43 Tropicana Resort & Casino
44 Hotel San Remo
45 Mandalay Bay

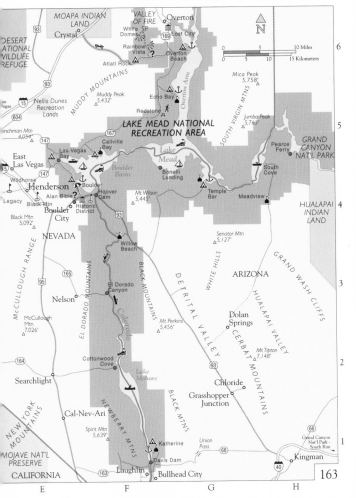

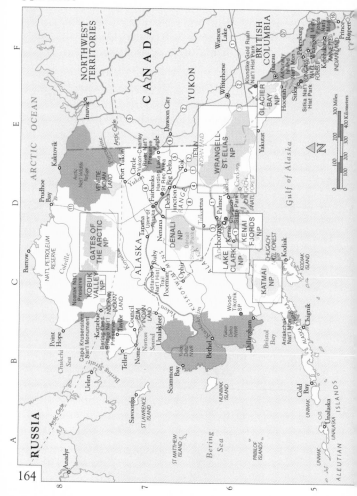

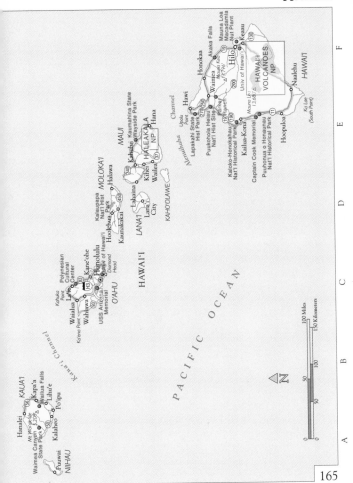

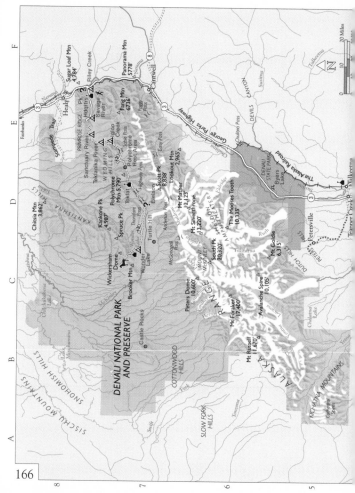

Denali NP ALASKA

166

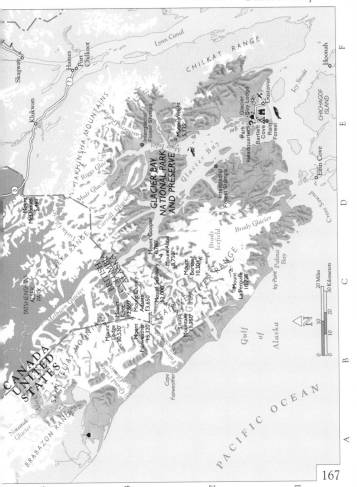

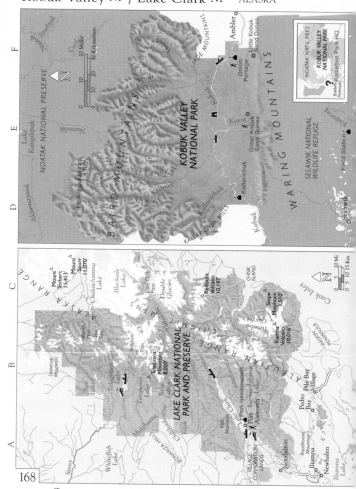

Kobuk Valley NP / Lake Clark NP   ALASKA

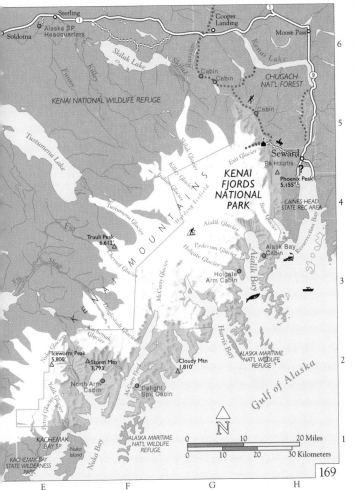

Wrangell-St. Elias NP   ALASKA

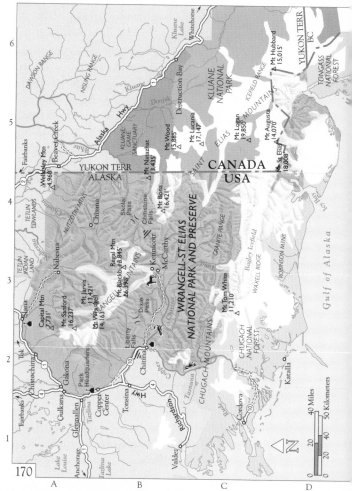

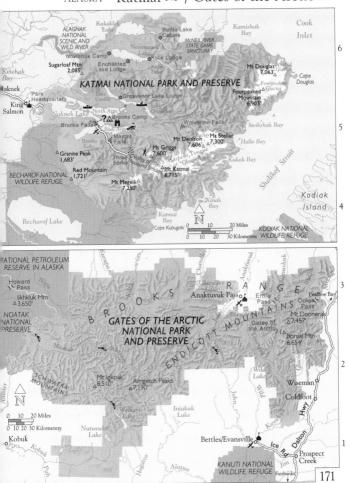

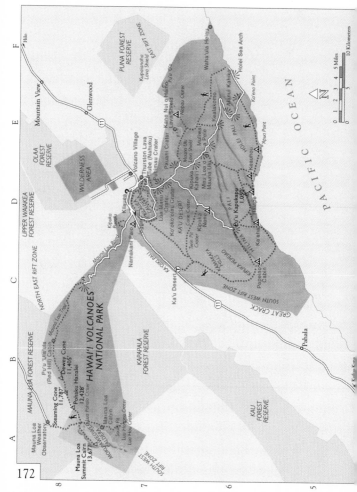

172

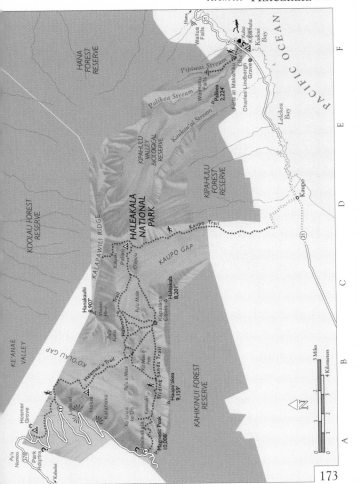

PACIFIC OCEAN

Hana

Wailua Falls

Kukui Bay

Kipahulu

Kalahu Point

Charles Lindbergh Grave

Ohe'o

Falls at Makahiku

Waimoku Falls

Pipiwai Stream

Palikea 2,224

Palikea Stream

HANA FOREST RESERVE

Kaukini at Stream

Lelekea Bay

Kaupo

KIPAHULU VALLEY BIOLOGICAL RESERVE

KIPAHULU FOREST RESERVE

KOOLAU FOREST RESERVE

KE'ANAE VALLEY

KO'OLAU GAP

KALAPAWILI RIDGE

HALEAKALA NATIONAL PARK

KAUPO GAP

Kaupo Trail

Hanakauhi 8,907

Mauna Hina

Paliku

O'ilipo'e

Paliku Trail

Halemau'u Trail

Pu'u Maile

Pu'u Kumu

Kapalaoa Cabin

Haleakala 8,201

KAHIKINUI FOREST RESERVE

Halemau'u Trail

Pu'u o Maui

Sliding Sands Trail

Pu'u Nole

Ka Lu'u o ka 'O'o

Kamoali'i

Holua

Kalahaku

Haupa'akea 9,159

Halemau'u Trail

Magnetic Peak 10,008

Hosmer Grove

Pu'u Nianau

Park Hdqtrs

Kahului

KOOLAU FOREST RESERVE

N

0   1   2   3   4 Kilometers
0   1   2   3 Miles

173

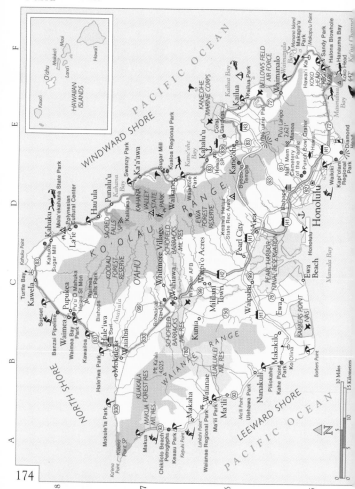

Oahu HAWAII

HAWAIIAN ISLANDS

Kaua'i
O'ahu
Moloka'i
Lana'i
Maui
Hawai'i

PACIFIC OCEAN

174

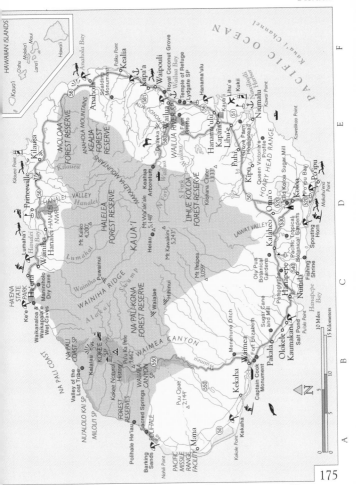

HAWAIIAN ISLANDS

Kaua'i
Ni'ihau
O'ahu
Moloka'i
Lāna'i Maui
Hawai'i

PACIFIC OCEAN

Kaua'i Channel

175

DESIGNATIONS

National Forest: Large acreage managed for the use of forests, watersheds, wildlife, and public recreation. Managed by the USFS.

National Lakeshore: Area of pristine, natural freshwater lakeshore designated to protect its natural form and appearance and provide public recreation. All four national lakeshores are on the Great Lakes. Managed by the NPS.

National Marine Sanctuary: Coastal waters protected for their natural, cultural, or historic resources. Restricted fishing, boating, and diving allowed. Managed by the NOS.

National Park: Spacious primitive or wilderness area with scenery and natural wonders so outstanding it has been preserved by the federal government for public recreation. Managed by the NPS.

National Recreation Area: Site established to conserve and develop for recreational purposes an area of national scenic, natural, or historic interest. Powerboats, dirt and mountain bikes, and ORVs allowed with restrictions. Managed by the NPS.

National Seashore: Area of pristine undeveloped seashore designated for conservation and public recreation. Camping and ORVs permitted. Managed by the NPS.

National Trails: Nationwide, a series of trails have been designated for special management by the National Park Service, the Forest Service, or the Bureau of Land Management. National Scenic Trails are continuous protected scenic corridors providing access to unique natural environs for outdoor recreation. National Historic Trails honor past routes of passage, migration, exploration, and military campaigns. These trails are not continuous and may cross both public and private property.

National Wildlife Refuge: Public land set aside for wild animals; protects migratory waterfowl, endangered and threatened species, and native plants. Managed by the USFWS.

Nature Preserve: Tract of land formally dedicated to protect specific natural resources and remnants of high-quality ecosystems such as old-growth forests and prairies. Managed by individual state's Department of Natural Resources.

National Wild and Scenic River System: National program set up to preserve selected rivers in their natural free-flowing condition; stretches are classified as wild, scenic, or recreational, depending on the degree of development on the river, shoreline, or adjacent lands. Management shared by the BLM, NPS, and USFWS.

Wilderness Area: State land managed to protect wildlife. Aside from seasonal restrictions, hunting, fishing, and public access are allowed. Managed by individual states.

Wildlife Management Area: Natural area owned, protected, and maintained for recreation; hunting, fishing, trapping, and cross-country skiing permitted. Managed by each state's wildlife division.

NATIONAL PARKS

Acadia National Park

Bar Harbor, Maine 04609
Established February 26, 1919
46,000 acres. Open all year. Fees May to November.
207-288-3338 www.nps.gov/acad (*see page 16*)

SPECIAL FEATURES AND PLACES: Acadia comprises portions of Maine's Schoodic Peninsula, the Isle au Haut, and the most visited destination, Mount Desert Island. On the island, the Park Loop Road provides access to carriage roads leading to trailheads, tide-pools, beaches, Jordan Pond, the granite outcropping known as the Beehive, and the magnificent overlook on Cadillac Mountain. The park offers visitors dense forests, isolated ponds, and a spectacular rocky coast.

WILDLIFE: White-tail deer, red fox, harbor seal, eider duck, great blue heron, and 21 nesting warblers.

PLANT LIFE: White, red, pitch and jack pines; white birch, red spruce, balsam fir, tamarack, blueberry, harebell, sheep laurel, rugosa rose, and bunchberry dogwood.

MARINE LIFE: Rockweed, Irish moss, kelp, Atlantic rock crab, green sea urchin, blue mussel, dog whelk, barnacles, and northern starfish.

ACTIVITIES: Carriage rides, bird watching, camping, rock climbing, sea kayaking, swimming, fishing, boating, canoeing, bicycling, hiking, cross-country skiing, ranger-led programs.

INSIDER'S TIPS: No backcountry camping. Beware of slippery algae-covered rocks and strong storm waves in spring and fall. Islandwide free shuttle bus late June – Labor Day. Carriage rides and boat trips are available.

DIRECTIONS: Take Maine 3 to Mount Desert Island, Maine 186 to Schoodic Peninsula, Maine 15 to the passenger ferry at Stonington to Isle au Haut. Nearest airport: Bangor.

Arches National Park

Moab, Utah 84532
Designated as a national monument April 12, 1929
Established as a national park November 12, 1971
76,519 acres. Open all year. Fee.
435-719-2299 www.nps.gov/arch (see page 125)

SPECIAL FEATURES AND PLACES: Time-driven extremes of water, wind, and temperature have molded over 2,000 arches in the park. Easy access is gained from the main park road to short trails (most less than 3 miles round-trip) leading to Balanced Rock, as well as the most famous arches: Delicate, Landscape, Sand Dune, Double, Skyline, North and South Window, and Broken.

WILDLIFE: Mule deer, jack rabbit, kangaroo rat, coyote, collared lizard, golden eagle, red-tailed hawk, turkey vulture, scrub and pinyon jay, and canyon wren.

PLANT LIFE: Evening primrose, Indian paintbrush, jimsonweed, rabbit-brush, yucca, prickly pear cactus, pinyon pine, juniper, tamarisk, and cottonwood.

ACTIVITIES: Hiking, photography, bird watching, 4-wheel driving, mountain biking, and rock climbing (no permit required).

178

INSIDER'S TIPS: Plan for 1 gallon of water per person per day when hiking to avoid dehydration. Sandstone crumbles and is slippery. Rock climbing is permitted except on most named features – inquire at visitor center for regulations. Mountain biking only on established roads. Accommodations are limited: a single campground (no wood gathering) and no lodging in the park.

DIRECTIONS: From Moab take US 191 5 miles northwest to the park. Nearest airports: Grand Junction, CO; there is a small airport with commercial service 10 miles north of Moab, UT.

Badlands National Park

Interior, South Dakota 57750
Established November 10, 1978
244,300 acres. Open all year. Fee: May to September.
605-433-5361 www.nps.gov/badl (see page 95)

SPECIAL FEATURES AND PLACES: An open landscape of pinnacles, prairie, and steep canyons defines this sparsely populated region. The White River Badlands of South Dakota are considered the world's richest mammal fossil beds and were once home to prehistoric rhinoceroses, three-toed horses, and saber-toothed cats. Half of the park is located on Pine Ridge Reservation, home to the Oglala Lakota Nation, an area steeped in American Indian history as well as the US military past. The most accessible overlooks are in the North Unit, which includes the Badlands Loop Road (SD Highway 240). Over a dozen overlooks provide glimpses into the area's geology, ecology, and history. The more remote South Unit is largely unroaded and undeveloped and includes the Stronghold and Palmer Creek areas. Access to the South Unit is extremely limited due to the lack of roads and the exclusion of off-road vehicle travel.

WILDLIFE: Black-footed ferret, bison, bighorn sheep, mule deer, pronghorn, coyote, black-tailed prairie dog, prairie rattlesnake, golden eagle, turkey vulture, meadowlark, and mountain bluebird.

PLANT LIFE: Big bluestem, buffalo, western wheat, prairie cordgrass, and needle-and-thread grasses; textile onion, mariposa lily, death camas, narrowleaf penstemon, salsify, yucca, wild rose, chokeberry, currant, cottonwood, and Rocky Mountain juniper. In total, Badlands National Park has over 460 plant species, including nearly 60 species of prairie grasses alone.

ACTIVITIES: Summer naturalist programs, camping, backcountry camping (currently, no permits are required), wildlife watching, hiking, bicycling, star gazing, horseback riding, and nature or fossil study.

INSIDER'S TIPS: The best weather and least crowded conditions can be found in the months of April and early May or late September through October. The Cedar Pass Lodge in Badlands National Park is operated by the Oglala Sioux Tribe and is open from April through October. Contact the lodge at 605-433-5460 to make reservations for rustic cabins. The Badlands Wilderness Area, located in the park's northwestern corner, is over 64,000 acres of prairie and badland formations and receives very little visitation. However, backcountry explorers must carry at least one gallon of water per person because there is no water in the Badlands backcountry.

DIRECTIONS: From Interstate 90, take exit 131 (Cactus Flat) from the east or exit 109 (Wall) from the west to visit the North Unit. To visit the South Unit, take South Dakota 44 east from Rapid City to the community of Scenic. At Scenic, head south to BIA Route 27. Nearest bus service: Wall, South Dakota. Nearest airport: Rapid City.

Big Bend National Park

Big Bend National Park, Texas 79834
Established June 12, 1944
801,146 acres. Open all year. Fee.
915-477-2251 www.nps.gov/bibe (see page 105)

SPECIAL FEATURES AND PLACES: The Rio Grande River forms a winding oasis strip through this desert and mountain region. The river forms an eastern, southern, and western border to the park, as well as the international US/Mexico border. Texas 118 runs through the park northwest from the river overlook at the Rio Grande Village, providing access to Hot Springs, Dugout Wells, and a side trip down the Ross Maxwell Scenic Drive. The latter winds southwest between the Chisos Mountains and the Burro Mesa, where it leads to Sotol Vista, Burro Mesa Pouroff overlook, and Mule Ears Peaks overlook, before reaching the river overlook at the mouth of Santa Elena Canyon.

WILDLIFE: Blue, Channel, and flathead catfish; Big Bend gambusia (a mosquito fish), Couch's spadefoot toad, Texas banded gecko lizard, leopard frog, Mojave rattlesnake, copperhead, road-runner, mountain blue-

180

bird, white-winged dove, peregrine falcon, collared peccary, coyote, mule deer, and Carmen Mountains white-tailed deer.

PLANT LIFE: Big Bend bluebonnet, rock nettle, lechuguilla, century plant, ocotillo, Coahuila, yucca, cresote bush, chinquapin oak, quaking aspen, Arizona cypress, ponderosa pine, and Douglas fir.

ACTIVITIES: Backcountry camping (permit required), horseback riding, bird watching (400+ species), fishing, and river rafting.

INSIDER'S TIPS: Bring sun protection. Watch for cacti and bring tweezers. Ground fires are prohibited in the backcountry. Beware of water crossings, which flood seasonally, and, for the same reason avoid camping in arroyos or washes. Rock climbing is discouraged because rock is fragmentary.

DIRECTIONS: From El Paso it is 323 miles: take I-10 east to Van Horn: take US 90 southeast; at Marathon take Texas 385 to Panther Junction. From San Antonio it is 410 miles: I-10 west; at Fort Stockton take US 385 south to Panther Junction. Nearest airport: El Paso, Midland.

Biscayne National Park

Homestead, Florida 33090
Established as Biscayne National Monument October 18, 1968
Established as Biscayne National Park June 28, 1980
172,924 acres (mostly water). Open all year. No entrance fee – fees charged for overnight docking and camping.
305-230-7275 www.nps.gov/bisc (see page 66)

SPECIAL FEATURES AND PLACES: Biscayne's 44 keys and coral reefs are boarded by hardwood forests and a narrow shoreline lined with mangroves. The park's shore overlooks a shallow bay in a pristine tropical wilderness along Florida's eastern coast. The main attractions are below the surface in the relatively shallow reefs – abundant fish, crustaceans, and live corals. The Intracoastal Waterway runs through the center of the park between the coast and Elliott Key.

WILDLIFE: American crocodile, mangrove cuckoo, white-crowned pigeon, white ibis, snowy egret, bald eagle, osprey, peregrine falcon, Schaus swallowtail, manatee, dolphin, golden orb spider, and loggerhead, hawksbill and green sea turtles.

PLANT LIFE: Red and black mangrove, mahogany, wild lime, buttonwood, strangler fig, gumbo-limbo, lignum vitae, torchwood, pigeon plum, Jamaican dogwood, and poisonwood.

MARINE LIFE: Brain, star, and smooth-branched fire corals; orange crinoid, queen angelfish, bonefish, sharp-beaked parrot fish, filefish, blue-striped grunt, Nassau grouper, procupinefish, spiny lobster, loggerhead sea turtle, manatee, sea fan, and turtle grass.

ACTIVITIES: Boating, canoeing, kayaking, island camping, fishing, scuba diving, and snorkeling.

INSIDER'S TIPS: No backcountry camping. The most comfortable time to visit is January – April, with cooler temperatures and fewer mosquitoes. The reefs are best seen in the summer, when there are brief, drenching showers in the afternoon. Bring sun protection. $15.00 charge per night for berthing a boat. Visit the park's islands, especially Boca Chita Key and Elliott Key, on windy days (generally December – April). Visit the reefs on calm, sunny days (generally late April – August). For those comfortable in the water, snorkeling is the preferred way to see the reef. A glass-bottomed boat tour is available. Reserve trips early, especially during peak summer season, Christmas week, and Presidents' Day weekend.

DIRECTIONS: From Miami, take the Florida Turnpike south to exit 6 (Speedway Boulevard), south on Speedway to 328th Street, east on 328th Street to end of road and park entrance (on left). From US 1 in Homestead, take SW 328th east to the park entrance. Nearest airport: Miami.

Black Canyon of the Gunnison National Park

Gunnison, Colorado 81230
Established as a national monument in 1933
and as a national park in October 1999
30,300 acres. Open all year. Fee.
970-641-2337 www.nps.gov/blca (see page 123)

SPECIAL FEATURES AND PLACES: The Black Canyon of the Gunnison's unique and spectacular landscape was formed slowly by the action of water and rock scouring down through hard Precambrian crystalline rock. No other canyon in North America combines the narrow opening, sheer walls, and startling depths offered by the Black Canyon of the Gunnison.

WILDLIFE: Beaver, black bear, blue grouse, bull snake, chipmunk, cicada, coyote, German brown trout, great horned owl, mountain bluebird, mountain lion, mule deer, porcupine, rainbow trout, raven, ringtail, rock squirrel, smooth green snake, Steller's jay, stone fly, western fence lizard, and yellow warbler.

PLANT LIFE: Boxelder, Gambel oak, lupine, pinyon pine, juniper, fendler bush, mountain mahogany, mule's ears, narrowleaf cottonwood, poison ivy, sagebrush scarlet gilia, serviceberry.

ACTIVITIES: Spectacular drive-up viewing, short walks to many canyon overlooks, hiking trails and routes, wildlife viewing, birding, camping, picnicking, photography, fishing (physically demanding access), bouldering, inner-canyon hiking and climbing. Camping is first-come/first-served; no reservations are accepted. Backcountry permits (free) are required for all inner-canyon travel, the routes to the river, for kayaking and for bouldering and rock climbing. When snow closes the South Rim Road, the NPS plows to the South Rim visitor center only, to allow cross-country skiing activity. Previously closed in winter, the visitor center is now open all year.

INSIDER'S TIPS: South Rim: Open every day, limited access in winter. North Rim: Open every day; North Rim Road and ranger station are closed in winter. During winter, the North Rim can be accessed by hiking, cross-country skiing, or snowshoeing. 230,000 visitors per year. The majority of people visit the South Rim, between Memorial Day and Labor Day. Weather can vary greatly between the canyon rim and canyon floor. Summer daytime temperatures range from 60 to 100 degrees F (15 to 38 degrees C), nights 30 to 50 degrees F (-1 to 10 degrees C). Winter daytime temperatures range between 20 and 40 degrees F (-6 to 4 degrees C), nights -10 to 20 degrees F (-23 to -6 degrees C). Precipitation is minimal; brief afternoon thunderstorms can occur during the summer. Layered clothing appropriate for the season is recommended.

DIRECTIONS: The park is located approximately 250 miles SW of Denver. South Rim: East of Montrose on US Hwy 50, 8 miles; north on CO Hwy 347 then 6 miles to park entrance. North Rim: CO Hwy 92 to Crawford, follow signs to North Rim Road, North Rim Road (unpaved) to park, 11 miles (North Rim Road closed in winter). Nearest airports: Montrose, Gunnison, Grand Junction.

Bryce Canyon National Park

Bryce Canyon, Utah 84717
Established September 15, 1928
35,835 acres. Open all year. Fee.
435-834-5322 www.nps.gov/brca *(see page 126)*

SPECIAL FEATURES AND PLACES: Bryce Canyon's beautifully colored and exotically shaped limestone and sandstone rock formations reveal a 95-million-year geologic history, carved by rain, snow, and ice. Ascending from the bottom of the Grand Canyon (in height as well as geological time) is a series of cliffs referred to as the "Grand Staircase," with the Pink Cliffs of Bryce Canyon forming the top of this magnificent, lithic "staircase." The 20-mile Rim Road winds along the eastern edge of the Paunsaugunt Plateau. On the north end of the drive is the geologic wonder known as the main amphitheater. Here breathtaking overlooks (e.g., Sunrise, Sunset, Inspiration and Bryce points) and world-famous day hikes like the Navajo Loop, Queen's Garden, and Peek-a-Boo Loop trails can be accessed. Followed south, the road increases in elevation and leads to additional trails and vistas such as Farview Point, Agua Canyon, and Rainbow Point.

WILDLIFE: Utah prairie dog, chipmunk, golden-mantled ground squirrel, mule deer, elk, mountain lion, porcupine, coyote, gray fox, bobcat, raven, red-tailed hawk, Steller's jay, peregrine falcon, golden eagle, Clark's nutcracker, swallows, and juncos.

PLANT LIFE: Aspen, ponderosa pine, oak, pinyon pine, juniper, bristlecone pine, limber pine, blue spruce, white and Douglas fir, manzanita, black sagebrush, mountain lilac, barberry, evening primrose, elderberry, bitterbrush, rabbitbrush, sego lily, scarlet gilia, Oregon grape, and paintbrush.

ACTIVITIES: Hiking, backcountry camping (permit required), horseback riding, biking, cross-country skiing, and snowshoeing.

INSIDER'S TIPS: Early morning light provides the best illumination of the park's formations. Sunset Point is the busiest place in the park – walk 5 minutes south towards Inspiration Point to avoid the crowds. Bring a warm jacket for cool summer nights. Winter visitors are offered free use of snowshoes by the National Park Service.

DIRECTIONS: From Las Vegas use Interstate 15; at Cedar City, follow Utah 14 east to US 89. Go north to Utah 12 and turn east. At Utah 63 turn south to the park. From Salt Lake City, take Interstate 15 south to Utah 20. Turn east and continue to US 89, go south to Utah 12 and follow east to Utah 63. Go south to the park. Nearest airports: Bryce Canyon (charter service available from Las Vegas to Bryce Canyon), Cedar City, Las Vegas, Salt Lake City, and Phoenix.

Canyonlands National Park

Moab, Utah 84532
Established September 12, 1964
337,570 acres. Open all year. Fee.
435-259-7164 www.nps.gov/cany (see page 129)

SPECIAL FEATURES AND PLACES: Located in the heart of the Colorado Plateau, wind and water have carved canyons, mesas, buttes, arches, spires, and fins into this land. Of the park's three districts, Needles, Maze, and Island in the Sky, the latter is most visited. There, at the Grand View Point overlook, stone columns rise 300' from the confluence of the Green and Colorado rivers 2,000' below. An easy hike offers a view of Mesa Arch. In the Needles District a short walk leads to the ruin of a small Anasazi granary, another provides a view of shrimp in a sandstone pothole. The remote Horseshoe Canyon unit contains the Great Gallery, an 80'-long mural with larger than life-sized pictographs, reachable on a 6¹/₂-mile round-trip hike.

WILDLIFE: Fairy and tadpole shrimp, mule deer, bighorn sheep, coyote, white-tailed antelope, ground squirrel, kangaroo rat, collared lizard, gopher snake, and midget faded rattlesnake.

PLANT LIFE: Mountain mahogany, prickly pear and beavertail cactus, pinyon pine, juniper, Gambel oak, Mormon tea, gooseberry, snakeweed, globemallow, skyrocket gilias, and maidenhair fern.

ACTIVITIES: Backcountry camping (permit required), hiking, boating, canoeing, rafting, and 4-wheel driving.

INSIDER'S TIPS: Bring 1 gallon of water per person per day and sun protection; use caution near overlook edges. Rainfall is scarce but hazardous for hikers and campers in low areas. Plan well ahead for river permits.

DIRECTIONS: From Moab it is about 30 miles to the Island in the Sky District: Take US 191 north; at the junction of Utah 313 go southwest. From Moab it is about 80 miles to the Needles District: Take US 191 south; at the junction of Utah 211 go west for 48 miles and follow signs. A 4-wheel-drive vehicle is required in order to reach the Maze District. Nearest airport: Grand Junction, CO.

Capitol Reef National Park

Torrey, Utah 84775
Established December 18, 1971

241,094 acres. Open all year. Fee.
801-425-3791 www.nps.gov/care *(see page 127)*

SPECIAL FEATURES AND PLACES: "Capitol" refers to the white-domed sandstone peaks and "reef" refers to the rock ridges that form a land barrier. The area is part of the Colorado Plateau, a dramatic regional upthrust caused by plate tectonics. Surface geology features the Waterpocket Fold, a hundred-mile-long "wrinkle" in the earth's crust. The Capitol Gorge and Grand Wash trails access canyons; another trail east of the petroglyphs goes through desert to Hickman Natural Bridge; the Sunset Point trail overlooks cliffs and domes. Each is 2 miles or less round-trip.

WILDLIFE: Mule deer, yellow-bellied marmots, red fox, ground squirrels, snakes, lizards, chukars, and ravens.

PLANT LIFE: Cottonwood, sage, yucca, four-winged saltbush, rabbit-brush, buffaloberry, globemallow, primrose, scarlet gilia, and Historic Fruita orchards.

ACTIVITIES: Hiking, backpacking (free permit required), sight-seeing, 4-wheel driving, ranger activities.

INSIDER'S TIPS: Best times to visit are late spring and early fall. Water from natural sources is scarce and unsafe for drinking. Potable water is available at the visitor center, picnic area, and Fruita campground. Flash floods, possible July through September, can result in dangers to hikers and backcountry users.

DIRECTIONS: From Salt Lake City take I-15 south to I-70; go east to exit 48. Take Utah 24 southeast to the park. From Arches, go west to Green River via I-70; continue west; at exit 147 (the intersection of Utah 24) go southwest to the park. From Bryce Canyon take Utah 12 northeast to Torrey; take Utah 24 and head east to the park. Nearest airport: Salt Lake City.

Carlsbad Caverns National Park

Carlsbad, New Mexico 88220
Established May 14, 1930
46,766 acres. Open all year. Fee.
505-785-2232 www.nps.gov/cave *(see page 112)*

SPECIAL FEATURES AND PLACES: Geologic forces have created gigantic caverns housing beautiful limestone rock formations: massive stalagmites and stalactites, draperies, popcorn, lily pads, and cave pearls. Of the more than 90 caves, only Carlsbad Cavern, Slaughter Canyon Cave, and Spider Cave are open to the general public. The Big Room in Carlsbad Cavern can be reached by descending 750 feet in an elevator. It is part of the two $1\frac{1}{4}$-mile tours, as is the Natural Entrance route. A $9\frac{1}{2}$-mile loop called the Walnut Canyon Desert Drive provides access to the dramatic scenery above ground.

WILDLIFE: Cave swallow, rock wren, golden eagle, Mexican freetailed bat, raccoon, hog-nosed skunk, western diamondback and banded rock rattlesnake, vermilion flycatcher, scaled quail, lesser nighthawk, red-tailed hawk, and black-chinned hummingbird.

PLANT LIFE: Prickly pear cactus, agave, yucca, sotol, ocotillo, desert grass, Texas black walnut, pinyon and ponderosa pines, juniper, Douglas fir, desert willow, and hackberry.

ACTIVITIES: Backcountry camping (permit required), caving, hiking, and horseback riding.

INSIDER'S TIPS: Experienced cavers may apply for permits to 10 other caves. Wear a sweater or flannel shirt with slacks, as the temperature inside the cave remains at 56 degrees, although Slaughter Canyon Cave is a little warmer (62 degrees). Nonskid shoes are recommended because the paths may be slippery. Bring a flashlight to explore Slaughter Canyon Cave. No campgrounds.

DIRECTIONS: From Carlsbad travel 16 miles southwest on US 62; at Whites City head 7 miles west on New Mexico 7 to the park. Nearest airport: El Paso, TX.

Channel Islands National Park
Ventura, California 93001
Established March 5, 1980
248,515 acres. Open all year. No fee.
805-658-5730 www.nps.gov/chis (see page 157)

SPECIAL FEATURES AND PLACES: Visible from the coast of California near Santa Barbara, five mountainous islands offer homes to numerous marine and mammal species. These islands harbor the largest seal and sea lion breeding colony in the US along with about 50 endemic species of plants and animals. Arch Rock, hollowed out by wind and sea, stands 40' above the ocean near Anacapa Island.

WILDLIFE: Santa Cruz gopher snake, island spotted skunk, island fox (smallest in North America), and Santa Cruz scrub jay ($^1/_3$ larger than those on the mainland). Many other seabirds and landbirds.

PLANT LIFE: Coreopsis, ironwood, torrey pine, and island oak.

MARINE LIFE: Brown pelicans, storm petrels, Xantus' murrelet, garibaldi, seal, sea lion, orca, blue whale, gooseneck barnacle, and kelp.

ACTIVITIES: Backcountry beach camping (permit required), hiking, camping, swimming, boating, kayaking, scuba diving, and snorkeling.

INSIDER'S TIPS: Access to the islands is available from park concessionaires located next to the visitor center in Ventura or at the Santa Barbara harbor. Private boat landings are available for certain islands at specific places. Because weather varies, bring warm clothing.

DIRECTIONS: From Los Angeles take 101 north; at the Victoria exit in Ventura follow the Channel Island signs for the visitor center. Nearest airports: Santa Barbara and Los Angeles.

Crater Lake National Park

Crater Lake, Oregon 97604
Established May 22, 1902
183,277 acres. South and west entrances open all year; north entrance mid-June to mid-October. Fee: May to early October.
541-594-2211 www.nps.gov/crla *(see page 147)*

SPECIAL FEATURES AND PLACES: When the summit of Mt. Mazama erupted and collapsed over 7,700 years ago, its caldera filled with rainwater and snow melt to form the deepest lake in the US. The Rim Drive provides wonderful overlooks of the lake 1,000' below. Also visible are canyons carved from pumice and cooled lava flows. The lake is reached only via the steep Cleetwood Cove Trail (2 miles round-trip). Rising out of the lake is a 700' cinder cone known as Wizard Island.

WILDLIFE: Goshawks, red-tailed and marsh hawks, golden and bald eagles, Steller's jay, Clark's nutcracker, raven, water ouzel, redbreasted nuthatch, red crossbill, great-horned owl, stocked rainbow trout, Kokanee salmon, ground squirrel, pika, yellow-bellied marmot, mule and black-tailed deer, Roosevelt elk, and black bear.

PLANT LIFE: Shasta red, white, and Douglas firs; ponderosa and lodgepole pines, mountain hemlock, western pasqueflower, common monkeyflower, Newberry knotweed, pussy paw, phantom orchid, sulfur flower, Indian paintbrush, rabbitbrush, and huckleberry.

ACTIVITIES: Backcountry camping (permit required), horseback riding, fishing, biking, cross-country skiing, and boat touring.

INSIDER'S TIPS: Wildflowers are best in late July and Early August. Summer temperatures can be hot at the lake. The first of the 1 3/4-hour boat tours leaves at 10 a.m. and the last is at 4:30 p.m. Be aware that volcanic rock is unstable and dangerous to climb. Roads along the lake's rim are unplowed in the winter where there may be 40' + of snow, passable only for those with skis or snowshoes. The lake rarely freezes as winter temperatures generally range from 20 to 40 degrees F.

DIRECTIONS: From Medford, head northeast on Oregon 62 for 65 miles to the west entrance. From Klamath Falls, go north on US 97 to the intersection of Oregon 62; travel northwest to the south entrance. Nearest airports: Medford, Klamath Falls.

Death Valley National Park

Death Valley, California 92328
Established February 11, 1933 as a national monument and October 31, 1994 as a national park
3.3 million acres (largest park outside of Alaska). Open all year. Fee.
760-786-2331 www.nps.gov/deva (see page 158)

SPECIAL FEATURES AND PLACES: Amid the vast Mojave Desert, the Valley is the hottest place in the US, bounded on the east by the Amargosa Range and on the west by the Panamint Range. Known for extremes, the park contains the lowest point in the Western Hemisphere, known as Badwater (282' below sea level), a point accessed from the east entrance. Also nearby is Zabriskie Point, providing a panoramic view of Badlands and the valley beyond. Panamint Valley, Emigrant Canyon, and Charcoal Kilns (about 7,000') are all reached from the east entrance as well. At the north entrance, roads lead to geologic formations such as Ubehebe Crater and Stovepipe Wells.

WILDLIFE: Bighorn sheep, chuckwalla, sidewinder, bobcat, coyote, kit fox, desert pupfish, desert banded gecko, raven, roadrunner, golden eagle, killdeer, rock wren, and great blue heron.

PLANT LIFE: Pinyon pine, juniper, 3,000-year-old bristlecone pine, mountain mahogany, mesquite, creosote bush, arrow weed, pickle-weed, salt grass, and desert holly.

ACTIVITIES: Backcountry camping (free voluntary permit), hiking, horseback riding, and biking.

INSIDER'S TIPS: Summer temperatures may exceed 120 degrees F; a broad-rimmed hat and other sun protection are advised. Radiator water is available in storage tanks along the roads. Be alert for open mine shafts and prospect holes while exploring. Make reservations far in advance since facilities are limited.

DIRECTIONS: There are two easy routes from Las Vegas: take State Route 160 to Pahrump, then turn west on Bell Vista/State Line Road; at Death Valley Junction take California 190 west to the park; or take US 95 to Nevada 373 and California 127; at Death Valley Junction take California 190 west to the park. Nearest airports: Las Vegas, Bakersfield, Los Angeles.

Denali National Park

Denali Park, Alaska 99755
Established February 26, 1917 as Mt. McKinley National Park
6,028,091 acres. Open all year. Fee.
907-683-2294 www.nps.gov/dena *(see page 166)*

SPECIAL FEATURES AND PLACES: Denali means "the High One" to native Athabaskans, who first named what is now Mt. McKinley, the highest point in North America. Set in the Alaska Range, the mountain's peak measures 20,320', rising 18,000' above the vast tundra below and sur-rounded by Mt. Brooks, Mt. Mather, Mt. Silverthrone, and Mt. Russell. Down the flanks are huge glaciers; at the base, tundra and taiga begins. Timberline is at 2,700' as compared to 11,000 – 12,000' in the Rockies.

WILDLIFE: Dall's sheep, moose, caribou, grizzly bear, weasel, wolverine, beaver, vole, lemming, lynx, martin, snowshoe hare, collared pika, arctic grayling, lake trout, golden and bald eagles, hawk owl, gyrfalcon, goshawk, sandhill crane, gray jay, spruce grouse, varied thrush, snow bunting, Lap-land longspur, arctic warbler, northern wheatear, golden plover, common redpoll, Bonaparte's and mew gulls, arctic tern, long-tailed jaeger, and white-tailed, rock and willow ptarmigans.

PLANT LIFE: Paper birch, larch, balsam poplar, dwarf birch, dwarf fireweed, mountain avens, dwarf rhododendron, bog blueberry, bearberry, lowbush cranberry, crowberry, cloudberry, arctic poppy, and Alaska cottongrass.

ACTIVITIES: Mountain climbing (permit required; to register to climb Mt. McKinley and Mt. Foraker, climbers must register 60 days in advance of their climb), backcountry camping (permit required), hiking, bicycling, mountain climbing, horseback riding, snowshoeing, cross-country skiing, dog sledding, fishing, and hunting.

INSIDER'S TIPS: With nearly continuous summer daylight to extend wildlife viewing, the 85-mile shuttle bus voyage is recommended (11 hours round-trip). Follow ranger advice regarding bears and glacial streams.

DIRECTIONS: From Anchorage take Alaska 1 north to Alaska 3; go 205 miles north to the park. In the summer the train to Fairbanks stops daily at the park; in the winter it runs only on weekends. From Fairbanks take Alaska 3 west and then south 120 miles to the park.

Dry Tortugas National Park

Key West, Florida 33041
Established as Fort Jefferson National Monument on January 4, 1935 and as a national park on October 4, 1992
64,700 acres (mostly water). Open all year. No fee.
305-242-7700 www.nps.gov/drto *(see page 62 – 63)*

SPECIAL FEATURES AND PLACES: A tropical aquatic park located 70 miles west of Key West, Dry Tortugas is an undersea wonder. Originally named by Ponce de Leon after the turtles found there, this cluster of seven islands is surrounded by shallow coral reefs. Located on land at Garden Key is Fort Jefferson, the largest 19th century American Coastal fort. Now a wildlife refuge for endangered birds and turtles, the park attracts snorkelers, divers, photographers, and boaters. Numerous shoals, keys, and shallow reefs create abundant wildlife-viewing opportunities.

WILDLIFE: Sooty tern, brown and black noddies, masked and brown boobies, magnificent frigatebird, and painted bunting.

MARINE LIFE: Green, loggerhead, and hawksbill turtles, small-mouth grunt, amberjack, grouper, wahoo, tarpon, bigeye, angelfish, butterflyfish, spotted eagle ray, parrot fish, sea anemone, turtlegrass, and spiny lobster.

ACTIVITIES: Backcountry camping (permit required), swimming, boating, snorkeling, scuba diving, underwater photography, and sport sea fishing.

INSIDER'S TIPS: Accessible only by boat or seaplane. All water, food, and supplies must be brought from the mainland. Overnight camping only on Garden Key. Bush Key is reserved for birds from February through September, and Hospital and Long Keys are closed year-round. The pier at Loggerhead Key is closed to the public.

DIRECTIONS: Several boat and air taxi services provide transport to the park from Key West. Nearest airport: Key West.

Everglades National Park
Homestead, Florida 33034
Established December 6, 1947
1,509,000 acres. Open all year. Fee.
305-242-7700 www.nps.gov/ever *(see page 62)*

SPECIAL FEATURES AND PLACES: Everglades is a shallow, freshwater river about 50 miles wide. The river bottom is limestone, deposited over time by plants and animals and covered by sand and peat. The park also includes saltwater areas, mangrove swamps, coastal prairies, cypress stands, freshwater sloughs, freshwater marl prairies, pinelands, and hardwood hemlocks. Varied ecosystems may be viewed from the central main road, accessing the Anhinga, Gumbo Limbo, Pineland, Pahayokee Overlook, and Coastal Prairie trails. Stop at Mahogany Hammock to see the oldest mahogany tree in the US and at Flamingo for a 2-hour backcountry cruise. The Tram Tour Road at Shark Valley is ideal for bicycling and offers an opportunity to get out into the heart of the freshwater marsh. Several nature trails can be found there as well. The maze of mangrove islands in the Gulf Coast/Ten Thousand Island area (park entrance at Everglades City) harbors an abundance of birds, plants, and marine life. In addition, it's the northern gateway to the Wilderness Waterway, a 99-mile route connecting Everglades City and Flamingo.

WILDLIFE: American alligator, American crocodile; Florida red-belly, soft-shell, and loggerhead turtles; green tree and leopard frogs; apple snail, Florida panther, zebra butterfly, snail kites; limpkin, roseate spoonbill, brown pelican, anhinga, great white and green-backed herons; wood stork, snowy egret, white ibis, purple gallinule, barred owl, black vulture, and bald eagle.

PLANT LIFE: Saw grass, swamp lily, bull thistle, strap fern, air plant, gumbo limbo, slash pine, royal palm, saw-palmetto, strangler fig, cypress, spatterdock, and red mangrove.

MARINE LIFE: Manatee, bluegill, mangrove snapper, largemouth bass, mosquitofish, Florida gar, crayfish, blue crab, coon oyster, and pink shrimp.

ACTIVITIES: Hiking, kayaking, birding, camping, backcountry camping (permit required), swimming, boating, canoeing, fishing, biking, and wildlife viewing.

INSIDER'S TIPS: Fees vary depending upon the entrance. Bring insect repellent; insects can make camping and hiking unbearable, especially during the summer rainy season. The most popular period to visit is mid-November to mid-April.

DIRECTIONS: From Miami and points north: take the Florida Turnpike south until it ends, merging with US 1 in Florida City. Take State Road 9336 and follow the signs to the main park entrance, 10 miles west of Florida City. Nearest airport: Miami.

Gates of the Arctic National Park

Bettles Field, Alaska 99726
Established December 2, 1980
8,500,000 acres. Open all year. No fee.
907-692-5494 www.nps.gov/gaar *(see page 171)*

SPECIAL FEATURES AND PLACES: The park gets its name from the Frigid Crags and Boreal Mountain, two peaks forming the gates from the Brooks Range (an extension of the Rockies) into the northern arctic regions. The southern slopes of the Brooks Range are covered with taiga, a scraggly forest of black spruce growing only 10 – 15' tall at a treeline of only 2,100' elevation – the extreme northwestern limit for trees on earth. The northern slopes are a treeless tundra. Six rivers have been designated "national wild rivers": the Kobuk, Noatak, Alatna, North Fork Koyukuk, Tinayguk, and the John. These waterways serve as the main travel routes through the park as there are no developed hiking trails. This park is so remote that some lakes and rivers remain unnamed.

WILDLIFE: Snowy owl, lemming, caribou, moose, Dall's sheep, wolverine, gray wolf, and grizzly and black bears.

PLANT LIFE: Black and white spruces, dwarf willow, dwarf and resin birches, alder, arctic cottongrass, reindeer moss, mountain aven, moss campion, and purple saxifrage.

ACTIVITIES: Backcountry camping (permit required), hiking, mountain climbing, boating, kayaking, rafting, fishing, and hunting.

INSIDER'S TIPS: There are no roads leading to or within the park. Supplies are limited in Bettles. Firearms may be carried for protection. Pack extra food in the event that air taxi service is delayed. Bring insect repellent in late June and July as well as warm clothing, since freezing temperatures occur unpredictably. Camping on gravel bars is recommended but be alert for flash floods and respect the property of native Nunamiut and Athabascan people.

DIRECTIONS: Fly from Fairbanks to Bettles on scheduled flights, and from there charter a small aircraft to Coldfoot or Anaktuvuk pass, which are closer to the park.

Glacier National Park
Waterton-Glacier International Peace Park

Glacier National Park, established May 12, 1910
Waterton-Glacier International Peace Park, established June 18, 1932
West Glacier, Montana 59936
1,013,572 acres. Open all year. Fee.
406-888-7800 www.nps.gov/glac
Waterton Lake National Park, Alberta, Canada TOK 2M0
525 square kilometers. 403-859-2224 (see page 136)

SPECIAL FEATURES AND PLACES: Straddling the US and Canadian border are two adjoining parks forming the world's first international Peace Park – one spectacular region of high mountain peaks, glacial valleys, cathedral-like forests, alpine meadows, prairies, tundra, pristine lakes, and abundant wildlife. The Continental Divide bisects the parks along the Lewis and Livingston Ranges. Peaks vary from 7,000' to 10,000'+, including some with active glaciers. Known best for its population of grizzly bears, the park's wildlife is as varied as any imaginable. Glacier National Park has six National Historic Landmarks (the Going-to-the-Sun Road, Sperry Chalet, Granite Park Chalet, Lake McDonald Lodge, Many Glacier Hotel, and the Two Medicine Campstore) and over 350 other properties listed on the National Register of Historic Places. An unforgettable 50-mile drive along Going-to-the-Sun Road winds past Lake McDonald, numerous waterfalls, overlooks, trailheads, and glaciers, finally reaching St. Mary's Lake at the eastern entrance to Glacier. Over 700 miles of hiking and backpacking trails traverse Glacier Park but paved roads are few; Waterton is smaller and more accessible by car.

WILDLIFE: Rainbow, lake, eastern brook, bull, and cutthroat trout; pike, whitefish, gray wolf, lynx, grizzly and black bears, bighorn sheep, mountain goat, elk, moose, gray wolf, mountain lion, wolverine, beaver, river otter, hoary mamot, white-tailed and mule deer, bald and golden eagles, osprey, blue grouse, Canadian jay, ptarmigan, kingfisher, water ouzel, harlequin duck, and Clark's nutcracker.

PLANT LIFE: Western and subalpine larch, Englemann spruce, Douglas and subalpine firs, lodgepole pine, western red cedar, hemlock, black cottonwood, beargrass, glacier lily, penstemon, buttercup, calypso orchid, heather, gentian, pasque flower, lupine, and Indian paintbrush.

ACTIVITIES: Backcountry camping (fee and permit required), hiking, boating, fishing, horseback riding, bicycling, cross-country skiing, and rock scrambling.

INSIDER'S TIPS: Temperatures are mildest from late June through August. Varied and unpredictable weather conditions increase the potential for hypothermia, so carry extra layers of clothing and rain gear. Follow park guidelines for minimizing interactions with bears.

DIRECTIONS: There are three eastern entrances to the park – Many Glacier, Two Medicine, and St. Mary. All three eastern entrances may be reached via US 89, the western entrance via US 2 from Kalispell. Waterton is accessible from Calgary. Take Highway 2 to Cardston, then west on Highway 5 to the park. Nearest US airports: Kalispell and Great Falls. Nearest Canadian airports: Lethbridge, Calgary. Amtrak stops in West Glacier and East Glacier.

Glacier Bay National Park

Gustavus, Alaska 99826
Established December 2, 1980
3,280,198 acres. Open all year. No fee.
907-697-2230 www.nps.gov/glba (see page 167)

SPECIAL FEATURES AND PLACES: Bounded on the north and northeast by the Takhinsha and Saint Elias mountains, spectacular Glacier Bay is accessible only by boat or plane. The Fairweather Range on the western arm of the park is separated from the Chilkat Range on the eastern arm by the bay. Each of these mountain ranges bears fine examples of tidewater glaciers; however, the highest mountains and the most active glaciers are on the western arm. Huge icebergs are born when glaciers break off at the edge of the sea. Native Americans called these sharp explosions "white thunder." Because of the recession of glaciers, there are wonderful examples of plant succession: spruce and hemlock trees have taken root within the last 200 years.

WILDLIFE: Salmon, krill, brown and black bears, mountain goat, red squirrel, red phalarope, blue grouse, bald eagle, humpback and killer whales, harbor seal, sea lion, and harbor porpoise.

PLANT LIFE: Hemlock, Sitka spruce, alder, black cottonwood, and dryas.

ACTIVITIES: Backcountry camping (permit required), hiking, mountain climbing, boating, kayaking, fishing, and hunting.

INSIDER'S TIPS: Visit between May and mid-September for the best weather. The park is most easily reached via a commercial cruise ship, from which kayakers and campers are dropped off at several sites. They are picked up at a later date, or go to Bartlett Cove to catch a bus and a plane. Good camping spots are easily available. Avoid mussels and clams which may contain a natural neurotoxin.

DIRECTIONS: From Juneau, travel by plane on a scheduled flight to Gustavus; then take a bus 10 miles to Glacier Bay Lodge or Bartlett Cove campground in the southeastern portion of the park. The park may be reached by boat, but permits are required in advance.

Grand Canyon National Park

Grand Canyon, Arizona 86023
Established February 26, 1919
1,218,375 acres. Open all year. Fee.
928-638-7888 www.nps.gov/grca (see page 116)

SPECIAL FEATURES AND PLACES: Up to 18 miles separate the rims of this immense canyon at its widest extent. From the South Rim, it is 4,700' deep; 5,700' from the North Rim. The Colorado River is far below, an 8-mile hike down the Bright Angel trail. An excellent view of the gorge may be observed from Mather Point off the Grand Canyon Village Loop. For other spectacular vistas, including Bright Angel Canyon, take the

East Rim Drive, stopping at Yavapai, Yaki, Grandview, and Lipan points, and finally at Desert View. At sunset, the colors of the rocks forming the walls of the canyon are breathtaking. In the summer, the West Rim Drive is open only to buses and hikers.

WILDLIFE: Kaibab squirrel, pink rattlesnake, mule deer, coyote, gray and kit foxes, ringtail cat, beaver, river otter, Grand Canyon rattlesnake, chuckwalla, cactus mouse, golden eagle, western tanager, larkspur, hermit thrush, summer tanager, cactus wren, perigrine falcon, spotted sandpiper, great blue heron, and fulvia checkerspot butterfly.

PLANT LIFE: Cliffrose, fernbrush, Indian paintbrush, skyrocket gilias, spotted coralroot, blackbrush, chollas, cresote bush, century plant, mesquite, tamarisk, seep willow, Gambel oak, mountain mahogany, ponderosa and pinyon pines, juniper and quaking aspen.

ACTIVITIES: Backcountry camping (permit required), mountain climbing, horseback riding, mule trips, fishing, white-water rafting, airplane and helicopter rides, and cross-country skiing.

INSIDER'S TIPS: Apply sunscreen and carry plenty of water when hiking in the canyon; evenings can be chilly. Backcountry permits are still in great demand in spring and fall, which are pleasant times to hike the canyon. In the winter, travelers to the South Rim should be prepared for snow and possible road closures. The North Rim is 8,000' high and temperatures there are generally 30 degrees colder than on the bottom of the canyon. It is closed from mid-October until mid-May.

DIRECTIONS: To the South Rim entrance: From Flagstaff, go north on US 89 to Cameron, take Arizona 64 west to the entrance near Desert View; or travel north on US 180 to South Rim entrance. To the North Rim entrance: From Flagstaff, take US 89 north to US alternate 89, then turn south on Arizona 67. Nearest airports: Flagstaff, Las Vegas.

Grand Teton National Park

Moose, Wyoming 83012
Established February 26, 1929
310,516 acres. Open all year. Fee.
307-739-3300 www.nps.gov/grte (see page 133)

SPECIAL FEATURES AND PLACES: The Snake River flows from the north through a vast plain with rugged peaked mountains rising behind it to the west. Between the river and the mountains are Jenny and Jackson lakes, immediately accessible from Teton Park Road. Short trails lead from Jenny Lake to Hidden Falls, Inspiration Point, and String and Leigh lakes. Picnic areas along Jackson Lake provide stunning views of glaciers on Nez Perce, Middle and Grand Teton, Mount Owen, and Teewinot Mountain. The Teton Range was formed over two million years ago by geologic upthrust forces, creating peaks rock-climbers dream of scaling.

WILDLIFE: Yellow-bellied marmot, porcupine, coyote, elk, pronghorn, bighorn sheep, moose, bison, river otter, bobcat, lynx, marten, black and grizzly bears, marsh hawk, common merganser, osprey, prairie falcon, bald eagle, trumpeter swan, spotted sandpiper, killdeer, yellow warbler, belted kingfisher, pine grosbeak, Cassin's finch, and blue butterfly.

PLANT LIFE: Douglas fir, balsamroot, sagebrush buttercup, western spring beauty, skyrocket gilia, wild buckwheat, alpine forget-me-not, mule's ear, and glacier lily.

ACTIVITIES: Backcountry camping (permit required), swimming, boating, fishing, mountain climbing, and cross-country skiing.

INSIDER'S TIPS: Fall colors are best seen in mid-September. Be sure to have proper footwear in the backcountry as talus slopes can be quite slippery. Picking wildflowers is not permitted.

DIRECTIONS: From I-80, travel north on 189 or 191 to Jackson and follow signs. The park is directly south of Yellowstone via 89/287. Nearest airport: Jackson.

Great Basin National Park

Baker, Nevada 89311
Established October 27, 1986
77,109 acres. Open all year.
Fees only for ranger-led cave tours.
772-234-7331 www.nps.gov/grba (see page 161)

SPECIAL FEATURES AND PLACES: Geologically, this young park in the South Snake Range contains 13 peaks taller than 11,000' and some of the oldest trees on earth. A visit to the 3,000-year-old bristlecone pines requires a 2.8-mile round-trip hike from the Wheeler Peak parking lot; add another 1.8 miles to reach the glacier at Wheeler Cirque. Lehman Caves is actually a single cavern that extends for a quarter mile, housing well-known types of cave formations such as columns, soda straws, and draperies, as well as unusual shields.

WILDLIFE: Golden eagle, sharp-shinned hawk, pinyon jay, rock squirrel, wood rat, chipmunk, gopher, and jackrabbit.

PLANT LIFE: Bristlecone pine, Engelmann spruce, mountain mahogany, Parry's primrose, sagebrush, prickly pear cactus, and blue columbine.

ACTIVITIES: Backcountry camping (no permit required), swimming, fishing, mountain climbing, caving, horseback riding, and cross-country skiing.

INSIDER'S TIPS: Wheeler Scenic Drive is closed from November to May and is not recommended for large motor homes or vehicles pulling trailers. Headaches or nausea may result from altitude sickness while climbing. Hikers should respect the fragile nature of alpine vegetation by staying on established trails. Cave tours are given daily, except on Thanksgiving, Christmas, and Labor Day.

DIRECTIONS: From Salt Lake City, take I-80 west to 93 south and follow signs to the park. Nearest airports: Salt Lake City, Reno, and Las Vegas.

Great Smoky Mountains National Park

Gatlinburg, Tennessee 37738
Established June 15, 1934
520,004 acres. Open all year. No fee.
865-436-1200 www.nps.gov/grsm (see page 52)

SPECIAL FEATURES AND PLACES: Great Smoky refers to fog that covers the rich forests and gives the mountains their distinctive appearance. The park contains 16 peaks higher than 6,000'. Freezing and thawing, not glaciers, have carved these mountains, separating huge pieces of rock which have fallen into the valleys below. The Appalachian Trail runs through the park, forming part of the border between Tennessee and North Carolina. The 11-mile Cades Cove Loop Road in the western part of the park leads to structures built in the late 1800s. To the south, Newfound Gap Road provides access to Chimney Tops and Clingmans Dome overlooks.

WILDLIFE: Black bear, wild boar, white-tailed deer, raccoon, red squirrel, salamander, and dark-eyed junco.

PLANT LIFE: Cucumber magnolia, red maple, red spruce, eastern hemlock, Fraser fir, yellow birch, buckeye, yellow poplar, Catawba rhododendron, cherry, silverbell, rhododendron, orange jewelweed, white trillium, bluet, and spring beauty.

ACTIVITIES: Backcountry camping (permit required), horseback riding, fishing, hiking, and cross-country skiing.

INSIDER'S TIPS: The busiest park in the US is increasingly visited in the spring and fall. Crowds are best avoided midweek and in September, April, and May. In any season prepare to dress both for wet and cold, since rainfall and temperature vary widely throughout the park.

DIRECTIONS: Numerous roads provide access to the park from Tennessee and North Carolina. Nearest airports: Knoxville, TN and Asheville, NC.

Guadalupe Mountains National Park

Salt Flat, Texas 79847
Established September 30, 1972
86,416 acres. Open all year. No fee.
915-828-3251 www.nps.gov/gumo *(see page 104)*

SPECIAL FEATURES AND PLACES: Once a gigantic ocean reef, the sea receded and the sea basin lifted, cracking the enormous reef. One piece of the reef, 40 miles long, is now called the Guadalupe Mountains. They form a V, the arms of which extend northward toward New Mexico. At the vertex of the V is another reef escarpment called El Capitan, with a summit of 8,085' which is visible from 50 miles away. Erosion formed canyons like McKittrick Canyon, 5 miles long and renowned for its display of fall colors.

WILDLIFE: Collared, crevice, spiny, side-blotched, and marble whiptail lizards; striped and hognosed skunks, gray-footed chipmunk, Texas antelope squirrel, black-tailed jackrabbit, desert cottontail, gray fox, rock and canyon wrens, black-throated and rufous-crowned sparrows, ladder-backed woodpecker, solitary vireo, Scott's oriole, mountain chickadee, and yucca moth.

PLANT LIFE: Big-toothed maple, bittersweet, chokecherry, striped coral-root, venushair fern, wild rose, yucca, cholla, prickly pear cactus, Douglas fir, Texas madrone, Rocky Mountain juniper, and pinyon, limber, and ponderosa pines.

ACTIVITIES: Backcountry camping (permit required), hiking, and horseback riding.

INSIDER'S TIPS: The road to historic Williams Ranch is limited to 4-wheel-drive vehicles. Though there is no open water in the backcountry, be prepared for flash floods. Watch for cactus, spiny plants, and rattlesnakes. Summer temperatures are extreme, but winter temperatures are normally above freezing with high winds common. Rocks are unstable and not recommended for climbing. Horses are allowed for day-use only.

DIRECTIONS: From El Paso, take 62/180 east to Pine Springs. Nearest airport: El Paso.

Haleakala National Park

Makawao, Maui, Hawaii 96768
Established August 1, 1916
30,183 acres. Open all year. Fee at the summit area;
none in the coastal area.
808-572-4400 www.nps.gov/hale *(see page 173)*

SPECIAL FEATURES AND PLACES: From the 10,023' summit of Mt. Haleakala the park extends down the southeast flank to the Kipahulu coast and the Pacific Ocean. Although it last erupted around 1790, Haleakala is considered an active volcano, currently not erupting. Thousands of years of volcanic activity and erosion have formed what is commonly called the "crater." The lava flows have provided unique environments for flora and fauna. The terrain is moonlike at the top, while the Kipahulu Valley near the bottom contains abundant waterfalls and a lush tropical rain forest.

WILDLIFE: Apa-pane, iiwi, amakihi, Nene, Hawaiian dark-rumped petrel, and white-tailed tropic bird.

PLANT LIFE: Silversword, mamane, ohia lehua, and koa.

ACTIVITIES: Backcountry camping (permit required), hiking, sightseeing, swimming, snorkeling, and scuba diving.

INSIDER'S TIPS: The summit is generally freer from clouds in the morning, and is about 30 degrees F cooler than the coast. Because oxygen concentrations are low at the summit, it should be avoided by pregnant women and those with heart conditions. Be prepared for both hot and cold temperatures by bringing sun and rain gear. Note that there are no food or gas facilities within the park.

DIRECTIONS: Summit: From Kahului, follow Hawaii 37 to 377 to 378. Kipahulu: From Kahului, follow 36, Hana Highway, to Hanatown. Nearest airport: Kahului.

Hawaii Volcanoes National Park

Hawaii National Park, Big Island, Hawaii 96718
Established August 1, 1916
217,000 acres. Open all year. Fee.
808-985-6000 www.nps.gov/havo *(see page 172)*

SPECIAL FEATURES AND PLACES: Mauna Loa (13,667' high) and Kilauea (over 4,000' and growing taller) are two of the most active volcanoes on earth. Each was built when lava fountained and flowed, either from the top of the caldera or from vents on the sides. Crater Rim Drive provides fine views of Kilauea Caldera and passes through rain forest and desert. The road provides easy access to a short hike to the Thurston Lava Tube (cooled lava) and leads to the Chain of Craters Road. The latter offers views of the East Rift Zone, containing Mauna Ulu (a steaming dome-like hill) and Puu Huluhulu (a grass-covered cinder cone) overlook. The drive continues southwest, accessing the Kau Desert, Halemaumau Crater, and the Jagger Museum.

WILDLIFE: Hawk, nene, apa-pane, white-tailed tropic bird, amakihi, butterflies, bats, crickets, beetles, and sea turtles.

PLANT LIFE: Tree and false staghorn ferns, ohelo, lobelia, ohia lehua, koa, mamane, and coconut palm.

ACTIVITIES: Backcountry camping (permit required), hiking, horseback riding, and biking.

INSIDER'S TIPS: Supplies are available in the town of Volcano. Heat may be very intense, so bring long pants and shirts as well as sunscreen and a hat. Roads may close due to volcanic activity. Fumes may pose health risks to children, pregnant women, and people with heart or breathing problems. Avoid steam vents, earth cracks, and cliffs.

DIRECTIONS: On the island of Hawaii Big Island, take Highway 11, a 95-mile drive from Kona International Airport or a 30-mile drive from Hilo Airport.

Hot Springs National Park

Hot Springs, AR 71902
Established April 20, 1832 as Hot Springs Reservation
Established as a national park March 4, 1921
5,500 acres. Open all year.

Fee only for camping and commercially operated bathhouses.
501-624-2701 www.nps.gov/hosp *(see page 77)*

SPECIAL FEATURES AND PLACES: This smallest of the national parks is located in the Zig Zag Mountains of the Ouachita Range and surrounds the north end of a city. The park is uniquely famous for its pristine springs containing dissolved silica, calcium, bicarbonates, and traces of other minerals. The 143 degree F water has been under pressure deep in the earth and is more than 4,000 years old. As it reaches the surface, the carbon dioxide which is dissolved in it bubbles forth. This water, renowned for its alleged medicinal effects from both drinking and bathing, draws thousands of visitors who use 1920s-vintage bathhouses such as the Buckstaff. One such building, the former Fordyce Bathhouse, offers 23 completely restored rooms, and serves as the park visitor center. The building is open for tours daily except New Year's Day, Thanksgiving Day, and Christmas Day, and also offers an introductory park movie as well as a movie explaining the traditional bath routine. The collection of eight buildings known as Bathhouse Row is a National Historic Landmark. It holds this distinction for being the largest and best collection of bathhouses in the United States. The Grand Promenade, built as a transition from the Bathhouse Row area to the wooded hillside behind, affords a leisurely walk through the springs discharge area.

WILDLIFE: Gray and fox squirrels, red and gray fox, wild turkey, raccoon, opossum, white-tailed deer, chipmunk, and various songbirds.

PLANT LIFE: Redbud, dogwood, short-leaf pine, white oak, red maple, southern magnolia, black cherry, fire pink, birdsfoot violet, bergamot, wild phlox, coreopsis, and various algae species in the hot springs.

ACTIVITIES: Camping in the campground, hiking, picnicking, and bathing.

TRAVEL TIPS: The scenic mountain drives are designed for slow sightseeing travelers, so drive carefully. Hot Springs Mountain Drive is closed to vehicles more than 30' long.

DIRECTIONS: From Little Rock, take I-30 to US 70 west to Hot Springs. Nearest airport: Little Rock. Shuttle services from Little Rock airport and the Little Rock and Malvern Amtrak stations.

Isle Royale National Park
Houghton, Michigan 49931
Authorized March 3, 1931

134,400 acres. Open mid-April to October 31. No fee.
906-482-0984 www.nps.gov/isro *(see page 88)*

SPECIAL FEATURES AND PLACES: Isolated in the northwest corner of Lake Superior, the park is a 45-mile refuge of islands dominated by Isle Royale, a 37-mile-long island. The shoreline is composed of an unbroken rock wall to the north and narrow peninsulas and inlets flanked by reefs and rock clusters elsewhere. Siskiwit Lake is the largest lake on the island (7 miles long) and is the home of Ryan Island. At either end of Isle Royale are ports with information centers: Windigo to the west and Rock Harbor to the east. Both access nature trails, with the latter offering the 4-mile Stoll Loop trail, passing shallow mining pits where Native Americans began mining copper around 2,500 BC. Offshore is the America, one of 10 major wrecks explored by scuba divers.

WILDLIFE: Great-horned owl, bald eagles, gray jay, goldeneye and old squaw ducks, common loon, whistling swan, winter wren, song and white-throated sparrows, redpoll, pine siskin, ruby-crowned kinglet, muskrat, marten, red fox, eastern timber wolf, and moose.

PLANT LIFE: Beaked alder, green hazel, yellow and paper birches, mountain ash, sugar maple, red oak, thimbleberry, blueberry, raspberry, skunk cabbage, hepatica, marsh marigold, hawkweed, fireweed, pearly everlasting, gaywing, and lady slipper.

ACTIVITIES: Backcountry camping (permit required), rock climbing, boating, scuba diving, and fishing.

INSIDER'S TIPS: The most pleasant time to visit is late June through September. Insects are most abundant in June and July. The park is accessible only by boat or floatplane; reservations required. Because of rough water, do not cross Lake Superior in a boat less than 20' long. All water should be filtered or boiled before drinking. Medical and phone services are unavailable.

DIRECTIONS: Boat service is available from Houghton, Copper Harbor, or Grand Portage. Floatplane service from Houghton. Nearest airport: Houghton.

Joshua Tree National Park
Twentynine Palms, California 92277
Established as a national monument in August 1936
and as a national park on October 31, 1994

792,828 acres. Open all year. Fee.
760-367-5500 www.nps.gov/jotr *(see page 159)*

SPECIAL FEATURES AND PLACES: Giant spiked Joshua trees mark the high desert within this part of the Mojave Desert. Low desert vegetation provides contrast within southern and eastern park sections of the Colorado Desert. From California 62, the 49 Palms Oasis can be reached via a steep trail. Further east, Park Boulevard leads to Jumbo Rocks and a Joshua tree forest, as well as a desert with yucca and unusual, softly rounded rock formations. Still further east, the Pinto Basin Road leads to the Cholla Cactus Garden, Ocotillo Patch, Cottonwood Spring, and Wonderland of Rocks – 12 sq. miles of disordered masses of granite near the Lost Horse Valley. Remnants of early ranchers and miners remain.

WILDLIFE: Bighorn sheep, mountain lion, bobcat, coyote, jackrabbit, roadrunner, desert tortoise, sidewinder rattlesnake, kangaroo rat, burrowing owl, yucca night lizard, and tarantula.

PLANT LIFE: Joshua tree, fan palm, pinyon pine, cottonwood, creosote bush, smoke tree, mesquite, ironwood; ocotillo, Palo Verde, barrel, Bigelow cholla, and dozens of other cacti; sand verbena, desert dandelion, and evening primrose.

ACTIVITIES: Backcountry camping (permit required), hiking, rock climbing, and bicycling.

INSIDER'S TIPS: Most popular time to visit is during the wildflower season, February through April (depending on the rainfall), and after summer temperatures decline from October through November. Campers marvel at star-gazing opportunities. Flash flooding may occur after even brief rain showers. In all seasons, carry plenty of water (1 gallon per day per person). Watch for open mine shafts and prospect holes.

DIRECTIONS: From I-10 (LA to the west, Indio to the east), take 62 to the north and follow the signs to the park entrances. Nearest airport: Palm Springs.

Katmai National Park
King Salmon, Alaska 99613
Established as a national monument in 1918,
as a national park on December 2, 1980
4,090,000 acres. Open all year. No fee.
907-246-3305 www.nps.gov/katm *(see page 171)*

SPECIAL FEATURES AND PLACES: A wild and rugged stage is set by 15 active volcanoes in the Aleutian Range lining the Shelikof Strait. Steam plumes occasionally rise from Mts. Mageik, Martin, and Trident, the last of which erupted as recently as 1968. At least 10 major eruptions have occurred during the past 7,000 years, depositing ash throughout the Katmai area. Ash deposits have been cut by rivers to form steep-walled gorges, creating an ideal habitat for bears and fish. In 1912 the Novarupta Volcano erupted, blowing out pumice and ash into what is known as the Valley of Ten Thousand Smokes. Bus and van tours from the Brooks Camp Visitor Center travel 23 miles through bear country to the Three Forks overlook. Descending 200' on a short trail, it is possible to see the Ukak River roaring through a bedrock canyon crowned by cliffs of volcanic ash. From the visitor center, a 1¹/₂-mile trail climbs up Dumpling Mountain to an 800' overlook, where Naknek Lake lies below.

WILDLIFE: Grizzly and Alaska brown bears, moose, gray wolf, lynx, wolverine, red fox, river and sea otters, mink, marten, weasel, porcupine, rock ptarmigan, red-necked grebe, tundra swan, arctic tern, bald eagle, rainbow trout, sockeye and red salmon, hair seal, and beluga, killer, and gray whales.

PLANT LIFE: White spruce, birch, alder, willow, balsam, poplar, Sitka spruce, blue joint grass, bluegrass, fireweed, yellow paintbrush, yarrow, lupine, and wild geranium.

ACTIVITIES: Backcountry camping (permit required), mountain climbing, kayaking, canoeing, boating, fishing, bear watching, and hunting (preserve only).

INSIDER'S TIPS: Bring rain gear, warm clothing, and insect repellent and be prepared for high winds. Stay at least 50 yards from individual bears and 100 yards from sows with young.

DIRECTIONS: The park is 290 miles southwest of Anchorage. Flights leave from Anchorage to King Salmon daily. Travel from King Salmon to Brooks Camp is by floatplane; other areas of the park are reached by charter aircraft.

Kenai Fjords National Park
Seward, Alaska 99664
Established December 1, 1980
580,000 acres. Open all year. User fee at Exit Glacier.
907-224-3175 www.nps.gov/kefj (see page 169)

SPECIAL FEATURES AND PLACES: Steep-sided glacial valleys now filled by sea water define Kenai Fjords along the Gulf of Alaska. The collision of 2 tectonic plates (the Pacific and North American) caused the land to submerge, and in so doing, glacier-carved cirques have become half-moon bays with mountain peak islands. Sitting on top of the Kenai Mountains to the north is the Harding Icefield. Over 700 square miles of ice up to a mile deep and feeding over 30 glaciers which carved out this coastal ecosystem, the Harding Icefield is the largest icefield totally within US boundaries. At Exit Glacier, the only part of the park accessible by road, visitors can walk easy trails through recently deglaciated landscapes to view a living laboratory of plant succession. A more challenging trail to the edge of the Harding Icefield requires a 3,000' climb along a 7-mile round-trip trail.

WILDLIFE: Bald eagle, peregrin falcon, horned and tufted puffins, common and thick-billed murre, rhinoceros and parakeet auklets, marbled and Kittlitz's murrelets, pigeon guillemots, northern fulmars, sooty shearwaters, parasitic jaeger, black-legged kittiwake, sea ducks, shorebirds, songbirds, salmon, halibut, lingcod, rockfish, mountain goat, moose, wolverine, red fox, hoary marmot, black and brown bears, Dall porpoise, sea otter, Steller sea lion, harbor seal, and gray, humpback, killer, minke and fin whales.

PLANT LIFE: Sitka spruce, Lutz spruce, black cottonwood, feltleaf willow, Sitka alder, mountain hemlock, fireweed, nootka lupin, devil's club, twisted stalk, yellow dryas, lovage, oyster leaf, beach pea, pyrola, bunchberry, blueberry, fucus, and bull kelp.

ACTIVITIES: Kayaking/backcountry camping, boating, fishing, sailing, sea kayaking, diving, cross-country skiing, snowshoeing, and dogsledding.

TRAVEL TIPS: Most visits to the park are by boat via private companies that take visitors on glacier/wildlife cruises to Holgate, Aialik, and Northwestern, tidewater glaciers that calve into the sea, and to the Chiswell Islands, home to tens of thousands of sea birds. The only area of the park accessible by car is Exit Glacier, about 12 miles northwest of Seward. Nights are cool along the coast of this temperate rain forest. Heavy rain can be expected.

DIRECTIONS: 130 miles south of Seward via the Seward Highway. Boat, ferry, train, or plane trips may be arranged in Anchorage, Seward, or on the internet.

Kobuk Valley National Park

Kotzebue, Alaska 99752
Established December 2, 1980
1,750,000 acres. Open all year. No fee.
907-442-3760 www.nps.gov/kova (*see page 168*)

SPECIAL FEATURES AND PLACES: Located entirely above the Arctic Circle and enclosed by the Baird and Waring mountains, the park includes the central section of the Kobuk River, the Great Kobuk sand dunes (25 sq. miles), and the Little Kobuk and Hunt River sand dunes. The grinding of glaciers produced the sand, which was carried to the valley by the wind. The boreal forest reaches its northernmost limit in Kobuk Valley, where pockets of tundra blend into dwarf spruce and birch. The Kobuk River is a wide, pleasant river, excellent for canoe, kayak, or motor boat. To travel the park on the Kobuk from Ambler west to Kiana is a 50-mile trip and takes less than a week. The water winds past the Onion Portage, where caribou cross the river. The more remote Salmon River, which flows from the north, provides more challenges.

WILDLIFE: Grizzly and black bears, caribou, gray wolf, wolverine, arctic fox, weasel, and lemming.

PLANT LIFE: White and black spruces, balsam, poplar, willow, alder, cottonwood, dwarf birch, sedge, blueberry, and lichen.

ACTIVITIES: Backcountry camping (no permit required), hiking, boating, fishing, kayaking, canoeing, rafting, and snowmobiling.

INSIDER'S TIPS: There are no roads or trails. Prepare for high winds, snow, and rain and guard against potential hypothermia. Water should be filtered or boiled before drinking. Bring protection from mosquitoes, gnats, and biting flies. Avoid subsistence camps and fishnets, and respect private property, much of which is owned by Native Americans.

DIRECTIONS: Travel to the park must be arranged through air taxi or charter aircraft services based in Fairbanks and Anchorage. Lists of services are available from the park.

Lake Clark National Park

Park Headquarters – Anchorage, Alaska 99508
Established December 2, 1980
4,045,000 acres. Open all year. No fee.

907-781-2218 (Field Office at Port Alsworth) www.nps.gov/lacl (*see page 168*)

SPECIAL FEATURES AND PLACES: Rugged mountains, deep forests, and picturesque lakes and rivers await visitors to the Cook Inlet region of Alaska. Where the Alaskan and the Aleutian ranges meet, two active volcanoes, Iliamna and Redoubt, vent steam and rise more than 10,000'. Only one short trail, Tanalian Falls trail (2 miles long), is maintained in the park at Port Alsworth. From it, Tanalian Mountain can be reached after leaving the trail and climbing strenuously 3,600' up a ridge – a hike of 7 miles round-trip. North of Lake Clark are ever more remote lakes: Lachbuna, Portage, Twin, Turquoise, and Telaquana, all about 15 miles apart. Kayakers may explore Mulchatna, Chilikadrotna, Kijik, and Tlikakila rivers within the park.

WILDLIFE: King, chum, coho, humpback, and sockeye salmon; Dolly Varden trout, northern pike, grayling, moose, Dall's sheep, caribou, Alaska brown and black bears, arctic ground squirrel, gray wolf, lynx, red fox, puffin, cormorant, and kittiwake.

PLANT LIFE: Black, Sitka, and white spruces; yellow birch, alpine bearberry, blueberry, and fireweed.

ACTIVITIES: Wilderness camping (no permit required), hiking, mountain climbing, kayaking, rafting, boating, fishing, hunting, limited snowmobiling, and cross-country skiing.

INSIDER'S TIPS: Hiking is easiest above 2,000' in the interior and on the coast due to snow conditions above the brush line. Try to stay on dry tundra, avoiding heavy brush, and carefully choose river crossings. Watch out for sudden winds while boating. Bring warm clothing, rain gear, insect repellent, a head net, and an insect-proof tent. Be aware of bears.

DIRECTIONS: There are no roads to the park. Most visitors charter a plane from Anchorage to lakes within Lake Clark. Less expensive is a scheduled flight from Anchorage to Port Alsworth or Iliamna followed by an air taxi into the park. Air taxis also fly from Homer and Kenai.

Lassen Volcanic National Park
Mineral, California 96063
Established August 9, 1916
106,000 acres. Open all year. Fee.
530-595-4444 www.nps.gov/lavo (*see page 152*)

SPECIAL FEATURES AND PLACES: On May 22, 1914, Lassen Peak erupted spectacularly, blowing ash and debris 7 miles high, and continuing sporadically for the next 7 years. Sulfur vents are still steaming. The surrounding landscape was forever altered by great lava pinnacles, mountains created by lava flows, and newly formed craters, creating a unique ecosystem. The Park Road leads to a 3-mile round-trip hike on the Bumpass Hell trail to the largest geo-thermal site in the park: 16 acres of boiling mud, pyrite pools, steam vents, and odoriferous fumaroles. Nearby is Lake Helen and farther east, the road leads to Summit Lake, a pristine alpine lake. Two other lakes, Reflection and Manzanita, are just inside the park's northwest entrance station. The Pacific Crest Trail runs through the center of the park.

WILDLIFE: Mule deer, black bear, coyote, Douglas' and flying squirrels, pika, blue grouse, wood duck, treefrog, and June bug.

PLANT LIFE: Snow plant, alpine shooting star, skyrocket gilia, Indian paintbrush, and lodgepole pine.

ACTIVITIES: Backcountry camping (permit required), horseback riding, swimming, canoeing, and cross-country skiing.

INSIDER'S TIPS: Motorized boats are prohibited in park waters. Around hot springs or steaming areas, stay on established trails. Ground crusts that appear stable may be dangerously thin.

DIRECTIONS: From I-5, exit east at Redding or Red Bluff to reach the park. Nearest airports: Redding, Chico.

Mammoth Cave National Park

Mammoth Cave, Kentucky 42259
Established July 1, 1941
52,830 acres. Open all year. No fee, except
for cave tours and camping.
270-758-2251 www.nps.gov/maca (see page 80)

SPECIAL FEATURES AND PLACES: Surveyors at Mammoth Cave have mapped more than 350 miles to date in what is believed to be the longest cave system in the world. Beneath ridges capped with sandstone is limestone, which is being dissolved slowly by acidic rainwater. Over millions of years caves and underground rivers were formed. Visitors use six entrances: Historic, New, Frozen Niagara, Violet City, Carmichael, and the Elevator. From the Historic entrance the Main Cave leads to underground passages such as Broadway, Audubon, Scot's Mans Trap, and Fat Man's Misery, off of which are rooms such as Great Relief Hall, Mammoth Dome, and Side Saddle Pit. Forces of erosion that formed the cave system also shaped bluffs, sinkholes, and ridge tops on the surface. The Green River flows through the park, dividing 60 miles of hiking trails to the north and 10 miles of trails to the south.

WILDLIFE: Eyeless fish and crayfish, cave shrimp, snails, flatworms, white spiders, and 6 types of beetles are some of the 30 species of permanent cave dwellers. Non-permanent dwellers include the cave salamander, cave cricket, and 7 species of bat. Species that inhabit the secondary growth forest around the cave are phoebe, great blue heron, kingfisher, wood duck, wild turkey, muskie, white perch, catfish, white-tailed deer, chipmunk, and raccoon.

PLANT LIFE: Eastern redbud, tulip poplar, beech, sugar maple, black oak, hemlock, sycamore, umbrella magnolia, holly, bladderwort, arrowroot, early spiderwort, and lance-leafed violet.

ACTIVITIES: Backcountry camping (permit required), horseback riding, canoeing, boating, camping, and fishing. Special programs are held throughout the year as part of the park's "Earthspeak" program.

INSIDER'S TIPS: Cave tours are given every day except Christmas – reservations are not required, but strongly recommended. Cave tour and campground reservations may be made by calling Biospherics at 800-967-2283. Specific tour information is available by calling the park directly at 270-758-2328. Tours can and do sell out in summer, on off-season weekends, holidays, and during spring break season (mid-March through mid-April). In the summer bring a light sweater or jacket, as the temperature in the cave is 54 degrees F and humidity may reach 100 percent. Some of the cave tours require stooping and walking over uneven terrain. Proper footwear is important, since some trails are slippery and wet.

DIRECTIONS: The park is a short drive from I-65. From Louisville, take exit 53 at Cave City and follow signs. From Nashville, take exit 48 at Park City and follow signs. Nearest airports: Louisville, Nashville.

Mesa Verde National Park
Mesa Verde, Colorado 81330
Established June 29, 1906

52,074 acres. Open all year. Fee.

970-529-4465 www.nps.gov/meve (see page 122)

SPECIAL FEATURES AND PLACES: Part of a large plateau rising above the Montezuma and Mancos valleys, the park contains remains of the thousand-year-old ancestral Puebloan culture. Many types of archeological sites are accessible to visitors, such as cliff dwellings, mesa top pithouses, and pueblos. Most famous are the Cliff Palace, Spruce Tree House, Balcony House, and Far View Community. Access to the Long House and the Badger House Community is from Wetherill Mesa 12 miles from the visitor center. The architectural variations of the ruins reflect the evolution of the culture. The first structures were pithouses and pueblos, but unknown factors encouraged the people to relocate to the cliffhouses in canyon walls at a later time. As agriculturally based people, they were dependent upon rainfall; a long drought is one factor that may have forced them from the region.

WILDLIFE: Collared, northern plateau, sagebrush, and shorthorned lizards; yellow-bellied marmot, rock and Abert squirrels, desert and mountain cottontail, Colorado chipmunk, white-tailed prairie dog, valley pocket gopher, Mexican and white-throated woodrats, prairie rattlesnake, bull snake, yellow-bellied racer, striped skunk, mountain lion, mule deer, coyote; scrub, pinyon, and Steller's jays; black-billed magpie, common poorwill, Townsend's solitaire, broad-tailed hummingbird, ash-throated flycatcher, blue-gray gnatcatcher, yellow-rumped and black-throated warblers, mountain bluebird, black-headed grosbeak, western tanager, violet-green swallow, white-throated swift, sharp-shinned hawk, and great-horned owl.

PLANT LIFE: Cliff fendlerbush, Mormon tea, Utah serviceberry, rabbitbrush, snowberry, yucca, prickly pear cactus, big sagebrush, skunkbush, sumac, mariposa lily, globemallow, Indian paintbrush, scarlet gilia, skyrocket penstemon, Utah juniper, mountain mahogany, pinyon and ponderosa pines, and Gambel oak.

ACTIVITIES: Hiking, camping, and cross-country skiing.

INSIDER'S TIPS: No backcountry camping is permitted. Bring adequate footgear for strenuous climbs into cliff dwellings. (Except for Balcony House, all cliff dwellings may be viewed from overlooks.) Hiking is permitted on 5 trails in the park. Mountain bikes are not allowed on the trails; bicycles are not allowed on Wetherill Mesa roads.

212

DIRECTIONS: From Cortez, take Highway 160 east to the park entrance. Nearest airports: Cortez, Durango.

Mt. Rainier National Park

Ashford, Washington 98304
Established March 2, 1899
235,625 acres. Open all year. Fee.
360-569-2211 www.nps.gov/mora *(see page 144)*

SPECIAL FEATURES AND PLACES: Located at the southern end of the Washington Cascades, Mt. Rainier is a million-year-old volcano with 14,410' of rock built by eruptions and lava flows. Because of a massive system of 25 glaciers combined with unpredictable weather, it is both hazardous and inviting to climbers. The snowfall toward the upper part of the mountain averages 620 inches a year and set a world's record of 1,022 inches the winter of 1971-72; the corresponding rainfall has created rain forests below. Paradise is a subalpine meadow in the south-central portion of the park. The park's main visitor center is there, as is the mountain climbing school, and the historic mountain lodge, Paradise Inn. Ohanepecosh Visitor Center in the park's southeast corner provides scenic views of the river of that name. Sunrise Visitor Center at 6,400' is the highest point to which a car can be driven in the park, and it is an excellent place to view glaciers. Longmire Museum, established in 1928 in the southwest corner of the park, is one of the oldest museums in the national park system. It is the only visitor information facility open daily year-round.

WILDLIFE: Black bear, black-tailed deer, elk, mountain goat, yellow-bellied marmot, chipmunk, ground squirrel, pika, Steller's and gray jays, Clark's nutcracker, rosy finch, mountain bluebird, red-tailed and Swainson's hawks, northern harrier, golden eagle, and banana slug.

PLANT LIFE: Indian paintbrush, fireweed, aster, lupine, arnica, monkeyflower, parrot's beak, gentian, avalanche lily, bear grass, huckleberry, mountain ash, crinkle-barked spruce, mountain hemlock, western red cedar, and Douglas fir.

ACTIVITIES: Scenic drives, backcountry camping (permit required), mountain climbing, horseback riding, fishing, cross-country skiing, and snowshoeing.

INSIDER'S TIPS: The trails are usually free of snow from mid-July through September. Though the road to Paradise is kept open all year, the inn is only open May through October, while the National Park Inn at Longmire, in the southwest corner of the park, is open all year. Parking is nearly impossible to find on sunny summer weekends and holidays in popular areas of the park (Paradise, Longmire, Sunrise, Grove of the Patriarchs, and Ohanapecosh). Plan your visit for mid-week if possible. Carpool and arrive early. Obtain a copy of *The Tahoma News: A Visitor's Guide to Mount Rainier National Park* at an entrance station or visitor center. It contains important information and updates that will help you make the most of your visit.

DIRECTIONS: From Seattle, take I-5 south to Washington Highway 7 and 706, following signs to the park. Nearest airports: Seattle, Portland.

North Cascades National Park

Sedro-Woolley, Washington 98284
Established October 2, 1968
684,000 acres. Open all year. No fee.
360-856-5700 www.nps.gov/noca *(see page 143)*

SPECIAL FEATURES AND PLACES: Amid one of the world's largest mountain ranges stretching from Canada into Oregon, the park offers steep peaks, snowfields, waterfalls, glaciers, and wildflower meadows. There are over 300 glaciers and countless mountains to be explored among a web of hiking trails. The drive across Washington State 20, from the town of Marblemount to Washington Pass Overlook, includes views of alpine meadows, jagged mountains like Pyramid Peak (7,182'), and cascading waterfalls such as Gorge Creek Falls. Access is provided to the Happy Creek Forest trail, Gorge Overlook trail, and other trails, as well as the North Cascades Visitor Center, Diablo and Ross dams and lakes, and Rainy Pass, where the Pacific Crest Trail crosses the highway. Washington Pass Overlook, part of the Okanogan National Forest, has views of the Early Winter Spires and Liberty Bell Mountain. North of the highway is the North Unit, accessible via the Big Beaver trail beginning at Ross Dam; the South Unit can be reached by the Thunder Creek trail beginning at Diablo Lake.

WILDLIFE: Black-tailed and mule deer, mountain goat, black bear, hoary marmot, pocket gopher, Douglas' squirrel, Trowbridge shrew, Towsend's chipmunk, pika, Pacific jumping mice, pileated woodpecker, spotted owl, cougar, and more.

PLANT LIFE: Mountain and western hemlocks, western red cedar, Douglas fir, ponderosa pine, bigleaf and vine maples, alder, black cottonwood, red alder, huckleberry, salmonberry, thimbleberry, moss campion, stinging nettles, devil's club, fireweed, fern, amanita muscaria, columbine, bistort, lupine, etc.

ACTIVITIES: Backcountry camping (permit required), hiking, mountain climbing, horseback riding, fishing, and boating.

INSIDER'S TIPS: Before starting backcountry trips, check stream and trail conditions and verify whether special equipment is necessary to cross snowfields. Hang food out of the reach of bears. There is no backpacking in the winter due to heavy snowfall.

DIRECTIONS: From Vancouver or Seattle, I-5 leads to Burlington. Head east on Washington 20 to the park. Nearest airports: Vancouver (Canada) and Seattle.

Olympic National Park

Port Angeles, Washington 98362
Established June 29, 1938
922,000 acres. Open all year. Fee.
360-565-3130 www.nps.gov/olym (*see page 140*)

SPECIAL FEATURES AND PLACES: A sliver of land along the rugged and wild coast is combined with verdant forests surrounding Mt. Olympus to form the Olympic Peninsula, home of Olympic National Park. Extensive hiking trails allow visitors to reach 100+ locations in the high country, including 60 active glaciers. Four types of forest represent unique ecosystems. Temperate rain forests of Sitka spruce and western cedar in low-lying areas on the west side of the park ascend to stands of western hemlock and grand fir. Further up in elevation, montane forests of silver fir precede the short subalpine forests of mountain hemlock, subalpine fir, and Alaska cedar. Numerous streams dissect the landscape and several lakes dot the region. US 101 provides access to the Olympic National Park Visitor Center, the Storm King Information Station at Lake Crescent, Sol Duc Hot Springs Resort, and the Hoh Rain Forest Visitor Center.

WILDLIFE: Olympic marmot, banana slug, treefrog, mountain lion, black-tailed deer, Roosevelt elk, snowshoe hare, Oregon junco, winter wren, ruffed grouse, kingfisher, great blue heron, oyster catcher, periwinkle snail, limpet, starfish, sea anemone, sea urchin, mussel, barnacle, and tide-pool sculpin.

PLANT LIFE: Rockweed, bigleaf and vine maples; Douglas, grand, silver, and subalpine firs; black cottonwood, western red cedar, red alder, Pacific madrone, western and mountain hemlocks, Sitka spruce, licorice, bead-ruby, salmonberry, sorrel, chanterelle and amanita muscaria mushrooms, spike moss, sword, maidenhair, and lady ferns.

ACTIVITIES: Backcountry camping (permit required), mountain climbing, horseback riding, swimming, boating, fishing, biking, cross-country skiing, and snowshoeing.

INSIDER'S TIPS: Roads at higher elevations are usually open June through September. Be aware of tides where they come into the base of cliffs and headlands.

DIRECTIONS: From Seattle, cross the Puget Sound by ferry to connect with Highway 101 and follow signs to the park. Nearest airport: Seattle.

Petrified Forest National Park

Petrified Forest National Park, Arizona 86028
Established as a national monument December 8, 1906
Established as a national park December 9, 1962
93,533 acres. Open all year; closed Christmas day.
Park road closed if winter weather causes
dangerous road conditions. Fee.
928-524-6628 www.nps.gov/pefo (see page 114)

SPECIAL FEATURES AND PLACES: Pine-like trees grew about 225 million years ago, and when they fell, they were washed into a vast floodplain and covered with deposits of silt, mud, and volcanic ash. Without oxygen, decay was slowed. Gradually, silica replaced the cells of the trees, and quartz casts were all that remained. Varied colors of quartz now visible in the petrified trees are caused by minerals like carbon, manganese, and iron oxides. A 28-mile scenic road through the park passes the Rainbow Forest Museum in the southern part of the park. Short trails near the museum require less than a mile of hiking to reach the sites of Giant Logs and Long Logs, as well as Agate House, a pueblo believed to have been inhabited around AD 1100. The road continues north to the historic Painted Desert Inn and Painted Desert Visitor Center, with many pullouts and overlooks providing views of the desert, petrified logs, and Newspaper

Rock, where petroglyphs were pecked into the surface of the large sandstone boulders at the base of the cliff.

WILDLIFE: Kangaroo rat, packrat, turkey vulture, raven, red-tailed hawk, golden eagle, coyote, pronghorn, cottontail, jackrabbit, prairie dog, and collared lizard.

PLANT LIFE: Juniper, Indian paintbrush, globemallow. The park protects a rare shortgrass environment that supports over 1,000 species of plants.

ACTIVITIES: Backcountry camping (permit required), hiking, ranger programs, photography, special events as scheduled, and park film every half-hour at the Painted Desert Visitor Center.

INSIDER'S TIPS: Extended park hours in the summer months – dates and times vary depending on staffing. Call in advance for park hours. Petrified Forest is on Mountain Standard Time year round. Removal of petrified wood or cultural objects is strictly prohibited. Because of relatively high altitudes within the arid park, be aware of over-exertion and carry sufficient water.

DIRECTIONS: From the west: Take US Highway 180 from Holbrook to the south park entrance – the drive north through the park will end on Interstate 40. From the east: Take Interstate 40 to exit 311 at the northern park entrance, drive south and turn west on US Highway 180 to join Interstate 40 at Holbrook. Nearest airport: Flagstaff.

Redwood National and State Parks

Crescent City, California 95531
Established October 2, 1968
Open all year. No fee.
707-464-6101 www.nps.gov/redw *(see page 150 – 151)*

SPECIAL FEATURES AND PLACES: The world's tallest trees make unforgettable forests. Redwood National Park and the adjacent state parks contain nearly half of all remaining old growth redwood forests. Together with Prairie Creek, Del Norte Coast, and Jedediah Smith Redwoods state parks, these parks form a rain forest of coastal redwood trees which are taller and younger than their close relatives, the sequoias. US 101 dissects the region, providing access to the ocean and other sites. The Coastal Drive off of US 101 at the mouth of the Klamath River winds south through stands of redwoods, opening to panoramic views of the Pacific Ocean.

WILDLIFE: Roosevelt elk, black-tailed deer, black bear, California vole, mountain beaver, striped skunk, rough-skinned newt, steelhead and cutthroat trout, Chinook salmon, kestrel, raven, Steller's jay, meadowlark, California quail, sanderling, long-billed curlew, marbled murrelet, double-crested cormorant, brown pelican, sea urchin, giant green sea anemone, acorn barnacle, periwinkle snail, harbor seal, and gray whale.

PLANT LIFE: Coastal redwood, Douglas fir, vine maple, rosebay, western azalea, trillium, redwood sorrel, blue-blossom, lilac, Indian paintbrush, poison oak, morning glory, sand verbena, and maidenhair, lady, five-fingered, and sword ferns.

ACTIVITIES: Backcountry camping (permit required), hiking, horseback riding, swimming, boating, kayaking, fishing, biking, and wildlife watching.

INSIDER'S TIPS: Late winter to early spring is the best time to spot whales. There are 4 backcountry camps; campsites are also available in 3 state parks and 3 national forests nearby. Trailers are prohibited on Davidson Road and not advised on the Coastal Drive or Howland Hill Road.

DIRECTIONS: Highway 101 provides access to the park. Nearest airports: Medford, OR, Arcata and Crescent City, CA.

Rocky Mountain National Park

Estes Park, Colorado 80517
Established January 26, 1915
265,753 acres. Open all year. Fee.
970-586-1206 www.nps.gov/romo (see page 121)

SPECIAL FEATURES AND PLACES: This park is one of the only places in the continental US where tundra, the land above tree line, is readily accessible. Covering one third of the park, snowtopped mountains rise above subalpine valleys. The 48-mile Trail Ridge Road begins in Estes Park and crosses the Continental Divide, before ending at Grand Lake. Revealed along the way are stunning vistas, geologic features, and many trailheads, including the Tundra World Nature trail, a moderate half-mile hike. Notwithstanding its impressive height, Long's Peak (at over 14,000') is one of the easiest-to-climb tall mountains in the US, although it is still a strenuous 16-mile round trip. The ascent can be undertaken without equipment, once the ice has melted. Bear Lake Road accesses trails leading to various alpine lakes, including Bierstadt, Cub, Fern, Spruce, and Lake of Glass. The road also offers beautiful views of Andrews and Tyndall glaciers.

WILDLIFE: Elk, mule deer, yellow-bellied marmot, black bear, Wyoming ground squirrel, pika, red and Abert's squirrels, bighorn sheep, Steller's and gray jays, mountain bluebird, broad-tailed hummingbird, evening grosbeak, pygmy nuthatch, and golden eagle.

PLANT LIFE: Quaking aspen, Engelmann and blue spruces, lodgepole and ponderosa pines, Douglas fir, Colorado columbine, tansy aster, yellow aster, wood lily, shooting star, alpine buttercup, dwarf clover, alpine forget-me-not, big-rooted spring beauty, tall one-sided penstemon, and Indian paintbrush.

ACTIVITIES: Backcountry camping (permit required), mountain climbing, horseback riding, fishing, cross-country skiing, snowmobiling (west side only), and snowshoeing.

INSIDER'S TIPS: The park is crowded in the summer, the weather is unpredictable in all seasons. Bring extra layers of clothing and sun protection. The edges of steep snow slopes should be avoided. People with circulatory or respiratory problems should not travel on Trail Ridge Road, due to the low oxygen at 2 miles above sea level.

DIRECTIONS: From Denver, take US Highway 36 to Estes Park. From the west, use I-70 and take US 40 north to US 34 and follow the signs. Nearest airport: Denver.

Saguaro National Park

Tucson, Arizona 85730
Established October 14, 1994
91,327 acres. Open all year. Fee.
520-733-5153 www.nps.gov/sagu (see page 115)

SPECIAL FEATURES AND PLACES: In the heart of the Sonoran Desert, this park owes its name to a very unusual plant, the Saguaro cactus, which lives 175-200 years. After 15 years it may be less than a foot tall; after 30 it begins to flower; after 50 it may be 7'; after 75 it may sprout branches, and after 100 it may reach 25' tall. There are two separate park districts about 30 miles apart. Saguaro West: Tucson Mountain District has a 9-mile scenic drive. The Cactus Garden trail at the Visitor Center is about

200 yards long. The Desert Discovery trail is a $1/3$-mile loop located 1 mile from the visitor center. The Valley View Overlook trail is a $4/5$-mile round trip that begins 3 miles from the visitor center. Saguaro East: Rincon Mountain District is much larger, with an 8-mile scenic drive and 128 miles of hiking trials, including the short, paved Desert Ecology trail.

WILDLIFE: Gila woodpecker, gilded flicker, purple martin, Gambel's quail, cactus wren, western kingbird, Lucy's warbler, roadrunner, screech and elf owls, kestrel, red-tailed and Harris hawks, coyote, collared peccary, ground and rock squirrels, jackrabbit, cactus mouse, bobcat, ringtail cat, mountain lion, black bear, gila monster, desert tortoise, and western diamondback, northern blacktailed, sidewinder, mojave, tiger, and Arizona black rattlesnakes.

PLANT LIFE: Saguaro, barrel, teddybear cholla, prickly pear, hedgehog, fishhook, and night-blooming cereus cacti; mesquite, creosote bush, desert broom, Douglas fir, ponderosa and Apache pines, Palo Verde, jojoba, and scrub oak.

ACTIVITIES: Backcountry camping (only at Rincon Mountain District, permit required), horseback riding, biking, hiking, bird watching, and wildlife viewing.

INSIDER'S TIPS: Best time to visit is October through April when 70 degrees F is the high temperature, although at night it may drop below freezing. During the rest of the year, temperatures average 100 degrees F, dropping 30 degrees at night. Carry 1 gallon of water per person per day. Watch for rattlesnakes, scorpions, and gila monsters and bring a comb to remove cactus thorns.

DIRECTIONS: From I-10, both districts are reached by following signs. The city of Tucson divides the two areas. The turnoff for the west is Speedway or Ina Roads; Houghton Road for the east. Nearest airport: Tucson.

Sequoia-Kings Canyon National Parks

Three Rivers, California 93271
Established September 25, 1890; March 4, 1940
863,159 acres. Open all year. Fee.
559-565-3341 www.nps.gov/sequ
www.nps.gov/kica *(see page 155)*

SPECIAL FEATURES AND PLACES: Two vast tracts of wilderness in the heart of the Sierra Nevada offer a myriad of beautiful lakes, creeks, and 6 peaks over 14,000' high. The John Muir trail traverses the entire length on the eastern border of the adjoining parks. California 180 leads to General Grant Grove and the visitor center of that name on the far western side of Kings Canyon, and to interior Cedar Grove, from which many trails lead to the high country. South of Grant Grove in Sequoia, off the Generals Highway, is the most famous grove of sequoia trees in the Sierras, the Giant Forest, so named by John Muir. On its northern edge is the General Sherman tree, more than 270' tall and still growing. It has been alive approximately 2,100 years and the trunk alone weighs about 1,385 tons. Also off the Generals Highway are Lodgepole and Buckeye Flat campgrounds, beginning points for trails through Sequoia into the high country and across the Great Western Divide.

WILDLIFE: Clark's nutcracker, water ouzel, Douglas' (chickaree) and California ground squirrels, water shrew, porcupine, mule deer, pine marten, bobcat, mountain lion, long-tailed weasel, badger, striped and spotted skunks, fisher, and wolverine.

PLANT LIFE: Giant sequoia, black and live oaks, white fir, ponderosa and sugar pines, alpine willow, sky pilot, columbine, and primrose.

ACTIVITIES: Backcountry camping (permit required), mountain climbing, horseback riding, fishing, and downhill and cross-country skiing.

INSIDER'S TIPS: Drive slowly as many of the park roads are steep and curvy; use low gears to avoid overheating brakes. Visitors with respiratory and circulatory problems should avoid higher elevations. Beware of lightning on exposed peaks during storms.

DIRECTIONS: From Fresno, take California Highway 180 west and follow signs. From the south, go to Visalia and take 198; follow signs to the park. Nearest airport: Fresno.

Shenandoah National Park

Luray, Virginia 22835
Established December 26, 1935
194,630 acres. Open all year. Fee.
540-999-3500 www.nps.gov/shen (see page 47)

SPECIAL FEATURES AND PLACES: Cradled in the Blue Ridge Mountains, the park contains ridges and valleys covered by forests woven with beautiful streams and waterfalls. The 105-mile Skyline Drive begins in the northern part of the park, and leads to the Dickey Ridge Visitor Center before winding south along the crest of the mountains for about 50 miles to Harry F. Byrd, Sr. Visitor Center. The surrounding lands were previously logged and farmed before becoming a national park. Travel another 30 miles to the Loft Mountain Information Center, passing about 75 overlooks along the way. Special ones include Big Meadows, nearby Dark Hollow Falls (and its 70' cascade), and Limberloss, a grove of hemlocks about 500 years old. The Appalachian Trail roughly follows the same course as the Drive.

WILDLIFE: Tiger swallowtail and monarch butterflies, katydid, treefrog, eastern box turtle, crayfish, black bear, deer, raccoon, gray fox, opossum, turkey vulture, broad-winged hawks; blackburnian and chestnut-sided warblers, water-thrush, kingfisher, woodcock, red-breasted nuthatch, rose-breasted grosbeak, pileated woodpecker, wood thrush, and wild turkey.

PLANT LIFE: Tulip poplar, red oak, white pine, striped maple, shagbark hickory, hemlock, basswood, umbrella magnolia, redbud, witch hazel, hawthorn, wild cherry, dogwood, hepatica, coltsfoot, trillium, bloodroot, pink and yellow lady slippers, showy orchis, ladies' tresses, Virginia spiderwort, wild geranium, marsh marigold, arbutus, Indian pipe, dutchman's britches, serviceberry, partridgeberry, wild azalea, and pink and white mountain laurel.

ACTIVITIES: Backcountry camping (permit required), mountain climbing, horseback riding, fishing, and cross-country skiing.

INSIDER'S TIPS: Layered clothing is recommended, since the mountains are usually 10 degrees cooler than the valleys. It typically showers in the summer, so be prepared for rain. Snow tires or chains may be required in the winter. Under the best conditions the speed limit is 35 m.p.h. and the entire trip can take up to 5 hours.

DIRECTIONS: From Washington, DC, take I-66 to US 340, traveling south to the park. To begin at the southern entrance, take I-81/64 from Roanoke or I-64 from Charlottesville to the exit at Rockfish. Nearest airports: Washington, DC; Charlottesville.

Theodore Roosevelt National Park
Medora, North Dakota 58645
Established as Theodore Roosevelt National Memorial Park in 1947;

established as a national park November 10, 1978
70,477 acres. Open all year. Fee.
701-623-4466 www.nps.gov/thro *(see page 92)*

SPECIAL FEATURES AND PLACES: A young Theodore Roosevelt hunted and raised cattle in the Dakota Territory and today the park pays tribute to the 26th President's lasting leadership in conservation. Carved by rain, wind, and the waters of the Little Missouri River, the badlands are still undergoing change from these and other land-shaping forces. Their ruggedness and beauty fascinated Roosevelt. The park has three separate areas: the North Unit, the South Unit, and the Elkhorn Ranch site. Medora Visitor Center on the southern border of the South Unit is easily accessible from Interstate 94. From there, it is a 36-mile scenic loop to Skyline Vista, Boicourt Overlook, and North Dakota Badlands Overlook, where erosion has left a maze of buttes and canyons that offer a kaleidoscope of colors. Painted Canyon Visitor Center is about 7 miles east of Medora on the upper ridge of the badlands, with a panoramic view of ragged ridges and, occasionally, bison or wild horses. The North Unit is about 60 miles from Painted Canyon Visitor Center off US 85. The 14-mile scenic drive passes such pullouts as Slump Block, Cannonball Concretions, Bentonitic Clay, and Edge of Glacier, each demonstrating the power of geologic forces over the landscape.

WILDLIFE: Meadowlark, prairie falcon, mule and white-tailed deer, pronghorn, elk, bison, bighorn sheep, coyote, badger, prairie dog, and wild horse.

PLANT LIFE: Blue gamma, little bluestem, needle-and-thread, and buffalo grasses, cottonwood, green ash, prickly pear cactus, yucca, western wheatgrass, yellow Indian paintbrush, Wood's rose, and Rocky Mountain juniper.

ACTIVITIES: Backcountry camping (permit required), camping, horseback riding, wildlife viewing, and hiking.

INSIDER'S TIPS: The Painted Canyon Vistor Center is closed during the winter months (however, one can still walk through a gate and view the panoramic view from Painted Canyon). Boil water in the backcountry. Due to the slippery clays and soft sediments that may yield underfoot, hikers should watch their footing after a rain or storms.

DIRECTIONS: South Unit abuts I-94 at Medora; North Unit abuts US Highway 85. Nearest airports: Bismarck, Williston, and Dickinson.

Virgin Islands National Park

St. John, US Virgin Islands 00831
Established August 2, 1956
14,688 acres. Open all year, closed Christmas day. No fee.
340-776-6201 www.nps.gov/viis *(see page 70)*

SPECIAL FEATURES AND PLACES: Virgin Islands National Park, renowned throughout the world for its breathtaking beauty, covers approximately 3/5 of St. John, and nearly all of Hassel Island in Charlotte Amalie harbor on St. Thomas. In addition to its amazing natural resources are relics from the pre-Colombian Amerindian civilization, remains of the Danish colonial sugar plantations, and reminders of African slavery and the subsistence culture that followed during the 100 years after emancipation – all part of the rich cultural history of the park and its island home. The most frequently visited sites in Virgin Islands National Park are Trunk Bay – one of many beautiful beaches along the north shore of St. John – and the ruins of Annaberg Plantation, once a sugar factory that played an important role in the island's colonial and post-emancipation eras. Virgin Islands National Park, authorized in 1956, includes 9,620 acres of land – over 5,000 of which were donated by philanthropist Laurance Rockefeller. In 1962, 5,600 acres of underwater environments were added to protect coral reefs and other marine environments.

WILDLIFE: Protected bays of crystal blue-green waters teeming with coral reef life, tropical birds.

PLANT LIFE: Seagrape trees, coconut palms, and tropical forests providing habitat for over 800 species of plants.

ACTIVITIES: Interpretive programs; guided walks through historical and natural areas; cultural heritage programs and demonstrations; evening campground programs; swimming, snorkeling and scuba diving, sailing, kayaking and windsurfing; camping, hiking and bird watching.

INSIDER'S TIPS: Visitation to Virgin Islands National Park is approximately one million annually, with greater visitation December through April. Lowest visitation occurs in September and October. Temperatures range in the low 70s to upper 80s, December through April, and are slightly higher (mid-80s to mid-90s), May through November. Usually there is more rainfall July through January, while spring and early summer can be quite dry. On any given day, however, brief light rain showers are not uncommon. Hurricane season extends from June through October. Park visitors may obtain ongoing information at the Visitor Contact Station or from any Park Ranger (including where to go in the event of a serious storm.) Throughout the year, cotton clothes that are light in color and weight are recommended in the daytime; a light jacket may occasionally be needed in the late evening and early morning during the winter season. Lightweight trousers help protect against insect bites on the denser hiking trails. Camping is permitted only at Cinnamon Bay campground. No backcountry or beach camping is permitted within Virgin Islands National Park.

DIRECTIONS: On St. John, access the park via North Shore or Centerline Roads. To the park: Hourly ferry service from Red Hook, St. Thomas (a 20-minute ride) is available to St. John and operates at 6:30 a.m., then on the hour from 7:00 a.m. to midnight. Ferry service from St. John to St. Thomas runs on the hour from 6:00 a.m. to 11:00 p.m. Less frequent ferries travel between Charlotte Amalie, St. Thomas and St. John (a 45-minute ride). In park: Most popular park areas are easily accessed by local taxis called safari buses. Rental vehicles are available in Cruz Bay and are necessary to travel to some of the more remote areas on St. John. Parking is limited at many park sites. Reef Bay and Cinnamon Bay trails and Salt Pond can be accessed by public bus service running from Cruz Bay to the Coral Bay area by way of Centerline Road (Route 10). Check the most current schedule posted near the Cruz Bay ferry dock. Boats are necessary to visit some park bays lacking road access. Bicycling is not recommended within the park, due to very steep, narrow and winding roads. Nearest airport: St. John.

Voyageurs National Park

International Falls, Minnesota 56649
Established April 8, 1975
218,054 acres. Open all year. No fee.
218-283-9821 www.nps.gov/voya (see page 93)

SPECIAL FEATURES AND PLACES: This water-based park in the southern portion of the Canadian Shield boasts some of the world's oldest exposed rock formations. At least four times in the past 100 million years, continental glaciers of ice 2 miles thick moved through the area. About

30 lakes now fill glacier-carved rock basins within land composed of ridges, knobs, bogs, marshes, and beaver ponds. The voyageurs were French-Canadian canoemen who paddled through the area in the late 18th and early 19th centuries on their way to and from the Canadian northwest territories in connection with the fur trade. The heart of the park is the 25-mile-long Kabetogama Peninsula, with Rainy Lake Visitor Center at the westernmost point. Chain of Lakes scenic trail, the major hiking trail on the peninsula, is accessible only by boat. To the south is Kabetogama Lake with a visitor center and boat ramps on the southern shore. Ramps are also available further east at Ash River Visitor Center, which also has a nature trail.

WILDLIFE: Pileated woodpecker, kingfisher, osprey, bald eagle, great blue heron, merganser, loon, cormorant, walleye, northern pike, smallmouth bass, perch, muskie, sauger, lake trout, river otter, beaver, coyote, black bear and timber wolf.

PLANT LIFE: Wild cranberry, wild rice, northern pitcherplant, waterlily, showy ladyslipper; white, jack, and red pines; and red spruce.

ACTIVITIES: Backcountry camping (no permit required), hiking, horseback riding, swimming, boating, canoeing, kayaking, fishing, bird watching, snowmobiling, and cross-country skiing.

INSIDER'S TIPS: Boaters should be familiar with navigation signs. Keep food and garbage stored properly away from bears. Remain at least 1/4 mile from bald eagle, osprey, and great blue heron nests.

DIRECTIONS: US Highways 71 and 53 go to International Falls; there Minnesota 11 leads to the park. Nearest airport: Winnipeg, Canada.

Wind Cave National Park

Hot Springs, South Dakota 57747
Established January 9, 1903
28,295 acres. Open all year.
No fee, except for cave tour and camping.
605-745-4600 www.nps.gov/wica *(see page 94)*

SPECIAL FEATURES AND PLACES: Located in the southern Black Hills, the park has two nature trails through its grasslands and ponderosa pine forests. About 60 million years ago the Black Hills were uplifted, producing cracks in the limestone that allowed acidic water to dissolve it and create an underground system of passages. Air moving through the cave can be detected as "wind" at the entrance of the cave. Wind Cave contains formations called frost-work, flowstone, popcorn, and helicites, but it is most famous for its thin protruding blades of calcite called "boxwork". The Natural Entrance Tour includes Roe's Misery, Devil's Lookout, and Methodist Church chambers, lasting about an hour. The Fairgrounds Entrance Tour goes to Monte Cristo's Palace, Bachelor's Quarters, and Chert Room, requiring 450 stairs to reach all chambers.

WILDLIFE: Mountain bluebird, rock wren, Townsend's solitaire, white-breasted nuthatch, red-headed woodpecker, sharp-tailed grouse, prairie falcon, wild turkey, prairie dog, prairie rattlesnake, bison, elk, mule deer, pronghorn, and coyote.

PLANT LIFE: Blue grama, western wheat, and little bluestem grasses; horsemint, bur oak, American elm, paper birch, ponderosa pine, and Rocky Mountain juniper.

ACTIVITIES: Backcountry camping (permit required), hiking, and caving.

INSIDER'S TIPS: Tours every day except Thanksgiving and Christmas day. Two special, longer cave tours are given from mid-June to mid-August. Wear proper footgear as the cave is dimly lit, uneven, and sometimes slippery and wet. A sweater or a jacket is recommended as the temperature is a constant 53 degrees F. Above ground, be aware of prairie dog burrows which may harbor rattlesnakes.

DIRECTIONS: From Rapid City, take 79 south to Hermosa. Follow 36 to 16A through Custer State Park to 87 south to the park. Nearest airport: Rapid City.

Wrangell-St. Elias National Park

Copper Center, Alaska 99573
Established December 2, 1980
13,188,000 acres. Open all year. No fee.
907-822-5235 www.nps.gov/wrst *(see page 170)*

SPECIAL FEATURES AND PLACES: By far the largest national park, Wrangell-St. Elias boasts four mountain ranges within its borders, including 9 of the 16 highest peaks in the US and three dormant volcanoes – Drum, Sanford, and Blackburn. A fourth volcano, Wrangell, is still active, erupting last in 1900. All four can be seen from highways hugging the park's northern boundaries. Two unpaved roads traverse the interior of the park: The Chitina-McCarthy Road travels east from the western border but is not regularly maintained and the Nabesna Road extends southeast from the northern border. The park contains some of the largest glaciers in North America – including the Malaspina, which flows out of the St. Elias Range and is bigger than the state of Rhode Island, and the Nabesna, the longest non-polar inland glacier at over 70 miles in length. The Tana, Miles, Hubbard, and Guyot glaciers are found in the remote southern region of the park. The largest of the park's many rivers, the Copper, flows out of the Wrangells and empties into the Gulf of Alaska.

WILDLIFE: Dall's sheep, caribou, moose, black and grizzly bears, salmon, trumpeter swan, northern wood frog, harbor seal, and sea lion.

PLANT LIFE: White and black spruces; birch, balsam poplar, aspen, willow, alder, and moss.

ACTIVITIES: Backcountry camping (no permit required), horseback riding, mountain climbing, boating, rafting, kayaking, fishing, hunting, biking, snowmobiling, and cross-country skiing.

INSIDER'S TIPS: Weather changes quickly so warm, layered clothing and rain protection are essential. Many streams and rivers are impassable; for those that are passable, hikers must be familiar with crossing techniques. Private lands (e.g., Kennicott, McCarthy, Chisana, and Nabesna) are interspersed with public lands. Airplanes, snowmobiles, horses, and dog teams may be used within the park.

DIRECTIONS: From Anchorage, take Alaska 1 to Glennallen and follow signs to the park. Charter aircraft and/or bus services are available from Anchorage, Valdez, McCarthy, and Gulkana. Nearest major airport: Anchorage.

Yellowstone National Park

Yellowstone National Park, Wyoming 82190
Established March 1, 1872
2,221,766 acres. Open all year. Fee.
307-344-7381 www.nps.gov/yell *(see page 132)*

SPECIAL FEATURES AND PLACES: The first national park remains the centerpiece of the National Park System, a geologic hotspot with enough modern infrastructure to make most of the famous sites easily accessible. Yellowstone is renowned for Old Faithful, one of more than 300 geysers. Surface water seeps into porous rock far below the surface where it is superheated, returning to the surface as geysers, hot springs, fumaroles, and mudpots. Mammoth Hot Springs has beautifully terraced limestone, and the Fountain Paint Pot is an area where hot gases belch up through mud-filled pits, creating a multicolored landscape of ever-changing foot-high cones and plate-sized craters. Specimen Ridge contains the petrified remains of redwoods, sycamores, magnolias, dogwoods, and other trees, which grew there 50 million years ago before they were covered by 27 different volcanic eruptions that spewed ash hundreds of feet thick on top of them. Exploring the park on foot is popular, using more than 1,000 miles of hiking trails. Hayden Valley is known for its herds of bison and abundant waterfowl. Just north, beautiful volcanic gray, yellow, and pink rocks can be seen in the Grand Canyon of the Yellowstone. In the park's center, frigid Yellowstone Lake offers fishing, boating, and scenic vistas.

WILDLIFE: Elk, bison, moose, grizzly and black bears, bobcat, wolf, coyote, Unita ground squirrel, pika, long-tailed weasel, yellow-bellied marmot, sandhill crane, trumpeter swan, bald eagle, osprey, Canada goose, green-winged teal, lesser scaup, cormorant, Wilson's warbler, cutthroat trout, and mountain whitefish.

PLANT LIFE: Rocky Mountain fringed gentian, Indian paintbrush, lupine, bluebell, alpine buttercup, fireweed, forget-me-not, phlox, lodgepole pine, quaking aspen, and Englemann spruce.

ACTIVITIES: Backcountry camping (permit required), horseback riding, boating, fishing, biking, snowmobiling, cross-country skiing, and snowshoeing.

INSIDER'S TIPS: Most of the roads in the park close from November through May, depending upon snowfall. Climbing in the canyon area is prohibited. Stay on trails in the thermal areas. Avoid feeding or approaching any wildlife.

DIRECTIONS: Five entrances are available for travelers approaching from Montana, Idaho, or Wyoming. For travel in spring, fall, or winter, consult local sources for road status. Nearest airports: Bozeman; Jackson.

Yosemite National Park

Yosemite, California 95389
Established October 12, 1890
761,757 acres. Open all year. Fee.
209-372-0200 www.nps.gov/yose (see page 154)

SPECIAL FEATURES AND PLACES: Yosemite's magnificent landscape is the result of erosion by water and glaciers. Famous for a stunning valley that is surrounded by towering cliffs, sheer walls, and marvelous granite domes, features like El Capitan and Half Dome are slowly peeling away in layers. Yosemite Valley is full of waterfalls: Bridalveil, Yosemite, Nevada, and Vernal falls are easily accessible. Free buses provide transport to famous spots such as Mirror Lake and Happy Isles. Sequoia trees can be seen in all their grandeur at Mariposa Grove in the southern part of the park. Some 500 trees remain, among them Yosemite Sequoia, the fifth largest and oldest of the sequoias – about 3,000 years. In the high country, accessible by California 120, is Tuolumne Meadows, the largest in the Sierra. It is a mecca for campers and backpackers, seeking the famous John Muir or Pacific Crest trails, or any of the dozens of day hikes in the area.

WILDLIFE: Yosemite toad, band-tailed pigeon, acorn woodpecker, great gray owl, Steller's jay, rosy finch, perigrine falcon, mule deer, bighorn sheep, coyote, California sister butterfly, black bear, mountain lion, pocket gopher, and California ground squirrel.

PLANT LIFE: Sequoia, incense cedar, western juniper, Jeffrey and ponderosa pines, white fir, California black and canyon live oaks, mountain dogwood, mountain azalea, black-eyed susan, bull thistle, cow parsnip, mountain goldenrod, bleeding heart, pussy paws, monkshood, fireweed, blue penstemon, sulphur flower, red columbine, groundsel, mistletoe, thimbleberry, snow plant, and meadow, scarlet, and pink monkeyflowers.

ACTIVITIES: Backcountry camping (permit required), mountain climbing, rock climbing, horseback riding, swimming, boating, fishing, biking, and cross-country skiing.

INSIDER'S TIPS: California 120 westbound from Lee Vining is closed during the winter. Carry tire chains for early or late season travel. Avoid bears and observe regulations on food storage.

DIRECTIONS: From Fresno, use California 41; from Merced, use 140 and, from Reno, take 395 to Lee Vining and follow signs to the Tioga Pass. Nearest airport: Fresno.

Zion National Park
Springdale, Utah 84767
Established November 19, 1919

145,551 acres. Open all year. Fee.
801-722-3256 www.nps.gov/zion *(see page 128)*

SPECIAL FEATURES AND PLACES: Defined by canyons so immense they dwarf all else, Zion proves the power of erosion by water. The park varies greatly in both elevation and terrain, ranging from Sonoran desert to subalpine forest. The canyon is made of Navajo sandstone 2,200' thick, one of the largest sedimentary formations in the world. An amazing example is Checkerboard Mesa with its interestingly eroded face. The Zion Canyon Scenic Highway and the Zion-Mt. Carmel Highway provide visitors paved routes to such monoliths as the Great White Throne, Angels Landing, and the Temple of Sinawava. From the highways, there are trails less than 2¹/₂ miles round-trip to Weeping Rock with its springs and wildflowers, to the Emerald Pools with waterfalls and a hanging garden, and to the Virgin River partway up Zion Canyon. At the northern extreme of the park, the world's largest natural rock arch, Kolob Arch, may be reached from I-15.

WILDLIFE: Zion snail, Gambel's quail, roadrunner, canyon wren, golden eagle, pinyon jay, western tanager, ringtail cat, chipmunk, jackrabbit, mountain lion, bobcat, red fox, mule deer, rock squirrel, side-blotched lizard, Great Basin rattlesnake, prairie lizard, red-spotted toad, and canyon treefrog.

PLANT LIFE: Cottonwood, box elder, juniper, ash, pinyon and ponderosa pines, Douglas and white firs, quaking aspen, wild grape, desert phlox, slitrock paintbrush, golden and western columbines, scarlet monkeyflower, shooting star, sego lily, sacred datura, maidenhair fern, yarrow, buffaloberry, yucca, and prickly pear, claret cup, hedgehog, and purple torch cacti.

ACTIVITIES: Backcountry camping (permit required), hiking, horseback riding, and biking.

INSIDER'S TIPS: Concessioner-guided horseback trips are offered from March to November. The Zion-Mt. Carmel tunnel near the east entrance was not build for vehicles larger than a car or pickup truck. Summer temperatures may reach 105 degrees F so carry sufficient water and sun protection; drink treated water only. During rainstorms, vacate canyons due to flash flood potential.

DIRECTIONS: Both the north and south entrances are accessible from I-15. For the latter, head east on Utah 9 to reach the entrance. Nearest airport: Cedar City.

NATIONAL TRAILS

Appalachian National Scenic Trail

Appalachian Trail Conference founded 1925
Trail established October 2, 1968 – Total authorized length 2,110 miles
Length of existing trail route 2,158 miles
National Park Service 304-535-6278
Appalachian Trail Conference 304-535-6331

The Appalachian Trail (A.T.) is a 2,158-mile, continuous, marked footpath that traverses the Appalachian Mountain chain from Maine to Georgia. The trail and its adjacent lands – about 270,000 acres – link more than 75 parks and forests in 14 states, including eight units of the national forest system and six other units of the national park system. Whether it's the rhododendron-painted slopes of Tennessee's Roan Mountain or the crystalline waters surrounding Maine's Bigelow Preserve, millions of visitors each year enjoy countless wild, scenic, and pastoral settings on the A.T. Many, including hundreds of would-be end-to-end hikers ("thru hikers"), seek a unique long-distance hiking experience; others come with a lighter agenda to hike for a day, bird-watch, photograph wildlife, or simply absorb a magnificent view.

The Appalachian Trail Conference is the nonprofit conservation and education organization that coordinates the volunteer efforts of thousands of individuals and affiliated clubs interested in constructing the A.T. and managing its protective corridor lands with the support of volunteer time and cash donations.

California National Historic Trail

Established 1992 – 5,665 miles
NPS Long-distance Trails Office 801-539-4094

Following the discovery of gold at Sutter's Mill in California, the 1849 goldrush followed many paths. Starting at several points along the Missouri River, gold seekers converged on the Great Platte River Road, overlapping with Oregon and Mormon emigrants, until they had crossed the crest of the Rockies. From there a variety of routes – determined by the availability of water and grass, the knowledge of guides, or the presence of Indians – were used to get to and cross various passes through the Sierra Nevada mountains. Over 70,000 crossed to California in 1849 and 1850 alone. Recent Oregon settlers used the newly opened Applegate Trail to go south into the California mountains. Today the trail's comprehensive management plan is being completed to outline auto tour routes, public land management policies, interpretive themes, and public-private partnerships essential to commemorating this important chapter in opening the American West.

Continental Divide National Scenic Trail

Established 1978 – 3,200 miles
Continental Divide Trail Alliance 303-838-3760

The Continental Divide Trail provides spectacular backcountry travel the length of the Rocky Mountains from Mexico to Canada. It is the most rugged of the long distance trails. The only section officially designated runs for 795 miles from Canada through Montana and Idaho to Yellowstone National Park. It is open to hikers, pack and saddle animals, and, in some places, off-road vehicles. Some segments are open for use in other states.

Florida National Scenic Trail

Established 1983 – 1,300 miles
USDA Forest Service 904-942-9305
Florida Trail Association 800-343-1882

The Florida Trail was conceived and initiated by James A. Kern, who formed the Florida Trail Association in 1964. The trail will eventually extend from Big Cypress National Preserve in South Florida through Florida's three national forests to Gulf Islands National Seashore in the western panhandle. It is especially delightful for winter hiking and camping, passing through America's only subtropical landscape. Side loop trails connect to nearby historic sites and other points of interest. More than

1,000 miles are completed and some 300 more are officially open for public use.

Ice Age National Scenic Trail

Established 1980 – 1,000 miles
National Park Service 608-441-5610
Ice Age Park and Trail Foundation 414-691-2776

At the end of the Ice Age, about 10,000 years ago, glaciers retreated from North America and left behind a chain of moraine hills which defined their southern edge. In Wisconsin, this band of hills zigzags across the state for 1,000 miles from Lake Michigan to the Saint Croix River. A trail along these hills was conceived by Ray Zilmer in the 1950s and publicized by Rep. Henry Reuss in his book, *On the Trail of the Ice Age*. Today, with help from the state of Wisconsin and the Ice Age Park & Trail Foundation, almost half the trail is open to public use. Certain sections are popular for marathons, ski races, and ultra running.

Iditarod National Historic Trail

Established 1978 – 2,450 miles, main route 900 miles
Bureau of Land Management 907-267-1207
Iditarod Trail Committee 907-376-5155

The Iditarod is a system of historic trails made famous by Alaska gold prospectors and their dog teams during the late 19th- and 20th-century gold rush. Most of the trail is usable only during Alaska's six-month winter, when rivers and tundra are frozen. Each year the renowned 1,150-mile Iditarod Sled Dog Race is run along the trail from Anchorage to Nome. Other events include the 210-mile Iditasport race for skiers, mountain bikers, and snowshoers, and the Alaska Gold Rush Classic Snowmachine Race. A network of shelters is being installed by the Bureau of Land Management and the Iditarod Trail Committee.

Juan Bautista de Anza National Historic Trail

Established 1990 – 1,200 miles
National Park Service 415-427-1438

In 1775, a party of Spanish colonists led by Col. Juan Bautista de Anza set out from Mexico to establish an overland route to California. They sought to build a presidio and mission overlooking the Golden Gate and secure it from threats by the Russians and British. This party of 30 families, a dozen soldiers, and 1,000 cattle, horses, and mules spent three months traversing the deserts of the Southwest before reaching the missions of the California coast. Another three months were spent traveling up the Pacific coast to the Golden Gate, where the city of San Francisco now stands. In 1975 and 1976, an expedition reenactment took place from Horcasitas, Mexico, to San Francisco.

Lewis and Clark National Historic Trail
Established 1978 – 3,700 miles
National Park Service 402-514-9311

In 1804, President Thomas Jefferson commissioned Meriwether Lewis and William Clark to explore the newly acquired Louisiana Territory and the "Oregon Country." Setting out in boats from what is today Wood River, Illinois, and following the Missouri River upstream, their expedition eventually reached the Pacific Ocean at the mouth of the Columbia River in 1805 and returned east the next year. In Idaho and western Montana, the route follows roads and trails as it crosses the Rocky Mountain passes. Along the route, state, local, and private interests have established motor routes, roadside interpretive markers, and museum exhibits telling the Lewis and Clark story.

Mormon Pioneer National Historic Trail
Established 1978 – 1,300 miles
National Park Service 801-539-4095

Mormon emigration was one of the principal forces of settlement of the West. Departing from Nauvoo, Illinois, in February 1846, thousands of Mormons crossed into Iowa seeking refuge from religious persecution. They spent the next winter in the Council Bluffs, Iowa, and Omaha, Nebraska, area. Early in 1847, Brigham Young led an advance party west along the Platte River, paralleling the Oregon Trail, to Fort Bridger, Wyoming, where they turned southwest and eventually came to the Great Salt Lake. The 1,624-mile auto tour route in five states is generally marked with the trail logo and closely follows the trail's historic route.

Natchez Trace National Scenic Trail

Established 1983 – 110 miles
National Park Service 662-680-4025

The Natchez Trace National Scenic Trail lies within the boundaries of the Natchez Trace Parkway, extending for 450 miles from Natchez, Mississippi, to Nashville, Tennessee. The Parkway commemorates the historic Natchez Trace, an ancient path that began as a series of animal tracks and Native American trails. It was later used by early explorers, "Kaintuck" boatmen, post riders, and military men, including General Andrew Jackson after his victory at the Battle of New Orleans. In the trail's 1987 comprehensive plan, four segments near Nashville, Jackson, and Natchez totalling 110 miles were selected for development as hiking and horseback trails.

Nez Perce (Nee-Me-Poo) National Historic Trail

Established 1986 – 1,170 miles
USDA Forest Service 208-843-2261

This trail route honors the heroic and poignant attempt by the Nez Perce Indians to escape capture by the US Army. In 1877, the Nez Perce were forced to leave their ancestral homelands and move to a reservation east of Lewiston, Idaho. During this journey, hostilities broke out between white settlers and some groups of the Nez Perce. The US Army was called in. The resisting bands headed east, crossed the Rocky Mountains, and hoped to find refuge in Canada. Led by several commanders, including Chief Joseph, they eluded capture for months, traveling through the newly established Yellowstone National Park and out onto the Great Plains. Just short of reaching the Canadian border in Montana, most of the party were overtaken near the Bearpaw Mountains.

North Country National Scenic Trail

Established 1980 – 3,200 miles
National Park Service 608-441-5610
North Country Trail Association 616-897-5987

Conceived in the mid-1960s, the North Country Trail links New York's Adirondack Mountains with the Missouri River in North Dakota. The trail journeys through a variety of environments: the grandeur of the Adirondacks, Pennsylvania's hardwood forests, the farmland and canals of

Ohio, the Great Lakes shorelines of Michigan, the glacier-carved forest, lakes, and streams of Wisconsin and Minnesota, and the vast plains of North Dakota. Today almost half of this trail is open for public use. Some of the longer segments cross nine national forests and two national park areas along the route.

Oregon National Historic Trail

Established 1978 – 2,170 miles
National Park Service 206-470-4060
Oregon-California Trails Association 816-252-2276

As the harbinger of America's westward expansion, the Oregon Trail was the pathway to the Pacific for fur traders, gold seekers, missionaries, and emigrants. Beginning in 1841 and enduring for more than 20 years, an estimated 300,000 emigrants followed this route from the Midwest to Oregon on a trip that took five months to complete. Today the trail corridor contains some 300 miles of discernible wagon ruts and 125 historic sites. The approximate route can still be followed by automobile, and opportunities are available to travel by foot, horse, or mountain bike in many places.

Overmountain Victory National Historic Trail

Established 1980 – 300 miles
National Park Service 404-562-3108

In the fall of 1780, upcountry patriots from Virginia, Tennessee, and North Carolina formed a militia to drive the British from the southern colonies. This trail marks their 14-day trek across the Appalachians to the Piedmont region of the Carolinas. There they defeated British troops at the Battle of Kings Mountain, setting in motion events that led to the British surrender at Yorktown and the end of the Revolutionary War. Each year history buffs commemorate this patriotic event. Much of the trail has become road and highway; only a small 20-mile portion remains as a foot trail across the mountains. In most places roadside signs indicate proximity to the trail. A guide to the seven walking sections is available.

Pacific Crest National Scenic Trail

Established 1968 – 2,638 miles
Pacific Crest Trail Association 916-349-2109

Lying along the spectacular shoulders of the Cascade and Sierra Nevada mountain ranges from Canada to Mexico, the Pacific Crest Trail is the West Coast counterpart to the Appalachian Trail. Inspired in the 1930s by the idea of a long-distance mountain trail, citizen activists worked with the USDA Forest Service to establish the trail. It passes through 25 national forests and seven national parks. The trail was completed in Oregon and Washington in 1987. Today, only 30 miles in California are not protected.

Pony Express National Historic Trail
Established 1992 – 1,855 miles
NPS Long-distance Trails Office 801-539-4094

Begun in 1860 as a vital mail route connecting the eastern United States to California, this privately financed operation lasted only 18 months before it was supplanted by telegraph. Dozens of wiry riders and hundreds of horses conducted the relay of mail through desert and plain, mountains and storm around the clock to get the mail through. Average travel time from St. Joe, Missouri to Sacramento, California was 10 days. Nearly 35,000 pieces of mail were transported, some containing the momentous news of Lincoln's election and the outbreak of the Civil War. The transcontinental railroad followed much of its route in later years. Today many portions of the route are marked by highway signs and reenactment rides – complete with souvenir mail – take place every year.

Potomac Heritage National Scenic Trail
Established 1983 – 700 miles
National Park Service 301-739-4200

The Potomac Heritage Trail recognizes and commemorates the unique mix of history and recreation along the Potomac River. Much is already in place: the 184-mile towpath of the Chesapeake and Ohio Canal in the District of Columbia and Maryland, the 18-mile Mount Vernon Trail in Virginia, and the 75-mile Laurel Highlands Trail in Pennsylvania. In western Maryland, members of the Potomac Heritage Trail Association have recommended a 55-mile hiking path from Cumberland, Maryland, north to Pennsylvania's Mount Davis and on to the Laurel Highlands.

Santa Fe National Historic Trail
Established 1987 – 1,203 miles

National Park Service 505-988-6888
Santa Fe Trail Association 316-285-2054

After Mexican independence in 1821, US and Mexican traders developed the Santa Fe Trail, using American Indian travel and trade routes. It quickly became a commercial and cultural link between the two countries. It also became a road of conquest during the Mexican and Civil wars. With the building of the railroad to Santa Fe in 1880, the trail was largely abandoned. Of the 1,203 miles of the trail route between Old Franklin, Missouri, and Santa Fe, New Mexico, more than 200 miles of ruts and trace remain visible; some 30 miles of these are protected on federal lands.

Trail of Tears National Historic Trail
Established 1987 – 2,052 miles
National Park Service 505-988-6888

After many years of pressure from white settlers, 16,000 Cherokee Indians from the southeastern states were moved by the US Army in the late 1830s to lands west of the Mississippi River. Various detachments followed different routes west to the Oklahoma Territory. Thousands died along the way. Today, the designated trail follows two of the principal routes: a water trail (1,226 miles) along the Tennessee, Ohio, Mississippi, and Arkansas rivers; and an overland route (826 miles) from Chattanooga, Tennessee, to Tahlequah, Oklahoma.

Alabama

Bureau of Tourism	800-ALABAMA
Dept. of Transportation	205-328-5820
State Parks	800-ALA PARK
National Forests	334-832-4470
Dept. of Fish & Game	334-242-3465
Robert Trent Jones Golf Trail	800-949-4444
Birmingham Visitor Bureau	800-458-8085

Alaska

Tourism Office	907-929-2200
Dept. of Transportation	907-456-7623
Marine Highway System	800-642-0066
National Forests	907-586-8863
Dept. of Fish & Game	907-465-2376
Alaska Public Lands Information Center	907-271-2737
Southeast Alaska Discovery Center	907-228-6234
Fairbanks Visitor Center	800-327-5774
Juneau Visitor Center	907-586-2201 888-581-2201

Arizona

Tourism Office	602-230-7733
State Parks	602-542-4174
National Forests	505-842-3300
Dept. of Fish & Game	602-942-3000
Bureau of Land Management	602-417-9200
Golf Arizona	800-942-5444

Flagstaff Visitor Bureau	520-779-7611
Phoenix Valley of the Sun Visitor Bureau	602-254-6500
Metro Tucson Visitor Bureau	800-638-8350
Lake Havasu Visitor Bureau	800-242-8278

Arkansas

Tourism Office	800-NATURAL 501-682-7777
Dept. of Transportation	501-569-2000
State Parks	888-AT PARKS
National Forests	404-347-4177
Dept. of Fish & Game	501-223-6300 800-364-GAME
Corps of Engineers	501-968-5008
Hot Springs Visitor Center	501-623-1433
Arkansas River Valley Tri-Peaks Region	800-561-6508

California

Tourism Office	916-322-2881
Dept. of Transportation	916-654-2852
Road Condition Info.	916-654-2852
State Parks	916-653-6995 530-525-7232
National Forests	707-562-8737
Dept. of Fish & Game	916-227-2244
Bureau of Land Management	916-978-4400
Private Camping	888-STAY CTPA

Downhill & Cross-Country
Ski Information 415-543-7036

San Diego
Visitor Center 619-276-8200

Los Angeles
Visitor Center 213-624-7300

San Francisco
Visitor Bureau 888-782-9673

Napa Valley
Visitor Bureau 707-226-7459

Sonoma County
Visitor Bureau 707-996-1090

Monterey Peninsula
Visitor Bureau 831-649-1770

Lake Tahoe
Visitor Authority
North 530-583-3494
South 530-544-5050

Colorado

Tourism Office 800-COLORADO

Dept. of Transportation 800-999-4997

State Parks 303-866-3437

National Forests 303-275-5350

U.S. Fish & Wildlife 303-236-7904

Bureau of
Land Management 303-239-3600

Assn. of Campgrounds 888-686-8549

Ski Country 303-825-SNOW

Bicycle Colorado 719-530-0051

Denver Visitor Bureau 303-892-1112

Southeast Colorado
Travel Bureau 800-338-6633

Connecticut

Tourism Office 860-270-8080

Dept. of Transportation 860-594-2000

Mystic Seaport Info. 860-572-5315

State Parks 860-424-3200

Campground
Owners Association 860-521-4704

State
Golf Association 860-257-4171

Delaware

Tourism Office 800-441-8846

Dept. of Transportation 302-760-2080

State Parks 302-739-4702

Department of
Fish & Wildlife 302-739-3441

Division of
Parks and Recreation 302-739-4702

Bike Trail Information 302-760-2453

District of Columbia

Tourism Office 202-638-3222

Smithsonian Visitor
Information Center 202-357-2700

National Gallery of Art 202-737-4215

U.S. Capitol 202-225-6827

White House
Visitor Center 202-208-1631

National Parks Service 202-619-7222

Arlington
National Cemetery 703-607-8052

Florida

Tourism Office	888-7-FLA USA
Dept. of Transportation	850-414-4590
State Parks	850-488-9872
National Forests	850-942-9300
Attractions Association	850-222-2885
Association of RV Parks and Campgrounds	850-562-7151
Department of Natural Resources	850-488-3701
Orlando Visitor Bureau	800-551-0181
Disney Information	407-824-4321
Tampa Visitor Association	800-44-TAMPA
Miami Visitor Bureau	800-283-2707
Key West Information Center	800-352-5397
Sanibel & Captiva Islands Chamber of Commerce	941-472-1080

Georgia

Tourism Office	800-VISIT GA
	404-656-3590
Dept. of Transportation	404-656-5267
State Parks	800-864-7275
National Forests	706-864-6173
Dept. of Fish & Game	404-679-7319
Savannah Visitor Center	912-944-0460
Atlanta Welcome Center	404-521-6688

Hawaii

Tourism Office	808-923-1811
Dept. of Transportation	808-587-2160
State Parks	808-974-6200
Oahu Visitor Association	808-524-0722
Kauai Visitor Bureau	808-245-3971

Idaho

Tourism Office	800-847-4843
	208-334-2470
Dept. of Transportation	208-334-8000
Dept. of Parks & Rec.	208-334-4199
National Forests	801-625-5306
Dept. of Fish & Game	800-635-7820
Bureau of Land Management	208-373-4000
Outfitters & Guides Association	800-635-7820
Hell's Canyon National Recreation Area	541-426-4978
Sawtooth National Recreation Area	208-726-7672

Illinois

Tourism Office	800-2-CONNECT
Dept. of Transportation	800-452-IDOT
National Forests	618-253-7114
Natural Resources	217-782-7454
Assn. of Park Districts	217-523-4554
Fish & Hunting	217-782-2965
Chicago Visitor Bureau	312-744-2400

Indiana

Tourism Office	800-291-8844
Dept. of Transportation	317-232-5533
State Parks	317-232-4124
National Forests	812-275-5987
Dept. of Fish & Game	317-232-4080
Indianapolis Visitor Association	317-639-4282

Iowa

Tourism Office	800-345-IOWA
	888-472-6035
Dept. of Transportation	515-239-1101
Department of Natural Resources	515-281-8368

Kansas

Tourism Office	785-296-2009
Dept. of Transportation	785-296-3585
State Parks, Fish & Game	785-296-2281
Kansas Historical Society	785-272-8681

Kentucky

Tourism Office	800-225-8747
Road Conditions	800-4-KY ROAD
State Parks	800-255-7275
National Forests	859-745-3100
Dept. of Fish & Game	502-564-4224
Lexington Visitor Bureau	800-845-3959

Louisiana

Tourism Office	800-98-GUMBO
Dept. of Transportation	225-379-1100
State Parks	888-677-1400
National Forests	318-473-7160
Department of Wildlife & Fisheries	225-765-2887
New Orleans Visitor Bureau	504-566-5011

Maine

Tourism Office	888-MAINE-45
Dept. of Transportation	207-287-2551
Bureau of Parks and Lands	207-287-3821
National Forests	603-528-8721
Dept. of Fish & Game	207-287-8000
Snowmobile Info.	207-622-6983
Campsite Information	207-782-5874
North Maine Woods Information	207-435-6213
Ski & Fall Foliage Information	888-MAINE-45

Maryland

Tourism Office	410-767-3400
Dept. of Transportation	888-713-1414
State Parks	410-260-8186
Dept. of Fish & Game	800-ASK FISH
Baltimore Visitor Association	800-343-3468
Assateague Island NS-Chincoteague NWR	410-641-3030

Massachusetts

Tourism Office	617-727-3201

Traffic Information	617-374-1234	Dept. of Transportation	601-359-7001
State Parks	617-727-3180	State Parks	800-GO PARKS
Dept. of Fish & Game	800-ASK FISH	National Forests	601-965-4391
Cape Cod Visitor Bureau	508-362-3225	Private Camping	228-875-2100
		Natchez Pilgrimage Tours	800-647-6742
Boston Visitor Bureau	888-SEE BOSTON	Natchez Trace Parkway	800-305-7417

Traffic Information 617-374-1234
State Parks 617-727-3180
Dept. of Fish & Game 800-ASK FISH
Cape Cod
  Visitor Bureau 508-362-3225
Boston
  Visitor Bureau 888-SEE BOSTON
Berkshires
  Visitor Bureau 800-237-5747
Freedom Trail 617-242-5642
Fall Foliage 800-227-6277

Michigan

Tourism Office 888-78-GREAT
Dept. of Transportation 517-373-2090
State Parks 517-373-9900
National Forests 906-786-4062
Department of
  Natural Resources 517-373-1204
Private Camping 800-44-PARKS
Golf Information 800-4-GOLF MI
Detroit Visitor Bureau 800-DETROIT

Minnesota

Tourism Office 800-657-3700
Dept. of Transportation 800-542-0220
State Parks &
  Natural Resources 651-296-6157
National Forests 218-335-8600
Minneapolis-St. Paul
  Visitor Bureau 800-445-7412

Mississippi

Tourism Office 800-WARMEST

Dept. of Transportation 601-359-7001
State Parks 800-GO PARKS
National Forests 601-965-4391
Private Camping 228-875-2100
Natchez Pilgrimage Tours 800-647-6742
Natchez Trace Parkway 800-305-7417
Natchez Visitor Bureau 601-268-3220
800-63-TOURS

Missouri

Tourism Office 800-877-1234
Dept. of Transportation 573-751-3322
State Parks &
  Natural Resources 800-334-6946
573-751-2479
National Forests 573-364-4621
Conservation Dept. 573-751-4115
Kansas City
  Visitor Bureau 800-767-7700
816-221-5242
St. Louis Visitor Bureau 800-916-0095
314-421-1023
Lake of the Ozarks
  Visitor Bureau 800-386-5253
573-348-1599

Montana

Tourism Office 800-VISIT MT
Dept. of Transportation 406-444-6200
National Forests 406-329-3511
Fish, Wildlife & Parks 406-444-2535
Glacier Country 800-338-5072

Nebraska

Tourism Office 800-228-4307

Dept. of Transportation	402-471-4567
State Parks	800-826-PARK
	402-471-0641
National Forests	308-432-0300

Nevada

Tourism Office	800-NEVADA-8
Dept. of Transportation	775-888-7000
National Forests	775-289-3031
Las Vegas Visitor Authority	800-332-5333
	702-892-0711
Lake Mead National Recreation Area	702-293-8907

New Hampshire

Tourism Office	603-271-2666
	800-386-4664
Dept. of Transportation	603-271-3734
State Parks	603-271-3556
National Forests	603-528-8721
Dept. of Fish & Game	603-271-3421
Private Camping	800-822-6764
Snowmobile Info.	603-224-8906
White Mountains Visitor Bureau	603-745-8720
Ski Information & Fall Foliage Report	800-258-3608

New Jersey

Tourism Office	609-633-2623
Dept. of Transportation	609-530-2000
State Parks	609-984-0370

Dept. of Fish & Game	609-292-2965
Atlantic City Visitor Bureau	609-348-7130

New Mexico

Tourism Office	800-545-2040
Dept. of Transportation	505-827-5100
State Parks	888-667-2757
National Forests	505-842-3300
Dept. of Fish & Game	505-476-8000
Bureau of Land Management	505-758-8851
Skiing Information	800-755-7669
Golf Information	505-897-0864
Santa Fe Visitor Bureau	800-777-CITY
Ruidoso Visitor Bureau	800-253-2255

New York

Tourism Office	800-CALL NYS
State Parks	518-474-0456
National Forests	607-546-4470
Private Camping	800-I LOVE NY
Long Island Convention & Visitor Bureau	877-FUN ON LI
Lake Placid Visitor Center	800-447-5224
Finger Lakes Association	800-KIT-4-FUN
	315-536-7488
New York City Visitor Bureau	800-NYC VISIT

North Carolina

Tourism Office	800-VISIT NC

Dept. of Transportation	919-733-2520
State Parks	919-733-4181
National Forests	828-257-4200
Wildlife Resources Commission	919-733-3391
Cape Hatteras National Seashore	252-473-2111
Cape Lookout National Seashore	252-728-2250
Ferry Information	800-293-3779

North Dakota

Tourism Office	800-HELLO ND 701-328-2525
Dept. of Transportation	701-328-2500
State Parks	800-807-4723
Dept. of Fish & Game	701-328-6300
Historical Society	701-328-2666

Ohio

Tourism Office	800-BUCKEYE
Dept. of Transportation	614-466-7170
Road Conditions	614-466-7170
National Forests	614-592-6644
Bicycle Transportation Information	614-644-7095
Cleveland Visitor Bureau	800-321-1001
Cincinnati Visitor Bureau	800-246-2987

Oklahoma

Tourism Office	800-652-6552
Dept. of Transportation	405-521-2554
Road Conditions	405-425-2385
State Parks	800-654-8240
National Forests	404-347-4177

Dept. of Fish & Game	800-275-3474
Department of Wildlife Conservation	405-521-3851
Hunting Information	405-521-2739
Route 66 Museum	580-323-7866

Oregon

Tourism Office	800-547-7842
Dept. of Transportation	503-986-4000
State Parks	800-551-6949
National Forests	503-326-2971
Dept. of Fish & Game	800-ASK FISH
Bureau of Land Management	503-952-6002
Private Camping	800-452-5687
Portland Visitor Assn.	877-678-5263
Oregon Coast Visitor Association	541-574-2679

Pennsylvania

Tourism Office	800-VISIT PA
Dept. of Transportation	717-787-2838
State Parks	800-63-PARKS
National Forests	814-723-5150
Fish & Boat Commission	717-705-7800
Private Camping	610-767-5026
Philadelphia Visitor Bureau	800-321-9563
Pittsburgh Visitor Bureau	800-366-0093
Pennsylvania DutchCountry Visitor Bureau	800-PA DUTCH
Gettysburg Visitor Bureau	717-334-6274
Delaware Water Gap	800-654-5984

Rhode Island

Tourism Office	401-222-2601
Dept. of Transportation	401-222-5826
State Parks	401-222-2632
Department of Fish & Wildlife	401-789-3094
Newport County Visitor Bureau	800-326-6030
	401-849-8048

South Carolina

Tourism, Recreation, & Parks	803-734-1700
National Forests	803-561-4000
Department of Natural Resources	803-734-3888
Charleston Visitor Bureau	800-868-8118
Myrtle Beach Visitor Bureau	800-356-3016
Hilton Head Visitor Bureau	888-741-7666

South Dakota

Tourism Office	800-S DAKOTA
Dept. of Transportation	605-773-3265
Road Conditions	605-394-2255
State Parks	605-773-3391
National Forests	303-275-5350
U.S. Army Corps of Engineers	605-845-2252
Private Camping	800-710-CAMP
Rapid City Visitor Bureau	800-487-3223

Tennessee

Tourism Office	800-836-6200
Dept. of Transportation	615-741-2848
State Parks	888-TN PARKS
National Forests	404-248-9142
Wildlife Resources Agency	615-781-6500
Bicycling Information	615-741-2331

Texas

Tourism Office	512-462-9191
	800-888-8TEX
Dept. of Transportation	512-832-7000
Road Conditions	800-452-9292
State Parks	800-792-1112
	512-389-4800
National Forests	404-248-9142
Private Camping	800-657-6555
San Antonio Visitor Center	800-447-3372
Austin Visitor Center	800-926-2282
	512-478-0098
Dallas/Ft. Worth Tourism Council	214-746-6677
Houston Visitor Bureau	800-365-7575
Corpus Christi Visitor Bureau	800-678-6232

Utah

Tourism Office	801-538-1030
	801-538-1467
Dept. of Transportation	801-965-4000
State Parks	801-538-7220
National Forests	801-625-5306
Department of Wildlife Resources	801-538-4700

Private Camping	800-322-3770	Civil War Information	888-CIVIL WAR

Bureau of
Land Management 801-539-4001

Bicycling Information 435-649-5806

Golf Information 801-538-1030

Skiing Information 801-534-1779

Dinosaur
National Monument 970-374-3000

Whitewater Rafting 800-231-2769

Vermont

Tourism Office 800-VERMONT

Dept. of Transportation 802-828-2657

State Parks 802-241-3655

National Forests 802-747-6700

Department of
Fish & Wildlife 802-241-3700

Skiing Information 800-VERMONT

Bicycling Information 800-425-8747

Snowmobile Info. 802-229-0005

Golf Information 800-639-1941

Fall Foliage Hotline 802-828-3239

Virginia

Tourism Office 800-VISIT VA

Dept. of Transportation 800-835-1203

State Parks 800-933-PARK

National Forests 540-265-5100

Department of Game
& Inland Fisheries 804-367-9369

State Ferry Information 800-VA FERRY

Bicycling Information 800-835-1203

Blue Ridge Institute 540-365-4416

Norfolk Visitor Bureau 757-441-1852

Washington

Tourism Office 800-544-1800

Dept. of Transportation 360-705-7000

Road Conditions 888-SNO INFO

State Parks 360-902-8844

National Forests 503-808-2971

Department of
Fish & Wildlife 360-902-2200

State Ferry Information 206-464-6400

Private Camping 360-902-8844

Skiing Information 206-525-4451

Bicycle Hotline 360-705-7277

Seattle Visitor Bureau 206-461-5840

Tacoma Visitor Bureau 800-272-2662

Mt. St. Helens National
Volcanic Monument 360-274-2100

West Virginia

Tourism Office 800-CALL WVA

Dept. of Transportation 304-558-3028

Road Conditions 304-558-2889

National Forests 404-347-4177

Department of
Natural Resources 304-558-2771

Mountain Bike Assn. 304-291-0780

Scenic Trails Assn. 304-755-4878

Rock Climbing 800-CALL WVA

Seneca Rocks
Visitor Bureau 304-567-2827

Wisconsin

Tourism Office 800-432-8747

Dept. of Transportation 608-246-3265

Road Conditions	800-762-3947	State Parks	307-777-6323
State Parks	608-266-2181	National Forests	303-275-5350
National Forests	414-297-3600	Dept. of Fish & Game	307-777-4600
		Bureau of Land Management	307-775-6256
Wyoming		Division of Cultural Resources	307-777-7013
Tourism Office	307-777-7777		
Dept. of Transportation	307-777-4437	Ski Information	800-225-5996

Notes

_____

_____

_____

_____

_____

_____

_____

_____

_____

_____

_____

TOLL-FREE NUMBERS

Airlines

Air Canada	800-630-3299
Alaska Airlines	800-426-0333
Aloha Airlines	800-367-5250
America West	800-235-9292
American, American Eagle	800-433-7300
Continental Airlines	800-525-0280
Delta Air Lines	800-221-1212
Midway Airlines	800-446-4392
Northwest Airlines	800-225-2525
Pan Am	800-359-7262
Southwest Airlines	800-435-9792
TWA	800-221-2000
United Airlines	800-241-6522
USAirways	800-428-4322

Hotels, Motels & Resorts

Best Western International	800-528-1234
Choice Hotels International	800-424-6423
Clarion Hotels & Resorts	800-252-7466
Comfort Inns & Suites	800-228-5150
Courtyard (by Marriott)	800-321-2211
Days Inns	800-325-2525
DoubleTree/Guest Quarters	800-424-2900
Econo Lodges	800-553-2666
Embassy Suites	800-362-2779
Fairmont Hotels	800-223-1818
Four Seasons Hotels	800-819-5053
Hampton Inns	800-426-7866
Helmsley Hotels	800-221-4982
Hilton Hotels	800-445-8667
Holiday Inn	800-465-4329
Howard Johnson Hotels	800-446-4656
Hyatt Hotels & Resorts	800-233-1234
Intercontinental Hotels	800-327-0200
Marriott Hotels & Resorts	800-228-9290
Motel 6	800-466-8356
Nikko Hotels International	800-645-5687
Novotel Hotels	800-668-6835

Omni International Hotels	800-843-6664
Quality Inns & Hotels	800-228-5151
Radisson Hotels	800-333-3333
Ramada Worldwide	800-228-2828
Red Roof Inns	800-843-7663
Renaissance Hotels	800-468-3571
Residence Inns by Marriott	800-331-3131
Ritz-Carlton Hotels	800-241-3333
Sheraton Worldwide	800-325-3535
Sleep Inns	800-753-3746
Westin Hotels & Resorts	800-228-3000
Wyndham Hotels & Resorts	800-822-4200

Car Rental

Alamo Rent-A-Car	800-327-9633
Avis Rent-A-Car	800-331-1212
Budget Car & Truck Rental	800-527-0700
Dollar Rent-A-Car	800-800-4000
Enterprise Rent-A-Car	800-325-8007
Hertz Rent-A-Car	800-654-3131
National Car Rental	800-227-7368
Payless Car Rental	800-237-2804
Thrifty Car Rental	800-367-2277

Courier Services

Airborne Express	800-247-2676
Federal Express	800-238-5355
UPS: United Parcel Service	800-742-5877

Credit Cards (Lost or Stolen)

American Express	800-528-4800
Diners Club/Carte Blanche	800-234-6377
Discover Card	800-347-2683
MasterCard International	800-826-2181
Optima Card	800-635-5955
Visa Worldwide	800-336-8472

Railways & Bus Lines

Amtrak-Metroliner	800-523-8720
Greyhound	800-231-2222
Trailways	800-858-8555

For additional toll-free listings, dial 1-800-555-1212 or check your local directory.

ABBREVIATIONS

AFB	Air Force Base	MEX	Mexico	Pres	Preserve
Amer	American	MI	Michigan	Pt	Point
AK	Alaska	Mil	Military	QU	Quebec
AL	Alabama	MN	Minnesota	Rec	Recreation
AR	Arkansas	MO	Missouri	Rd	Road
Ave	Avenue	Mon	Monument	Res	Reservoir/Reserve
AZ	Arizona	MS	Mississippi	RI	Rhode Island
BC	British Columbia	MT	Montana	SB	State Beach
Bldg	Building	Mt	Mount	SC	South Carolina
CA	California	Mtn(s)	Mountain(s)	SD	South Dakota
CAN	Canada	Muni	Municipal	SF	State Forest
Cem	Cemetery	Mus	Museum	SHM	State Historical Monument
CO	Colorado	NAS	Naval Air Station		
Commem	Commemorative	Nat'l	National		
Conv	Convention	Nat'l Mem	National Memorial	SHP	State Historical Park
Cr	Creek	NB	New Brunswick	SHS	State Historical Site
CT	Connecticut	NC	North Carolina	SM	State Monument
Ctr	Center	ND	North Dakota	SNA	State Natural Area
DC	District of Columbia	NE	Nebraska	SP	State Park
DE	Delaware	NF	National Forest	Sq	Square
Dept	Department	NH	New Hampshire	SPres	State Preserve
Dr	Drive	NHS	National Historic Site	SRA	State Recreation Area
For	Forest	NHP	National Historic Park		
FL	Florida	NJ	New Jersey	St	Saint
GA	Georgia	NL	National Lakeshore	Sta	Station
GC	Golf Course	NM	National Monument	Terr	Territory
Govt	Government	NM	New Mexico	TN	Tennessee
HQ/Hdqtrs	Headquarters	NMP	National Military Park	Tr	Trail
HI	Hawaii	Nat'l Pres	National Preserve	TX	Texas
Hist	Historic(al)	NP	National Park	U/Univ	University
HS	Historic Site	NRA	National Recreation Area	USVI	US Virgin Islands
Hwy	Highway	NRMA	Natural Resource Management Area	UT	Utah
IA	Iowa			VA	Virginia
ID	Idaho	NS	National Seashore	Vis	Visitor
IL	Illinois	NTC	National Training Center	VT	Vermont
IN	Indiana			WA	Washington
Info	Information	NV	Nevada	WA	Wilderness Area
Int'l	International	NWR	National Wildlife Refuge	WI	Wisconsin
Is	Island			Wild	Wilderness
KS	Kansas	NY	New York	Wild Ref	Wildlife Refuge
KY	Kentucky	OH	Ohio	WMA	Wildlife Management Area
LA	Louisiana	OK	Oklahoma		
Ln	Lane	ON	Ontario		
Lp	Loop	OR	Oregon	WV	West Virginia
MA	Massachusetts	PA	Pennsylvania	WY	Wyoming
MD	Maryland	Pk	Peak		
ME	Maine	Pkwy	Parkway		
Mem	Memorial	PR	Puerto Rico		

A

Abaco, BAHAMAS 67 **C4**
Abbeville, GA 50 **B2**
Abbeville, SC 50 **C4**
Abbie Gardner Cabin SHS, IA 97 **E6**
Abbotsford, WI 84 **B4**, 86 **D1**
Abbott Village, ME 15 **F3**
Abbottstown, PA 34 **D2**
Aberdeen, MD 35 **F2**, 43 **G5**
Aberdeen, MS 73 **E4**, 76 **B1**
Aberdeen, SD 90 **D3**
Aberdeen, WA 138 **B6**
Abiel Smith School, MA 24 **B3**
Abilene, TX 103 **E4**
Abingdon, VA 42 **B1**
Abington, MA 21 **F4**
Abiquiu Res, NM 110 **E8**
Abrahams, BAHAMAS 67 **F2**
Abram Hewit SF, NJ 35 **G4**
Absaroka Beartooth Wild, MT 132 **C6**
Acadia NP, ME 15 **G2**, 16
Ackerman, MS 76 **D6**
Acklins Is, BAHAMAS 67 **E1**, 71 **A4**
Acme, MI 89 **H4**
Acme, WA 142 **D6**
Acres, NC 54 **A5**
Adamana, AZ 114 **B4**
Adams, MA 20 **C6**, 25 **G5**
Adams, NY 29 **E4**
Adamstown, PA 36 **D7**
Addis, LA 74 **B5**
Addison, VT 14 **A4**
Adel, GA 50 **B1**
Adelaide, BAHAMAS 67 **C3**
Adeline, LA 74 **A4**
Adirondack Mtns, NY 30
Adirondack Mus, NY 29 **G4**
Adirondack Park, NY 29 **G6**, 30 **B4**
Admiral's Dock, RI 26 **A4**
Admiralty Is NM, AK 164 **F5**
Adrian, MO 98 **A5**
Aetna Springs, CA 153 **G6**
African Meeting House, MA 24 **B3**
Afton, OK 72 **B6**
Agassiz, MT 136 **B5**

Agate Fossil Beds NM, NE 96 **A5**
Agness, OR 146 **D2**
Agnew, WA 141 **F5**, 142 **A3**
Aguadilla, PR 68 **A8**
Aguadilla Bay, PR 68 **A8**
Ahern, MT 136 **C4**
Ahoskie, NC 43 **G1**, 55 **A7**
Aialik Bay, AK 169 **G3**
Aialik Glacier, AK 169 **G3**
Aibonito, PR 68 **D7**
'Aiea, HI 174 **D6**
Aiken, SC 50 **C3**
Aiken-Rhett Mansion, SC 59 **F6**
Ainsworth, NE 90 **C1**, 96 **C6**
Airpower Mus, IA 97 **F4**
Ajax Reef, FL 66 **C2**
Ajo, AZ 108 **B2**
Akamina-Kishinena Prov Park, BC, CAN 136 **A6**
Akron, CO 119 **G4**
Akron, IA 97 **E6**
Akron, OH 79 **G5**
Akta-lakota Mus, SD 90 **C2**
Alabama, 50, 60, 73, 76
Alagnak Nat'l Scenic & Wild River, AK 171 **E6**
Alakai Swamp, HI 175 **C3**
Alamo, NV 149 **F4**
Alamo, The, TX 103 **E2**, 107 **B3**
Alamo Heights, TX 107 **B4**
Alamodome TX 107 **B2**
Alamogordo, NM 102 **B4**, 109 **F2**, 113 **F2**
Alamosa, CO 119 **F2**
Alamosa, NM 109 **F6**
Alamosa NWR, CO 119 **F2**
Alaska, 164
Alaska Maritime NWR, AK 169 **G2**
Albany, GA 50 **B2**, 73 **G3**
Albany, NY 20 **B6**, 29 **H2**, 40 **C5**
Albany, OH 83 **G4**
Albany, OR 139 **B4**, 146 **B2**
Albany, TX 103 **E4**
Albemarle Sound, NC 55 **D6**
Albert Lea, MN 91 **F2**, 97 **F6**
Albert Town, BAHAMAS 67 **E2**
Alberta, can 130 **D6**, 136 **A6**
Alberton, MT 137 **F1**
Albion, CA 150 **B1**, 150 **C6**

Albion, NE 96 **D5**
Albion, NY 28 **C3**
Albion, PA 34 **A6**
Albuquerque, NM 109 **F4**, 110 **E5**
Alcorn, MS 76 **C2**
Alder Creek, NY 29 **F4**
Alenuihaha Channel, HI 165 **E2**
Alex H Stephens Mem SP, GA 50 **C3**
Alexander City, AL 73 **F4**
Alexander Valley, CA 153 **F6**
Alexandria, LA 72 **C2**, 103 **G3**
Alexandria, MN 91 **E4**
Alexandria, VA 43 **G4**, 45 **H5**
Alexandria Bay, NY 29 **E5**
Alford, MA 25 **E2**
Alfred, ME 15 **E1**
Alger, WA 142 **D6**
Algoma, WI 84 **D5**
Alhambra GC, FL 65 **G5**
Alibates NM, TX 102 **D6**
Alice, TX 103 **E2**
Alice Town, BAHAMAS 67 **C3**
Alkali Flat, NM 113 **E2**
Allagash, ME 17 **G6**
Allagash Wilderness Waterway, ME 15 **F5**, 17 **F4**
Allegany SP, NY 28 **B1**, 34 **C6**
38 **D6**
Allegheny NF, PA 34 **B5**, 38 **C3**
Allegheny Res, PA 38 **C5**
Allen, WA 142 **D5**
Allendale, SC 50 **C3**
Allentown, GA 57 **G1**
Allentown, NJ 35 **G3**
Allentown, PA 35 **F3**, 40 **D2**,
43 **H6**
Alley Is, ME 16 **A6**
Alley Spring, MO 97 **G1**
Alliance, NE 96 **A5**
Alligator, NC 55 **D6**
Alligator Lake, NC 54 **C5**
Alligator River NWR, NC 51 **G6**, 55 **D6**
Allis SP, VT 14 **B4**
Alluvial City, LA 75 **F4**
Alma, MI 85 **F2**
Alma, NE 96 **C4**
Alma, WI 84 **B3**
Almond, NY 32 **A1**

Bailey Beach, RI 26 **C1**
Bailey Is, ME 15 **F2**
Baileys Bay, PR 69 **D3**
Baileys Harbor, WI 84 **D4**
Bainbridge, GA 50 **A1**, 61 **E6**
Bainbridge, NY 29 **F2**, 35 **F6**
Bainbridge Is, WA 142 **C1**
Baird Mts, AK 168 **D7**
Baja California, MEX 149 **E1**
Baker, LA 74 **B6**
Baker, MT 131 **G4**
Baker, NV 161 **H5**
Baker City, MT 130 **A3**
Baker City, OR 139 **E4**
Baker Is, ME 16 **D3**
Baker Lake, NV 161 **E4**
Baker Lake, WA 143 **E4**
Bakersfield, CA 149 **C3**
Balboa Park, FL 61 **F3**
Balcones Heights, TX 107 **A4**
Bald Eagle Natural Area, WA
138 **C7**
Bald Eagle SF, PA 34 **D4**
Bald Porcupine Is, ME 16 **D5**
Baldwin, LA 74 **A3**
Baldwin, MI 85 **E3**
Baldwin Peninsula, AK 168 **F5**
Baldwinville, MA 20 **D6**
Baldwyn, MS 76 **A2**
Balesville, NJ 39 **H3**
Ball Buoy Reef, FL 66 **C1**
Ballinger, TX 103 **E4**
Balmorhea SP, TX 102 **C3**
Balsam Lake, WI 86 **A3**
Baltimore, MD 35 **E1**, 41 **F6**,
43 **G5**
Bamberg, SC 50 **D3**
Banco, VA 47 **H3**
Bancroft, NE 96 **D5**
Bandelier NM, NM 109 **F5**, 110
E7
Bandera, TX 106 **A3**
Bandera Falls, TX 103 **E3**
Bandon, OR 139 **A3**, 146 **C4**
Banes, BAHAMAS 67 **D7**
Bangor, ME 15 **G3**, 17 **G1**, 40 **B5**
Bannack HSP, MT 130 **C4**
Bar Harbor, ME 16 **B2-D5**
Bar Is, ME 16 **A3-B5-D6**
Baracoa, CUBA 71 **A4**

Baraga, MI 87 **G6**
Barataria Bay, LA 75 **E2**
Barbados, 71 **F2**
Barbers Pt NAS, HI 174 **C5**
Barboursville, VA 47 **G2**
Barbuda, ANTIGUA & BARBUDA 71 **F3**
Barceloneta, PR 68 **C8**
Barco, NC 55 **D8**
Bardstown, KY 79 **E2**
Bardwell, KY 82 **A1**
Barlow, KY 82 **A2**
Barnard Hall, GA 58 **A3**
Barnegat, NJ 35 **H2**
Barnegat Lighthouse SP, NJ
35 **H2**
Barnesville, GA 57 **E3**
Barnstable, MA 22 **D5**
Barnum & Bailey Mus, FL 61 **F3**
Barnumville, VT 19 **F5**
Barnwell, SC 50 **C3**
Barranquilla, COLOMBIA 71 **A1**
Barranquitas, PR 68 **D7**
Barre, MA 20 **D5**
Barre, VT 14 **B4**, 40 **A2**
Barren River Lake, KY 78 **D1**
Barrie, ON, CAN 28 **A5**
Barron, WI 86 **B2**
Barrow, AK 164 **C8**
Barryville, NY 31 **E2**
Barstow, CA 149 **E3**
Bartlesville, OK 97 **E1**, 103 **F6**
Bartlett, NH 18 **C3**
Bartlett Is, ME 16 **A5**
Barton Creek Wilderness Park,
TX 107 **D2**
Bartow, FL 61 **G3**
Bartow, WV 42 **D4**
Basalt, CO 120 **A3**
Baseball Hall of Fame, NY 29 **F2**
Baskett Slough NWR, OR
146 **B3**
Bass Harbor, ME 16 **B1-B2**
Bass Harbor Head, ME 16 **B2**
Bassett, NE 96 **C6**
Bassinger, FL 61 **G3**
Basswood Island, WI 88 **E6**
Bastian, VA 41 **G6**
Bastion Bay, LA 75 **F2**
Bastrop, LA 72 **C3**
Basye, VA 47 **F6**

Bat Cave, NC 46 **D2**
Batavia, NY 28 **C3**
Batesland, SD 90 **B1**
Batesville, AR 72 **C6**
Bath, ME 15 **F2**
Bath, NH 14 **C4**
Bath, NY 28 **D2**, 32 **C1**, 34 **D6**
Bath, NC 54 **B4**
Baton Rouge, LA 72 **C2**, 74 **B6**,
103 **H3**
Battery Carriage House Inn, SC
59 **G1**
Battle Creek, MI 85 **E1**
Battle Mtn, NV 130 **B1**, 149 **E6**
Battle of Athens SHS, MO
97 **G4**
Baudette, MN 91 **F6**
Baxley, GA 50 **C2**
Baxter SP, ME 15 **F5**, 17 **G4**,
40 **A6**
Bay City, IL 82 **C2**
Bay City, MI 85 **F2**
Bay City SP, MI 85 **F2**
Bay Lake, FL 65 **E4**
Bay of Quinte, CAN 28 **D5**
Bay St Louis, MS 75 **G6**
Bay Shore, NY 20 **C1**
Bayamo, CUBA 71 **A4**
Bayboro, NC 54 **B3**
Bayfield, WI 84 **B5**, 86 **D6**,
88 **B5-E5**
Bayfield Peninsula, WI 88 **D5**
Baylies Mansion, MA 24 **A2**
Bayou Cane, LA 74 **C3**
Bayview, NC 54 **B4**
Bayview Park, FL 62 **C6**
Beach Institute, GA 58 **C3**
Beach SP, RI 21 **E3**
Beacon, NY 31 **G3**
Beacon Hill, MA 24 **A3**
Bear Brook SP, NH 14 **C2**
Bear Glacier, AK 169 **H4**
Bear Island, ME 16 **C3**
Bear Island, WI 88 **E6**
Bear Lake, MI 89 **E1-E2**
Bear Lake, UT 118 **C6**
Bear Paw Battlefield NHP, MT
131 **E6**
Bear River Migratory Bird
Refuge, UT, 118 **B5**
Beardstown, IL 78 **B4**

C

Captiva FL 64 **B2**

Captiva Is, FL 61 **F2**, 64 **B2**

Captiva Pass, FL 64 **B3**

Capulin Volcano NM, NM 109 **H6**

Caracas, VENEZUELA 71 **D1**

Caratunk, ME 40 **A5**

Carbon Glacier, WA 144 **C7**

Carbondale, CO 119 **E4**, 120 **A3**

Carbondale, IL 78 **C2**

Carbondale, PA 35 **F5**

Card Sound, FL 66 **A1**

Cardiff by the Sea, CA 151 **G2**

Cardigan SP, NH 14 **C3**

Cardston, BC, CAN 136 **D6**

Cardwell Pt, CA 157 **A4**

Carey, ID 130 **C2**

Caribbean Sea, 60, 68 **C5**, 71

Caribou, ME 15 **G6**, 17 **H5**

Caribou NF, ID 130 **D2**

Carl Sandburg Home NHS, SC 50 **C5**

Carlin, NV 149 **E6**

Carlisle, LA 75 **E3**

Carlisle, PA 34 **D3**, 40 **C1**, 41 **E6**

Carlsbad, CA 151 **G2**

Carlsbad, NM 102 **C4**, 109 **G2**

Carlsbad Caverns NP, NM 109 **G2**, 112

Carlsborg, WA 141 **G5**, 142 **A3**

Carlton, NY 28 **C3**

Carlyle Lake, IL 78 **B3**

Carmel, CA 151 **E6**, 156 **D1**

Carmel, IN 78 **D4**

Carmel Art Association, CA 156 **C2**

Carmel Bay, CA 156 **C2**

Carmel City Beach, CA 156 **C2**

Carmel River SB, CA 156 **D1**

Carmel Valley, CA 151 **E6**

Carmi, IL 82 **D6**

Carnelian Bay, CA 160 **B5**

Caro, VENEZUELA 71 **C1**

Caroga Lake, NY 30 **B1**

Carolina Sandhills NWR, SC 50 **D4**

Carolina Yacht Club, SC 59 **H2**

Carpinteria, CA 151 **F1**, 151 **G6**

Carrabelle, FL 61 **E5**

Carrier Mills, IL 82 **B4**

Carrington, ND 90 **D5**

Carrington Pt, CA 157 **C4**

Carrizo Springs, TX 103 **E2**

Carrizozo, NM 113 **F5**

Carroll, IA 97 **E5**

Carroll Glacier, AK 167 **D3**

Carrollton, MO 97 **F3**

Carrsville, KY 82 **C3**

Carry Falls Res, NY 29 **F5**

Carry Nation House, KS 96 **C2**

Carson City, NV 148 **C5**

Carson NF, NM 109 **F5**, 110 **C8**

Cartagena, COLOMBIA 71 **A1**

Cartersville, GA 50 **A4**

Carthage, MS 76 **D4**

Carthage, MO 98 **A1**

Casa Grande, AZ 108 **C2**

Casa Grande NM, AZ 108 **C2**

Casa Navarro SHS, TX 107 **B2**

Cascade Head, OR 139 **A4**

Cascade Lake, CA 160 **B1**

Cascade Mtn, OR 147 **G6**

Casement Glacier, AK 167 **E3**

Caspar, CA 150 **B1**

Casper, WY 119 **E6**, 131 **F2**

Cass Scenic RR SP, WV 42 **D4**

Cassadaga, NY 34 **B6**

Cassoday, KS 97 **D2**

Cassville, WI 84 **B2**

Castaic Lake, CA 151 **H6**

Castillo De San Marcos NM, FL 61 **G5**

Castle Crags SP, CA 148 **B7**

Castle Harbour, BERMUDA 69 **E3**

Castle Hills, TX 107 **A4**

Castle Is, PR 69 **F3**

Castle Lake, WA 145 **F4**

Castroville, CA 150 **C1**

Castroville, TX 106 **A1**

Cat, BAHAMAS 67 **D3**

Cat Head Pt, MI 89 **G6**

Cat Is, WI 88 **F6**

Catfish Pt, FL 64 **A6**

Cathedral City, CA 159 **A2**

Cathedral Gorge SP, NV 149 **F5**

Cathedral of St John the Baptist, GA 58 **C3**

Cathedral of St John the Baptist, SC 59 **F2**

Cathedral Park, NM 111 **G3**

Cathedral SP, WV 42 **D5**

Catholic Mus, NM 111 **G3**

Catskill, NY 29 **G2**, 31 **G5**, 35 **H6**

Catskill Park, NY 29 **G1**, 31 **E5**, 35 **G6**, 40 **C4**

Cave City, KY 79 **E1**, 80 **F6**

Cave Junction, OR 146 **D1**

Cave-in-Rock SP, IL 78 **C2**

Cay Sal Bank, CUBA 67 **A2**

Cayey, PR 68 **D7**

Cayo Coco, CUBA 67 **B2**

Cayo Costa, FL 64 **A4**

Cayo Costa SP, FL 61 **F2**, 64 **A5**

Cayo Costa St Pres, FL 64 **A4**

Cayo Grande, CUBA 67 **A1**

Cayo Pelau, FL 64 **B6**

Cayucos, CA 151 **E4**

Cayuga, NY 33 **F5**

Cayuga Lake, NY 29 **E2**, 33 **F4**

Cayuga Lake SP, NY 28 **D2**

Cazenovia, NY 29 **E3**

Cebolla, NM 110 **E8**

Cedar, MI 89 **G4**

Cedar Breaks NM, UT 118 **B2**

Cedar City, UT 118 **B2**

Cedar Creek SP, WV 42 **C4**

Cedar Falls, IA 97 **F5**

Cedar Is, VA 48 **D4**

Cedar Is NWR, NC 51 **G5**, 54 **C3**

Cedar Keys, FL 61 **F5**

Cedar Keys Wildlife Refuge, FL 61 **F5**

Cedar Rapids, IA 78 **A6**, 84 **B1**, 97 **G5**

Cedar Spring, KY 80 **C5**

Cedarville, MA 22 **B5**

Ceiba, PR 68 **E5-F7**

Center, WA 142 **B3**

Center Sandwich, NH 18 **B2**

Centerville, IA 97 **F4**

Centerville, KY 81 **E4**

Centerville, LA 74 **A3**

Centerville, MD 43 **G4**

Centerville, MA 22 **C4**

Centerville, TN 76 **A5**

Central Burying Ground, MA 24 **B1**

Central City, CO 120 **D4**

East Lake, NC 55 **D6**
East Lake Tohopekaliga, FL 65 **H2**
East Las Vegas, NV 163 **E5**
East Liverpool, OH 42 **D6**
East Marion, MA 22 **A5**
East Marion, NY 27 **C4**
East Meredith, NY 31 **E6**
East Montpelier, VT 14 **B4**
East Orleans, MA 22 **F5**
East Otis, MA 25 **G2**
East Potomac Park, DC 44 **D5**
East Pt, CA 157 **C3**
East Quogue, NY 27 **A1**
East Rochester, NY 32 **C6**
East Rupert, VT 19 **F6**
East St Louis, IL 78 **B3**
East Sandwich, MA 22 **C5**
East Timbalier Is, LA 74 **D1**
East Waterboro, ME 15 **E1**
East Windsor, MA 25 **G4**
Eastern Bay, ME 16 **C6**
Eastern Colorado Historical Society Mus, CO 119 **H3**
Eastern Ear, ME 16 **D1**
Eastern Head, ME 16 **D1**
Eastham, MA 23 **F6**
Easton, MD 43 **G4**
Easton Bay, RI 26 **D5**
Easton Beach, RI 26 **D5**
Easton Pond, RI 26 **D6**
Eastport, MI 89 **H6**
Eastsound, WA 142 **B6**
Eastville, VA 43 **H2**, 48 **C3**
Eatonton, GA 50 **B3**, 57 **G4**
Eau Claire, WI 84 **B4**, 86 **C1**, 91 **G3**
Ebensburg, PA 34 **C3**
Echo Lake, PA 39 **E2**
Echo Lake SP, NH 14 **D4**
Eddyville, IL 82 **B3**
Eddyville, KY 82 **D2**
Eden, GA 56 **B6**
Eden, TX 103 **E3**
Eden, VT 14 **B5**
Edenton, NC 55 **B6**
Edgard, LA 74 **D4**
Edgartown, MA 21 **G3**, 22 **B2**
Edge Lake, ME 16 **C5**
Edgerton, KS 97 **E3**

Edinburg, TX 103 **E1**
Edison, WA 142 **C5**
Edmonds, WA 142 **D2**
Edmore, ND 90 **D5**
Edmunds Glacier, WA 144 **B7**
Edmundston, NB, CAN 15 **G6**, 17 **H6**
Edom, VA 47 **E4**
Edward, NC 54 **A4**
Edward King House, RI 26 **C4**
Edwards, MS 76 **C3**
Edwards AFB, CA 149 **D3**
Effigy Mounds NM, IA 97 **G6**
Effingham, IL 78 **C3**
Effingham Falls, NH 14 **C3**
Egmont Key SP, FL 61 **F3**
Eisenhower Lock, NY 29 **F6**
Eisenhower Nat'l Historic Site, PA 37 **E2**
El Centro, CA 149 **E1**
El Centro Shopping Ctr, NM 111 **F3**
El Dorado, AR 72 **C4**, 103 **G4**
El Dorado, KS 96 **D2**
El Dorado Hotel, NM 111 **F4**
El Dorado Springs, MO 98 **B4**
El Estero Park, CA 156 **D5**
El Malpais NM, NM 109 **E4**, 110 **B5**
El Morro NM, NM 109 **E4**
El Paso, TX 102 **B4**, 109 **F1**
El Portal, CA 154 **A2**
El Yunque Caribbean NF, PR 68 **E7**
Ela, NC 53 **E2**
Elbert Sq, GA 58 **A4**
Elberta, GA 57 **F1**
Elberta, MI 89 **E3**
Elberton, GA 50 **B4**
Eldon, MO 99 **E5**
Eldon, WA 141 **H1**, 142 **B1**
Eldorado, IL 82 **C5**
Eldorado NF, CA 160 **A3**, **C1**
Elephant Butte Res, NM 109 **F3**
Eleuthera, BAHAMAS 67 **D3**
Eleven Mile Canyon Res, CO 120 **D1**
Elfin Cove, AK 167 **D1**
Elgin, IL 78 **C6**
Elgin AFB, FL 60 **C6**

Elim Indian Land, AK 164 **C7**
Elizabeth, NJ 35 **H4**
Elizabeth City, NC 43 **H1**, 51 **G6**, 55 **C7**
Elizabeth Station, KY 81 **E4**
Elizabethton, TN 41 **G4**
Elizabethtown, IL 82 **D3**
Elizabethtown, KY 78 **D2**
Elizabethtown, NY 30 **D4**
Elizabethtown, NC 51 **E4**
Elizabethtown, PA 36 **B7**
Elk, CA 150 **B1-C6**
Elk, NM 113 **H2**
Elk City, ID 130 **B4**
Elk City, OK 103 **E6**
Elk Is, WY 133 **G4**
Elk Lake, MI 89 **H5**
Elk Lake, WA 140 **A6**
Elk Pt, NV 160 **C2**
Elk Rapids, MI 89 **H5**
Elk Silver, NM 113 **G2**
Elk Springs, CO 124 **F5**
Elk SF, PA 34 **C5**
Elkhart, IN 79 **D5**, 85 **E1**
Elkhorn Coral Reef, FL 66 **C2**
Elkins, WV 34 **A1**, 42 **D4**
Elko, NV 130 **B1**, 149 **E7**
Elkton, MD 43 **H5**
Elkton, OR 139 **A3**, 146 **D5**
Elkton, VA 47 **F3**
Ellenburg, NY 29 **G6**
Ellendale, ND 90 **D4**
Ellensburg, WA 138 **D6**
Ellenville, NY 29 **G1**, 31 **F2**
Ellicottville, NY 34 **C6**
Ellijay, GA 50 **A4**
Ellington, MO 97 **G2**, 99 **H2**
Elliott Key, FL 63 **H6**, 66 **C3**
Elliott Key Harbor, FL 66 **B3**
Ellipse,The, DC 44 **C7**
Ellis, ID 130 **C3**
Ellis Sq, GA 58 **B5**
Ellisville, MA 23 **B6**
Ellsworth, KS 96 **D3**
Ellsworth, ME 15 **G3**, 16 **B2**
Ellsworth, NE 96 **B5**
Elmira, NY 31 **D3**, 35 **E6**
Elmo, MT 137 **F5**
Elmore SP, VT 14 **B5**
Elms,The, RI 26 **C4**

Hopkinsville, KY 78 **C1**
Hoquiam, WA 138 **A6**
Horicon NWR, WI 84 **C2**
Hornell, NY 28 **C2**, 32 **A1**, 34 **D6**
Horse World, FL 65 **F1**
Horseshoe Beach, FL 61 **E5**
Horseshoe Canyon Unit, UT 127 **E6**, 129 **E5**
Horseshoe Curve, PA 34 **C3**
Horseshoe Lake, CA 152 **E6**
Hortense, GA 50 **C1**
Hot Indian Land, WA 140 **B2**
Hot Springs, AR 103 **G5**
Hot Springs, MT 137 **E4**
Hot Springs, NC 41 **G3**
Hot Springs, SD 90 **A2**, 96 **A6**, 131 **H3**
Hot Springs NP, AR 72 **B5**, 77
Hot Sulphur Springs, CO 120 **C5**
Houghton, MI 84 **C5**, 88 **B5**
Houghton, NY 28 **C2**
Houlton, ME 15 **G5**, 17 **H4**
Houma, LA 60 **A5**, 74 **C3**, 103 **H3**
Housatonic, MA 25 **E3**
Houston, MO 99 **F2**
Houston, TX 72 **A1**, 103 **F3**, 107 **C3**
Hovenweep NM, UT 118 **D2**
Howard, NY 32 **B1**
Howes, SD 90 **B2**
Hualapai Indian Land, AZ 108 **B5**, 116 **B2**, 163 **H4**
Hubbardston SF, MA 21 **E5**
Hubbardton SHS, VT 14 **A3**
Hubbart Res, MT 137 **E2**
Hubbell Trading Post NHS, AZ 108 **D5**
Hubble Corners, NY 31 **F6**
Huckleberry Hill Pres, CA 156 **B4**
Hudson, NH 14 **C1**, 20 **B5**, 29 **H2**, 31 **H5**, 35 **H6**
Hudson, WI 86 **A1**
Hudson Falls, NY 29 **H3**
Hueco Tanks SHP, TX 102 **B4**
Hugo, OK 103 **F5**
Hulls Cove, ME 16 **C6**
Humacao, PR 68 **7E**
Humansville, MO 98 **B3**

Humarock, MA 23 **A8**
Humboldt Bay, CA 150 **A4**
Humboldt NF, NV 149 **D5-D7-E6-E7-F6**, 161 **E6-H1**
Humboldt Redwoods SP, CA 148 **A6**
Humpback Ridge, VA 43 **E3**
Humphreys, LA 74 **C3**
Hundred, WV 34 **A2**
Hungry Horse, MT 136 **B2**
Hungry Horse Res, MT 136 **B1**, 137 **H6**
Hunter Dawson SHS, MO 97 **H1**
Hunters Hot Springs, OR 139 **D2**
Hunting Is SP, SC 50 **D2**
Huntingdon, PA 34 **C3**
Huntington, IN 79 **E5**
Huntington, MA 25 **H2**
Huntington, NY 20 **B1**
Huntington, WV 42 **B4**, 79 **G2**
Huntington Beach, CA 149 **D2**, 151 **G4**
Huntsville, AL 73 **F5**
Huntsville, TX 72 **A2**, 103 **F3**
Hurdsfield, ND 90 **C5**
Hurley, NY 31 **G4**
Hurley, WI 84 **B5**, 87 **E5**
Huron, SD 90 **D2**
Huron NF, MI 85 **F3**
Huron NWR, WI 87 **H6**
Hurricane Hole, USVI 70 **F7**
Huson, MT 137 **F1**
Hutchinson, KS 96 **D2**
Hutchinson, KY 81 **E3**
Hutchinson Is, GA 58 **C6**
Huttonsville, WV 42 **D4**
Hyannis, MA 21 **G3**, 22 **D4**
Hyannis, NE 96 **B5**
Hyde Park, NY 29 **G1**, 31 **G4**, 35 **H5**

I

Iberia, MO 99 **E4**
Ice Caves Mtn, NY 35 **G5**
Icy Bay, AK 170 **D4**
Icy Pt, AK 167 **C1**
Icy Strait, AK 167 **F1**
Ida Lewis Rock, RI 26 **B4**
Ida Lewis Yacht Club, RI 26 **A4**

Idaho, 118, 130, 132, 139, 149
Idaho Falls, ID 130 **D2**
Idaho Panhandle NF, ID 130 **B5**
Idaho Springs, CO 120 **D4**
Iditarod Nat'l Hist Trail, AK 164 **C7**
Idlewild Park, PA 34 **B3**
Iliamna, AK 168 **A5**
Iliamna Lake, AK 168 **A5**
Ilion, NY 30 **A1**
Iliuk Arm, AK 171 **F5**
Illinois, 78, 82, 84, 97
Imnaha, OR 134 **B4**
Imperial Palace Auto Collection, NV 162 **A3**
Incline Village, NV 160 **C5**
Independence, CA 155 **H4**
Independence, KS 97 **E1**
Independence, MN 86 **B6**
Independence, MO 97 **E3**
Independence, VA 42 **C1**, 46 **C6**
Independent Presbyterian Church, GA 58 **B4**
Indian City USA, OK 103 **E5**
Indian Echo Caves, PA 35 **E3**
Indian Glacier, AK 169 **G4**
Indian Lake, NY 29 **G4**, 30 **B3**
Indian Peaks Wild, CO 121 **G1**
Indian Pt, ME 16 **B5**
Indian Rock Paintings SP, WA 138 **D6**
Indian Springs, NV 149 **E4**
Indian Trail Conservation Area, MO 99 **G3**
Indian Well SP, CT 20 **C2**
Indiana, 78, 82, 85
Indiana, PA 34 **B3**, 43 **E6**
Indiana Dunes NL, IN 78 **D5**
Indianapolis, IN 78 **D4**
Indianapolis Motor Speedway, IN 78 **D4**
Indianola, IA 97 **F5**
Indio, CA 149 **E2**, 159 **B1**
Ingraham, NY 29 **H6**
Ingraham Glacier, WA 144 **C6**
Ingraham Pt, ME 16 **D3**
Institute of American Indian Arts, NM 111 **G4**
Institute of Texan Cultures, TX 107 **B2**
Intercession City, FL 65 **F1**

K

Loíza, PR 68 **E8**
Lola, NC 51 **G5**, 54 **C3**
Loleta, CA 150 **A4**
Lolo NF, MT 130 **C4- C5**, 137 **E2-E5-H2**
Loma, MT 131 **E6**
Lompoc, CA 149 **C3**, 151 **E2**
London, KY 79 **F1**
London, ON, CAN 85 **G2**
London Bridge, AZ 108 **A4**
Londonderry, VT 19 **H6**
Lone Cypress Tree, CA 156 **A2**
Lone Pine, CA 158 **A4**
Lone Pine SP, MT 130 **C6**
Lonepine, MT 137 **E4**
Long, ME 17 **H6**
Long Arsenicker, FL 66 **A2**
Long Beach, CA 149 **D2**, 151 **G4**, 157 **C1**
Long Beach, FL 62 **C2**
Long Beach, LA 75 **G6**
Long Beach, NY 20 **B1**, 35 **H4**
Long Branch, NJ 35 **H3**
Long Cay, BAHAMAS 67 **E2**
Long Island, BAHAMAS 67 **D2**
Long Island, NY 20 **C2**
Long Island, WI 88 **E5**
Long Island Sound, NY 20 **C2**, 27 **B4**
Long Key, FL 63 **F3**
Long Lake, MI 89 **G3**
Long Lake, NY 29 **G5**, 30 **B4**
Long Lake, ND 90 **C4**
Long Lake, WI 86 **B3**
Long Pond, ME 16 **B4**
Long Pond, MA 23 **B6**
Long Porcupine Is, ME 16 **D6**
Long Pt, MA 23 **E7**
Long Pt, NC 54 **D4**
Long Reef, FL 66 **D3**
Long Shoal, NC 54 **E5**
Long Shoal Pt, NC 54 **E5**
Long View, WA 138 **B5**
Long Wharf, MA 24 **D3**
Longview, TX 103 **G4**
Lookout Pt, ME 16 **G4**
Lopez, WA 142 **B5**
Lopez Is, WA 142 **B5**
Lopez Pt, CA 151 **E5**
Loradale, KY 81 **E4**

Lordsburg, NM 102 **A4**, 109 **E2**
Loretto Chapel, NM 111 **G3**
Loring, MT 131 **F6**
Lorman, MS 76 **C1**
Los Alamos, CA 151 **E2**
Los Alamos, NM 109 **F5**, 110 **E7**
Los Angeles, CA 149 **D2**, 151 **H4**, 157 **C1**
Los Angeles NF, CA 151 **H4**
Los Olivos, CA 151 **E2**
Los Padres NF, CA 149 **B4-C3**, 151 **F1-H6**
Lost Bay, MN 93 **C3**
Lost City Mus, NV 149 **F4**
Lostwood NWR, ND 90 **B6**
Lottsville, PA 38 **A5**
Loudonville, OH 79 **G4**
Loughman, FL 65 **E1**
Louisburg, NC 51 **E6**
Louisiana, 60, 72, 75, 76, 103
Louisville, GA 50 **C3**
Louisville, KY 79 **E2**
Louisville, MS 76 **D5**
Lovelaceville, KY 82 **B1**
Lovelock, NV 149 **D6**
Lover's Pt, CA 156 **B6**
Lovington, NM 109 **H2**
Lowell, MA 14 **C1**, 21 **F6**
Lowell, VT 14 **B5**
Lowell NHP, MA 21 **F6**
Lower Aldwell, WA 141 **F5**
Lower Brule Indian Land, SD 90 **C2**
Lower Chateaugay Lake, NY 30 **C6**
Lower Elwha Klallam Indian Land, WA 141 **F5**
Lower Red Lake, MN 91 **F5**
Lower Richardson Lake, ME 18 **D6**
Lower St Croix Nat'l Scenic Riverway, MN 86 **A4**
Lower St Croix Nat'l Scenic Riverway, WI 84 **A4**
Lowland, NC 54 **B4**
Lowville, NY 29 **F4**
Loxahatchee NWR, FL 61 **H2**
Lualualei Mil Res, HI 174 **B6**
Lubbock, TX 102 **D5**
Lubec, ME 15 **H3**
Lucas Theatre, GA 58 **C5**

Lucasville, OH 83 **E2**
Lucaya, BAHAMAS 67 **B4**
Lucedale, MS 60 **B6**, 73 **E2**
Lucerne, WA 143 **H1**
Lucile, ID 134 **D4**
Luckenbach, TX 106 **A4**
Ludington, MI 84 **E3**
Ludlow, PA 38 **C4**
Ludlow, VT 14 **B2**
Ludowici, GA 56 **A5**
Lufkin, TX 72 **A3**
Luling, TX 106 **D3**
Lumberman's Mus, ME 15 **G5**
Lumberton, NC 51 **E4**
Lummi Indian Land, WA 138 **B7**, 142 **C6**
Lunar Crater, NV 149 **E5**
Lund, NV 149 **F5**
Lupfer, MT 136 **D2**
Luquillo, PR 68 **F7**
Luray, VA 41 **F4**, 47 **G5**
Lusk, WY 131 **G2**
Lutheran Church of the Ascension, GA 58 **C5**
Lutherville, PA 34 **C4**
Lycoming Hist Soc Mus, PA 35 **E4**
Lynbrook, NY 20 **B1**
Lynch, PA 38 **C3**
Lynchburg, MO 99 **E2**
Lynchburg, VA 41 **F2**, 43 **E2**, 45 **E2**, 46 **B5**
Lynchs Corner, NC 55 **C8**
Lyndon B Johnson Mem, DC 44 **B5**
Lyndon B Johnson SHP, TX 103 **E3**
Lyndonville, VT 14 **C5**
Lynn, MA 21 **F5**
Lynn Canal, AK 167 **F3**
Lyons, CO 120 **D5**
Lyons, GA 50 **C2**
Lyons, KS 96 **D2**
Lyons, NY 28 **D3**, 33 **E6**
Lyons Ferry SP, WA 138 **E6**
Lytle, TX 106 **A1**
Lytton, CA 153 **E6**

M

ML King Park, TX 107 **C2**

287

O

303

RECORD OF PERSONAL DATA

Name:

Address:

Telephone:

Office Telephone: _____ Facsimile:

Passport No. _____ Social Security No.

E-Mail: _____ Frequent Flyer No.

NOTABLE NUMBERS

Emergency   Personal

_____   _____

_____   _____

_____   _____

_____   _____

_____   Financial/Credit

Medical   _____

_____   _____

_____   Legal

_____   _____

_____   _____

San Francisco Overland Limited

CHICAGO & NORTH WESTERN RY.
UNION PACIFIC SYSTEM
SOUTHERN PACIFIC LINES

RAINBOW COTTAGES
YOUR MODERN COTTAGE HOST
IN
Salida
"IN THE HEART OF THE ROCKIES"
CONVENIENTLY LOCATED ON HIGHWAY 5

Salida, Colorado

Hotel Benson

KELLER AND BOYD
OWNERS AND OPERATORS

Portland, Oregon

MOTEL
TRAVELERS WELCOME

THE BLACK

SOUTH MICHIGAN AVENUE

CAPITAL
MOTEL

OWNERS AND MANAGERS
THE DRAKE HOTEL CO.
TRACY C. DRAKE, PRES'T.
JOHN B. DRAKE, VICE-PRES'T.

CHICAGO

July

The Brown Palace Hotel

ABSOLUTELY FIREPROOF

Denver, Colo.

Magnolia Auto Court

ULTRA MODERN TOURIST CABINS • TELEPHONE 2-9681 • WILLIAM BLAZIE, MANAGER